CW00687956

New to the LSP classroom?

A selection of monographs on successful practices

Edited by

Martina Vránová
Brno University of Technology, Czech Republic

Series in Education

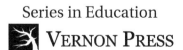

VERNON PRESS

Copyright © 2023 by the Authors.

All rights reserved. No part of this publication may be reproduced, stored in a retrieval system, or transmitted in any form or by any means, electronic, mechanical, photocopying, recording, or otherwise, without the prior permission of Vernon Art and Science Inc.
www.vernonpress.com

In the Americas:	*In the rest of the world:*
Vernon Press	Vernon Press
1000 N West Street, Suite 1200,	C/Sancti Espiritu 17,
Wilmington, Delaware 19801	Malaga, 29006
United States	Spain

Series in Education

Library of Congress Control Number: 2022947700

ISBN: 978-1-64889-150-2

Product and company names mentioned in this work are the trademarks of their respective owners. While every care has been taken in preparing this work, neither the authors nor Vernon Art and Science Inc. may be held responsible for any loss or damage caused or alleged to be caused directly or indirectly by the information contained in it.

Every effort has been made to trace all copyright holders, but if any have been inadvertently overlooked the publisher will be pleased to include any necessary credits in any subsequent reprint or edition.

Cover by Kristina Komárková.

Table of contents

List of figures

List of tables

List of appendices

List of abbreviations and acronyms

AWL	Academic Word List
BE	Business English
CALAT	Computer-Assisted Language Assessment and Testing
CALL	Computer-Assisted Language Learning
CALP	Cognitive and Academic Language Proficiency
CELTA	Certificate in Teaching English to Speakers of Other Languages
CEFR	Common European Framework for Languages
CercleS	European Confederation of Language Centres in Higher Education
CertTESOL	Trinity Certificate in Teaching English to Speakers of Other Languages
CLIL	Content and Language Integrated Learning
CODHUS	Centre for Corpus Related Digital Approaches to Humanities
DELTA	Diploma of Teaching English to Speakers of Other Languages
DDL	Data-Driven Learning
EAP	English for Academic Purposes
EBP	English for Business Purposes
ECTS	European Credit Transfer and Accumulation System
EFL	English as a Foreign Language
EFMD	European Foundation for Management Development
EGBP	English for General Business Purposes
EGP	English for General Purposes
ELP	English for Legal Purposes
ELT	English Language Teaching
EMI	English as a Medium of Instruction
EMP	English for Medical Purposes
EOP	English for Occupational Purposes
EQUIS	European Foundation for Management Development Quality Improvement System
ESBP	English for Specific Business Purposes
ESL	English as a Second Language
ESP	English Specific Purposes

EVP	English for Vocational Purposes
FSP	French for Specific Purposes
GB	General Business
GE	General English
GELS	Global Engineers Language Skills
GSE	Global Scale of English
GSL	General Service List
HE	higher education
HOTS	high-order thinking skills
ICT	information and communications technology
IMAT	International Medical Admissions Test
Inlato	Interactive Language Toolbox
L1	first language
L2	second language
LC CUT	Language Centre of the Cyprus University of Technology
LP	Language for the Professions
LSP	Language for Specific Purposes
M	mother tongue
MALL	Mobile-Assisted Language Learning
MIUR	Italian Ministry of Education, Universities and Research
ML	modern languages
RSA	Royal Society of Arts
TE	teacher education
TEFL	Teaching English as a Foreign Language
TELL	Technology-Enhanced Language Teaching
TESOL	Teaching English to Speakers of Other Languages
TFrench& GreekSOL	Teaching French and Greek for Speakers of Other Languages
TLU	target-language use
VE	vocational education
WTC	willingness to communicate

INTRODUCTION:
New to the LSP classroom?

Martina Vránová

Brno University of Technology, Czech Republic

Dita Gálová

Brno University of Technology, Czech Republic

Languages for Specific Purposes (LSP) have always been defined as learner-centered, communication-oriented, and content-based as the learner, the way of acquiring language, and its situational use are considered to be the main factors in the whole process of learning. The centrality of the student is reflected in the fact that LSP courses must be "tailored to meet the needs of specific students in specific circumstances" (Huckin 2003, 8). Thus, LSP practitioners should ideally know their students, including the level of their knowledge and skills at the beginning of the educational process and the target level at its end. They should be acquainted with job profiles, literary genres, and linguistic forms of those professions their students typically enter in order to prepare them to communicate effectively in their own particular scientific or professional contexts. The LSP practitioner should help students develop the essential skills of understanding, using, and presenting (in written and oral forms) authentic information in their fields and facilitate the use of the foreign language in a real context. Therefore, LSP practitioners are required to go beyond the general language methodology and consider the aspects related to different content areas. These features of LSP can be traced back to its humble origins in the 1950s in *The Language of Science* by Savory (1953).

LSP is an all-encompassing discipline. In the introduction to *Innovations in Languages for Specific Purposes: Present Challenges and Future Promises* (2017), the editors stress the "diversity of target learners and instructional contexts" (Sowa and Krajka 2017, 9) that LSP must deal with, which gave rise to a publication whose ambition is to be a "forum for the exchange of experiences of researchers and practitioners from a number of countries" (Sowa and Krajka 2017, 10). Such fragmentation of focus and a call for exchanging experiences underlies most, if not all, publications in the field of LSP. Some areas, however, are more pronounced than others. The needs analysis is the necessary starting point for any successful practice. For example, in *The Changing Face of ESP in*

Today's Classroom and Workplace (2020), two whole chapters are dedicated solely to needs analysis in particular geographical and business contexts. The analysis of learners' needs is also closely tied to the identity the learners construct of themselves and of their professional community. Belcher and Lukkarila (2011) argue that teachers have to find out more about their learners' imagined identities and imagined communities. This focus on the target community of language users has given rise to ethnographic approaches to LSP. An overview of ethnographic ESP research is provided by Dressen-Hammouda (2013), and ethnography-oriented research techniques in relation to EAP are also discussed by Paltridge and Starfield (2016).

The focus on communication has been reflected in an ongoing interest in the genre. The development of the genre in the field of ESP and its relation to discourse analysis, the multimodality of language, and social context can be found in a chapter by Brian Paltridge in *The Handbook of English for Specific Purposes* (2013). Genre is also widely discussed in the field of academic writing (in EAP). Several chapters in *English for Specific Purposes Instruction and Research: Current Practices, Challenges and Innovations* (2020) discuss academic writing from various viewpoints, including using corpus linguistics as a tool for analyzing students' papers. Also, Lillis and Curry in *Academic Writing in a Global Context* (2010) employ document analysis, interviews, and observations to examine the experiences of scholars publishing their work on English. However, when it comes to inspecting communication in LSP, an increasingly dominant space has been dedicated to technology, electronic communication, and the use of media. CALL (Computer-Assisted Language Learning) and MALL (Mobile-Assisted Language Learning) are investigated in several chapters in *Positioning English for Specific Purposes in an English Language Teaching Context* (2018). There is also a whole publication entitled *Languages for Specific Purposes in the Digital Era* (2016), which explores various issues connected with CALL. The benefits of wikis, blogs, and podcasts created by learners themselves and used in a language class as student-generated content are discussed in journal articles by, for example, Wheeler, Yeomans, and Wheeler (2008) and Snowball and McKenna (2017).

The content is another major area of LSP research, as already mentioned above. As LSP serves a diversity of disciplines, a great number of papers are dedicated to issues arising from teaching language for a particular discipline. Such a diversity of papers can be found, for example, in *Vistas of English for Specific Purposes* (2015) and *Convergence of ESP with Other Disciplines* (2018). The evergreens of material design, curriculum development, and CLIL (Content and Language Integrated Learning) are thoroughly discussed in *Key Issues of in English for Specific Purposes in Higher Education* (2018). However, Nalan, Isik-Tas, and Jian (2020) included in their edited volume also more specific deliberation on developing teaching material through cooperation with subject specialists and students.

As the survey of current literature showed, the learner, communication, and content have kept on having the upper hand. However, it is only through the carrier and performer of this specific educational process—the LSP practitioner— that these topics may become such dominant centers of practice. To counterbalance the aforementioned centrality, the goal of this volume is to shift the focus to the neglected agent of LSP instruction. This turn towards the instructor has been motivated by the fact that a great number of LSP practitioners enter their jobs without previous expertise. Most LSP practitioners undergo general language teacher training. They, however, lack LSP education or may not even have a background in applied linguistics. This motivation has proven valid as many of the volume's contributors faced this "sink-or-swim situation" (Feng 2009, 195) in their professional lives. They started from scratch and rediscovered the already discovered, as there is no solid theoretical canon that novice LSP practitioners can be equipped with.

The less pre-service education LSP practitioners receive, the more in-service education they need. For insights into the LSP field and guidelines on best practices, instructors have to rely on their colleagues who are willing to share their experiences through workshops, conferences, or papers. In her overview of LSP teacher education, Basturkmen concludes the same by saying that even though standardized core literature is very limited, "many of the LSP initiatives, courses and projects reported in the literature are written by experienced LSP teachers who faced a specific challenge or need in their teaching context" (2014, 27). All chapters in this volume have been written by LSP practitioners and researchers in higher education. In other words, it has been written by experienced LSP practitioners for aspiring LSP practitioners about how they see themselves and face the challenges of their jobs. This volume provides both guidance and self-reflection. It joins the initiative to form LSP support groups and networks, thus contributing to the ongoing professional self-development efforts.

As a proof that LSP practice is a global challenge, papers have been collected from many European countries, the USA and Uruguay. Even though most chapters are naturally concerned with English, being the lingua franca of today, the collection also features guidelines for teaching Spanish or French for specific purposes. Moreover, the target disciplines that these languages are taught for encompass business, engineering, sociology, or medicine, thus supporting the assumption of the universal character of problems with which LSP practitioners deal.

Chapters have been arranged so that they start with LSP practitioners' challenges and move on to successful examples of LSP practice. The first four chapters thus present considerations of problems and difficulties novice LSP instructors do not always expect to encounter. The dismal state of LSP practitioners' education may have a negative effect on their identity formation. An LSP practitioner's identity is made of a variety of often disparate roles, which is reflected in the terminological instability in this volume. Despite the widely used term "LSP practitioner" introduced by Hutchinson and Waters in 1987, some authors in this volume prefer other designations, such as LSP teacher or instructor. The remaining chapters comprise accounts of genuine LSP practice. They explore specific LSP programs, techniques, and activities with the aim of sharing lessons learned, providing inspiration and guidance to other LSP practitioners. It offers best practices with possible answers to questions LSP practitioners frequently ask themselves.

Chapter 1 by Kakoulli Constantinou and Papadima-Sophocleous starts with a motivation common to the whole volume: LSP/ESP teacher education has not been properly investigated, and opportunities for it are very few. Not only do the authors stress the necessity of ESP pre-service education but they also present results from their own research conducted among Cypriot and Greek ESP practitioners with the aim of finding out what input such undereducated teachers need. Their research participants either received no ESP teacher training or very little and were indeed unsatisfactory. The participants identified the most pressing responsibilities of ESP practitioners as analyzing the learners' needs, defining the course objectives, and deciding on the content of the course and the material to be used. In fulfilling these responsibilities, ESP practitioners cannot rely on their education or any seriously undertaken research but tend to rely on their own intellect, personality, and experience. Thus, the authors conclude that ESP practitioners with little pre-service education desperately need in-service training. Such LSP/ESP professional development programs should involve both a theoretical aspect of LSP/ESP and learning in general and a more practical aspect focusing on teaching methodology and curriculum design.

Bereczky, in Chapter 2, takes up the challenge to describe the various roles LSP practitioners must assume in their jobs that make up their professional identity. She conducted a survey among Hungarian higher-education ESP practitioners. To counterpoint the omnipresent student-centered aspect of LSP, Bereczky commences her chapter with a historical survey of approaches to the teacher as the main agent of education, differentiating general teacher's roles, language teacher's roles, and ESP teacher's roles. The ESP practitioner's roles seem rather diversified in the literature, yet the most outstanding one is that of a subject specialist. It is in the demands placed on the subject-specialist role that the author finds a possible identity crisis that ESP practitioners may feel. Many language teachers, including her research subjects, believe that they are unprepared to tackle the specific content they must teach in ESP. Yet, most literature on ESP denies the need for deep subject knowledge. The author thus identifies a clash of identities. The ESP practitioner's assigned identity—in the literature described under the roles of teacher, trainer, instructor, or coach—clashes in real-life conditions with the identity the ESP practitioners claim for themselves—the learning facilitator. Without specific subject knowledge, ESP practitioners tend to be perceived as "less worthy" than other subject teachers. Facilitating the learning process by teaching language skills does not seem equal to teaching hardcore science. Such is the heart of the identity crisis present in the transition process from a general language teacher, a true subject specialist, to the LSP practitioner, a learning facilitator.

Chapter 3, "Being a legal alien: Inspecting the (in)accessibility of specific professional communities to LSP teachers," identifies various challenges novice LSP teachers come up against in their careers that might discourage them from their efforts. The first one is, once again, the lack of pre-service education which has serious consequences for general language teachers thinking that LSP is only a question of specialist vocabulary and content. Another challenge is coping with not being perceived as true academics. In the university environment nowadays, the stress of doing research, particularly strategic research bringing financial incentives, has immensely devalued the teaching part of the job. Teaching an instrument, not hard science, is another reason for considering LSP practitioners a "necessary pendant" to true academic endeavors. In case LSP practitioners try to acquire specific subject knowledge or get information about the specific language skills their students need, they usually come up against a tall wall of resistance from the target community of professionals whose language they teach. Professional communities tend to be seclusive and guard their knowledge, which prevents successful co-teaching or team-teaching. The final challenge is the needs analysis. Teachers educated in language-related disciplines find themselves at a loss as it is based on ethnographic research of the target-language community. For such research, they are utterly unprepared. Nevertheless, Vránová does not only paint a bleak picture of the LSP practitioners' profession. She suggests that the immediate source of subject knowledge and the easiest access to the target-language community available to LSP practitioners is their students. Cooperation with students promotes an educational partnership that brings tangible rewards and satisfaction for both parties.

The reasons why many students lose motivation to study languages early into their university studies are presented in Chapter 4. However, the insights are presented from the point of view of the students' teachers (Hungarian LSP practitioners teaching English for business, tourism, and catering), who are themselves very much aware of the fact that motivating students to study languages is often a Sisyphean endeavor. Lazar starts with an overview of relevant literature on student motivation, reasons for losing it, and ways of regaining it. As the most powerful "demotive" is a lack of meaningful purpose and the most powerful "remotive" stems from the student's own ambitions, we can see that LSP courses may be a double-edged sword. If LSP courses do not properly address the working-life-related realities, students get demotivated; if a direct link between one's future professional career and mastering a foreign language is explicitly established and personally felt, students may gain or even regain motivation. Lazar's research yielded similar results to those of theoretical studies. When students feel true intrinsic motivation for the profession, their instrumental motivation to learn a foreign language intensifies as well. However, the research also revealed that motivation is not only a matter of students but also an organic part of the LSP practitioner's identity. Hungarian LSP practitioners embrace the role of motivational agents even though their task is to motivate their students for a professional career with which they themselves have very little experience.

Chapter 5, "Developing a language curriculum in a business institution," presents a possible attitude to one of the main areas of LSP—course and curriculum development. Responding to a great demand for Spanish for Specific Purposes, Rubio designed a Spanish for Business Minor at Bentley University. After tackling the university's curriculum policies, Rubio reflects on his own facilities to help him in curriculum design—his research background, cultural experience, and knowledge of business. Having been trained in literary and cultural studies, he found himself exactly in that situation we try to address in this volume. He thus allowed himself some flexibility to research business-related topics. At the same time, he also counted on his students to contribute to the learning process because of their strong business education. His curriculum has several goals, which include appreciation of business practices in Spanish cultures, understanding cultural differences, and gaining new knowledge of ethical practices in Spanish-speaking countries. Once again, we can see the strong tie between content and language, which can be turned from a disadvantage—the LSP practitioner's lack of subject knowledge—to an outright advantage—engaging students in the learning and teaching process and developing their soft skills in a particular cultural context. What follows is a description of three courses designed with an interdisciplinary approach and examples of classroom activities used in these courses.

Having proficient reading skills in English has become essential for any professional so that he or she can keep up with international news or the latest scientific findings. To respond to this demand, the Center for Foreign Languages at Universidad de la República (Uruguay) has been offering ongoing courses in English Reading Comprehension. The goal of these courses is to provide university students with the necessary strategies to tackle frequent genres in their disciplinary areas so that they can access specialized literature. Having this goal in mind, in Chapter 6, Rodríguez and Risso present three sociolinguistic tenets that guided the design and execution of the courses. First, they argue that monolingualism is not the normal state of humankind, stressing that languages do not have to be taught separately; students' native and other foreign languages are welcome and compared with the target language. Second, emphasizing that languages change over time, students may be led to see the target-language irregularities. The third tenet is particularly important for students speaking Romance languages and studying English. The fact that languages are in contact with each other paves the way to dealing with language borrowings and cognates. The reading comprehension courses based on these sociolinguistic principles are then regularly evaluated by students themselves so that they are kept relevant to their needs. These questionnaires proved that students indeed become aware of the sociolinguistic reading strategies, which will help them in the future.

In Chapter 7, a team of authors from European technical universities addresses the most common challenge novice LSP practitioners usually have—inadequate knowledge of the target domain. They propose strategies to develop the language instructor's technical terminology and concepts. Struggling with feelings of intimidation in an alienating environment of the technical English classroom led the authors to a realization that the best source of target-domain knowledge is their own students. Interacting with students and receiving and appreciating subject-matter input from them bridges the gap between LSP practitioners with humanistic training and their technology-oriented students. By creating the classroom culture of two sets of experts in cooperation to solve a problem, both the teachers and the students can symbiotically learn from each other. Such teacher-student cooperation will give novice LSP practitioners a considerable head start. Moreover, it ensures that course design and curriculum can be tailored to the students' needs. Such student-guided input will also make up for the intensely felt lack of contact between LSP instructors and experts teaching subject-matter courses. The reflections on the unenviable situation of LSP instructors in an environment where everybody else but them has the target-domain knowledge is then followed by a list of specific in-class and take-home activities that incorporate the student-domain expertise in the ESP classroom. All these activities can be adapted to any language, level of proficiency, or target domain.

In order to pass IMAT and successfully enter the studies of medicine in Italy, students have to have an excellent level of English-text comprehension as well as an in-depth knowledge of specialized terminology and target-language use. Such skills will enable them to predict language performance in the specific context of their future workplace. Preparation for IMAT implies the use of both EMI (English as a Medium of Instruction), which is increasingly present at educational institutions at non-English-speaking countries, and CLIL (Content and Language Integrated Learning), whose aim is dual—studying both subject matter and language in which it is conveyed. Abbate thus, in Chapter 8 entitled "Lexical approach and social reading in CLIL settings," suggests employing these two strategies to develop students' functional vocabulary and communication skills—the essentials for IMAT. The lexical approach focuses on the study of lexical structures, or "language chunks," such as collocations or institutionalized utterances. To assist the integration of the lexical approach into CLIL, the author suggests using online cloze-test creators and gap-fill generators, such as IdiomSearch. Since learning has recently been considered a social activity, Abbate, especially in the time of COVID-19, also recommends social reading— a shared reading practice in the Web environment. Specifically, collaborative annotation tools are useful as they offer a meta-reading opportunity and promote close reading. What follows is a guide to using some online tools, such as Vocabkitchen, eMargin, NowComment, or Learn Actively. This instructional chapter on teaching medical vocabulary can be easily altered to any other discipline.

Those who write in two different languages face several challenges. One of them is writing for two academic writing audiences with different genre expectations. Even though articles published in student journals by students at West University of Timișoara (Romania) are selected and edited by professors, the interference from Romanian into English has become an issue of discussion. In Chapter 9, Bercuci and Chitez analyze the influence of Romanian language traits and academic genre norms in order to suggest remedial practices which will make students aware of this interference. The traits of Romanian in English academic writing were analyzed on introductions in two student journals. Two learner corpuses—one English and one Romanian— were compiled, and specific traits of Romanian style in student English writing were identified. As such transformations from a mother tongue to a foreign language exist in all languages, the authors provide a guide on how to analyze student texts and identify these traits. Even though the corpus linguistic procedure is for advanced LSP practitioners and for those trained in linguistics, what this research proves is, once again, that the most readily available source of subject knowledge, research, and teaching materials is the students themselves.

Chapter 10 focuses on the development of a writing program in French for Dutch-speaking students of economy and sociology. Yet the strategies discussed could be applied to any language as the chapter is indeed conceived as instructions on how to develop a writing program/course. The advantage of the text is that it describes strategies for writing reports, summarizing texts, and presenting figures, which are daily tasks of most professions. This is in contrast to many academic writing textbooks whose content is mostly essay writing. First, an overall design of the training program is described with specific goals for enhancing writing competence, and then a detailed procedure with examples of activities and text samples is given in the section, "Developing writing activities, coaching tools, and materials." Also, post-writing activities in the form of correcting a created text are discussed. The program is strictly context-oriented ("specific" in the sense of LSP) and relies on blended learning (part in-class and part digital learning). Such a program needs continuous development to fit the changing needs of students, which means that activities are adapted, and language materials are revised based on the student writing production and questionnaires. The students' submissions for the course also become a basis for update and adaptation, emphasizing the role of students as an essential source of knowledge for the LSP teacher.

With an increasing emphasis placed on internationalization and employability, physical mobility programs have become key tools in their achievement. Recently, especially in the time of COVID-19, alternatives have been offered to both educators and students to gain international experience without leaving their classrooms. The digital space has become the medium for online collaboration, telecollaboration, and virtual exchange projects. In Chapter 11 "Twenty-first century methods for twenty-first century skills," Koris describes a virtual exchange project between Hungarian and American universities in the fields of international relations and international business communication. This virtual project aimed to develop students' intercultural competence, critical thinking, debating, online collaboration, and communication skills in virtual international teams, with an additional goal for the Hungarian students to practice professional communication in English. After the project, Koris interviewed her Hungarian subjects and realized that they had a very positive attitude towards intercultural and international online collaboration projects. Such learning experience increases their motivation, activates their creativity, and promotes learner autonomy. The students benefited from an exchange of individual perspectives and the idea of practice over theory. In their own opinions, content knowledge can be reinforced much better by participating in international collaboration projects. Venturing into virtual exchange projects which combine language and subject-matter learning is thus a meaningful effort to be tried by LSP practitioners.

In summary, the whole volume is not only a guide for starting LSP practitioners or those who look for advice. It also pays tribute to LSP practitioners as they enter their professional lives quite unprepared but continue facing struggle, often developing courses from scratch, so that their students can prosper.

References

Bárcena, Elena, Timothy Read, and Jorge Arus, eds. 2016. *Languages for Specific Purposes in the Digital Era.* Cham: Springer.

Basturkmen, Helen. 2014. "LSP Teacher Education: Review of Literature and Suggestions for the Research Agenda." *Ibérica* 28: 17–34.

Belcher, Diane, and Lauren Lukkarila. 2011. "Identity in the ESP Context: Putting the Learner Front and Center in Needs Analysis." In *New Directions in English for Specific Purposes Research,* edited by Diane Belcher, Ann M. Johns, and Brian Paltridge, 73–93. Ann Arbor: University of Michigan Press.

Dressen-Hammouda, Dacia. 2013. "Ethnographic Approaches to ESP Research." In *The Handbook of English for Specific Purposes,* edited by Brian Paltridge and Sue Starfield, 501–18. Malden: Wiley-Blackwell.

Dudley-Evans, Tony, and Maggie Jo St John. 1998. *Developments in English for Specific Purposes: A Multi-disciplinary Approach.* Cambridge: Cambridge University Press.

Huckin, Thomas N. 2003. "Specificity in LSP." *Ibérica* 5: 3–18.

Feng, Julan. 2009. "A Study on ESP Teacher Education Models in Chinese Context." *The Asian ESP Journal,* Special Edition: The 1st Asian ESP Conference. Chonquing University: 192–205.

Kırkgöz, Yasemin, and Kenan Dikilitaş. 2018. *Key Issues in English for Specific Purposes in Higher Education.* Cham: Springer.

Lillis, Theresa, and Mary Jane Curry. 2010. *Academic Writing in a Global Context: The Politics and Practices of Publishing in English.* London: Routledge.

Nalan, Kenny, Elvan Eda Isık-Tas, and Huang Jian, eds. 2020. *English for Specific Purposes Instruction and Research: Current Practices, Challenges and Innovations.* Basingstoke: Palgrave Macmillan.

Nalan, Kenny, and Linda Escobar, eds. 2020. *The Changing Face of ESP in Today's Classroom and Workplace.* S.l.: Vernon Press.

Paltridge, Brian. 2013. "Genre and English for Specific Purposes." In *The Handbook of English for Specific Purposes,* edited by Brian Paltridge and Sue Starfield, 347–66. Malden: Wiley-Blackwell.

Paltridge, Brian, and Sue Starfield. 2016. "Ethnographic Perspectives on English for Academic Purposes." In *The Routledge Handbook of English for Academic Purposes,* edited by Ken Hyland and Philip Shaw, 218–29. London: Routledge.

Savory, Theodore H. 1953. *The Language of Science: Its Growth, Character and Usage.* London: Andre Deutsch.

Snowball, Jen D., and Sioux McKenna. 2017. "Student-Generated Content: An Approach to Harnessing the Power of Diversity in Higher Education." *Teaching in Higher Education* 22 (5): 604–18. https://doi.org/10.1080/135625 17.2016.1273205.

Sowa, Magdalena, and Jaroslaw Krajka, eds. 2017. *Innovations in Languages for Specific Purposes: Present Challenges and Future Promises.* Frankfurt am Main: Peter Lang.

Stojković, Nadežda, ed. 2015. *Vistas of English for Specific Purposes.* Newcastle upon Tyne: Cambridge Scholars Publishing.

Stojković, Nadežda, ed. 2018. *Positioning English for Specific Purposes in an English Language Teaching Context.* S.l.: Vernon Press.

Stojković, Nadežda, Gabriela Chmelíková, and Ľudmila Hurjová, eds. 2018. *Convergence of ESP with Other Disciplines.* S.l.: Vernon Press.

Wheeler, Steve, Peter Yeomans, and Dawn Wheeler. 2008. "The Good, the Bad and the Wiki: Evaluating Student-Generated Content for Collaborative Learning." *British Journal of Educational Technology* 39 (6): 987–95. https://doi.org/10.1111/j.1467-8535.2007.00799.x.

ESP Teacher Education:
Examining the needs of ESP practitioners

Elis Kakoulli Constantinou

Cyprus University of Technology, Cyprus

Salomi Papadima-Sophocleous

Cyprus University of Technology, Cyprus

Abstract

English for Specific Purposes (ESP) has advanced significantly since its emergence in the 1960s with the design of many different ESP courses and the release of numerous publications, which has made the ESP field one of the most popular research areas in the broader field of Language for Specific Purposes (LSP). Despite this fact, the area of LSP Teacher Education (TE), and ESP TE in particular, remains neglected by research; as a result, opportunities for ESP teacher training are very limited, a fact expressed by many researchers in the last 35 years worldwide. The state of affairs in the Cypriot and Greek context is quite similar, since practitioners are mainly English as a Foreign Language (EFL) teachers with no specialization in ESP. This paper presents the current practices of ESP practitioners in Higher Education in Cyprus and Greece and analyses their needs in terms of ESP TE. More specifically, the paper reports on the findings of a study focusing on (a) the profile of ESP educators in Higher and Vocational education in Cyprus and Greece, (b) their views on the role of the ESP educator, (c) the ESP practitioners' needs in terms of in-service professional education, and finally (d) what an ESP TE program should include, according to the practitioners' opinions and needs. Findings reveal aspects of ESP teaching practices that need improvement and yield insights for future endeavors related to the creation of ESP TE programs.

Keywords: Language for Specific Purposes Teacher Education (LSP TE), English for Specific Purposes Teacher Education (ESP TE), ESP teaching, needs analysis

***

Introduction

The idea of language specialization is not new according to a recent edited volume on the history of Languages for Specific Purposes (LSP) in which Yeught claims that it appeared centuries ago in domains such as medicine, law, science, or business (2018, 6). Over the years, specialized varieties of different languages, such as English, French, German, Spanish, etc., evolved. In a recent definition of ESP, Paltridge and Starfield suggest that English for Specific Purposes (ESP) "refers to the teaching and learning of English as a second language where the goal of the learners is to use English in a particular domain" (2013, 2). This idea of ESP as it is known today emerged in the 1960s, in an era of change, due to developments in science, business, and technology, the growing number of university students in the UK, the USA, and Australia, and finally the increasing number of immigrants (Dudley-Evans and St John 1998, Richards 2001). Since then, the number of ESP courses has been constantly increasing and so has research in the area of ESP with more publications dedicated to ESP being released, more conferences being organized, and professional associations being established.

Despite the fact that research in ESP is developing, ESP Teacher Education (TE) is an area not investigated in depth yet, and the studies that focus on ESP practitioners' needs are not many. Opportunities for ESP TE are limited, and the majority of ESP practitioners are General English (GE) teachers with no specialized training in ESP. Hewings' review of *ESP* journal articles published since the 1980s illustrates a focus of ESP research mainly on topics such as text/discourse analysis and much less on issues such as ESP materials, methods, testing, or TE (2002). Johns' more recent historical account confirms this and simultaneously stresses the dominance of genre and corpus studies in ESP research today (2013). Similarly, other researchers claim that research studies in ESP concentrate on the needs of the learners as well as on the specialist discourse; in other words, on content rather than on method (Watson Todd 2003, Wu and Badger 2009, Basturkmen 2012). This lack of ESP TE and the need for more research on this issue and the analysis of ESP practitioners' needs have been expressed by many researchers around the globe in the last decades.

This chapter presents a study conducted in the context of higher and vocational education (HE and VE) in the Republic of Cyprus and Greece, concentrating on the practices of ESP practitioners and their needs in terms of ESP TE. The chapter describes (a) the profile of ESP educators in HE and VE in the Republic of Cyprus and Greece, (b) their views on the role of the ESP educator, (c) the ESP practitioners' needs in terms of in-service professional education, and finally (d) what an ESP TE program should include, according to the practitioners' opinions and needs.

1 The need for English for Specific Purposes Teacher Education

During the last 35 years, there have been scattered endeavors to touch upon the issue of ESP TE in different areas of the world; this signifies the necessity for more research into this field. The vast majority of the research studies conducted concur that English language teachers who wish to become ESP practitioners need to receive specialized education on the subject. Some of these studies even suggest certain parameters on which future ESP TE programs should be based (Dudley-Evans 1997; Chen 2000; Zavasnik 2007; Räsänen 2008; Chostelidou, Griva, and Tsakiridou 2009; Morgan 2009; Abdulaziz et al. 2012; Bezukladnikov and Kruze 2012; Cabrita, Mealha, and Queiroz de Barros 2014; Basturkmen 2014; Kniazian and Khromchenko 2019; Gaye 2020; Kavanoz 2020).

Literature pertaining to ESP TE goes back to 1983 when Kennedy observed that the focus on learners' needs led to the marginalization of the language teacher who was in need of TE in general and suggested that generally, TE programs should be viewed as ESP programs that integrate subject content, methodology, and language. More than a decade later, more publications in the field followed, all expressing the need for the creation of more opportunities for ESP TE based on the needs of ESP practitioners and the specialized nature of ESP (Howard 1997, Johnstone 1997, Master 1997, Jackson 1998). Along these lines, Bojović suggested that ESP teachers needed to "acquire certain knowledge" (2006, 490). In other words, ESP teachers should be appropriately educated and be equipped with "the necessary tools, frameworks, and principles of course design to apply them to new material" (Bojović 2006, 493).

In a different setting, Mahapatra (2011) published an article that could be regarded as a historical review of ESP TE programs in different countries, like the USA, the UK, Saudi Arabia, Chile, Malaysia, Thailand, Romania, Ivory Coast, etc. The article characterized ESP TE as "a neglected need" (Mahapatra 2011, 2). The review was divided into three periods: the time of Ewer's beginning of ESP training programs (1970s), the post-Munby times (Munby 1978), and the post-method era (1990s). The author concluded with the remark that research in ESP TE was not rich, and every TE program should concentrate on teachers in their specific context. The need for ESP TE and the view that research in the area had been poor was also expressed through the years by other researchers in various educational settings (Zavasnik 2007; Fortanet-Gomez and Räisänen 2008; Sava 2009; Basturkmen 2010; Rajabi, Kiany, and Maftoon 2012; Abdulaziz et al. 2012; Bezukladnikov and Kruze 2012; Chen 2012; Bracaj 2014; Latha 2014).

According to Mahapatra (2011), ESP TE should be context-specific, time-bound, and based on teachers' needs. This view was supported by Bocanegra-Valle and Basturkmen (2019), who asserted that any LSP TE endeavor must be founded on the needs of the practitioners. Nevertheless, cases of ESP practitioners' needs analyses are scantily reported in the literature.

2 ESP practitioners' needs in terms of ESP Teacher Education

Even though the necessity of investigating ESP and generally LSP practitioners' needs has been pointed out by researchers in the field (Mahapatra 2011, Basturkmen 2014, Bocanegra-Valle and Basturkmen 2019), there are not many studies that focus on this. In a study in Slovenia, Zavasnik (2007) emphasized that there had not been any attempt to establish ESP teacher training based on the needs of the ESP practitioners. Her research sheds light on ESP teacher-training needs evaluating ESP teacher (sub)competencies, comparing existing ESP teacher-training programs with the analyzed needs in Slovenia, and setting guidelines for future ESP teacher-training programs in the country. In a similar manner, Sifakis (2005) reported on the limited research on ESP practitioners' needs analysis in the Greek context and provided a brief "guide" for teaching English for Academic Purposes (EAP) and ESP in Greece. Sifakis' view that ESP practitioners in general and in Greece in particular face different challenges was confirmed by Chostelidou, Griva, and Tsakiridou's research (2009). Their study involved the identification and recording of the training needs of ESP teachers operating in the context of State Vocational Institutes in Greece. The researchers stressed the fact that ESP teacher training was essential and that ESP pre-service training in the country is insufficient. Their study concluded that ESP teacher training should consist of both theory and practice; it should include the use of technology in the ESP classroom and also focus on needs analysis. It could also involve short-term ESP teacher-training courses (e.g., two weeks long), preferably delivered by experts in the field. Additionally, as other researchers in the past, they argued in favor of ESP practitioners' collaboration with content instructors and team-teaching (Fortanet-Gomez and Räisänen 2008, Platt 1993).

Other research that revealed the need of ESP instructors for more TE was the study by Athanasiou et al. (2016). The study concentrated on the difficulties faced by language educators at the Language Centre of the Cyprus University of Technology (LC CUT) in the process of adapting a wide range of multidisciplinary ESP courses in accordance with the Common European Framework for Languages (CEFR). The HE ESP practitioners who participated in the study recognized how challenging and complicated teaching ESP can be. Furthermore, the participants in the study expressed the need for TE in aligning the CEFR with their ESP courses and suggested the creation of discipline-specific CEFR descriptors. In another context in Senegal (Gaye 2020), English as a Foreign Language (EFL) HE instructors were surveyed to explore their knowledge of ESP and their attitude toward its teaching. The findings of the study revealed that the instructors had limited knowledge of the dimensions of ESP and the skills to teach it. The researcher stressed the need for pre-service and in-service ESP TE.

Literature from different parts of the world revealed that there is an intense need for more research in the area of ESP TE, in-depth investigation of the needs of ESP practitioners in terms of TE, and also more ESP TE opportunities for future and current ESP practitioners. These needs constituted the impetus for this research study, the purpose of which is to examine the profiles of HE and VE ESP practitioners in the Republic of Cyprus and Greece, analyze their needs in terms of ESP TE, and highlight their preferences regarding what ESP TE should involve.

3 The research study

3.1 The purpose of the study

Drawing on the necessity for more research in the area of ESP TE, this research study aims at investigating the current practices of ESP practitioners in HE and VE in the Republic of Cyprus and Greece and analyze their needs in terms of ESP TE. More specifically, the purpose of the study, which was conducted during Spring 2016, is (a) to establish the profile of ESP educators in HE and VE in the Republic of Cyprus and Greece, (b) to outline their views on the role of the ESP educator, (c) identify the ESP practitioners' needs in terms of in-service professional education, and finally (d) establish what an ESP TE program should include according to the practitioners' opinions and needs.

3.2 The participants

A total of 58 ESP practitioners from HE and VE in the Republic of Cyprus and 108 ESP practitioners from public HE and VE in Greece were contacted by email to participate in the study. Eventually, 67 ESP practitioners participated in the research—29 from Cyprus and 38 from Greece.

3.3 The research method and data analysis

The data were elicited through the use of an electronic questionnaire that was administered using Google Forms. The question items included in the instrument were generated based on a review of the literature, previous research in the field of ESP TE, and language TE in general (Crocker 1981; Ur 1996; Dudley-Evans and St John 1998; Harmer 2001; Chostelidou, Griva, and Tsakiridou 2009; Thaine 2010) as well as the researchers' personal experience as ESP practitioners. The questionnaire consisted of 30 items in the form of close-ended questions (multiple response and Likert scale) and open-ended questions and was divided into four sections. Before its actual administration, the questionnaire was reviewed by three external reviewers who provided the researchers with feedback concerning its content and design. The questionnaire was also pilot-tested with eight HE ESP practitioners in Cyprus, and appropriate changes were made before it was administered to the participants.

The study employed mainly a quantitative methodology of data analysis. Data were analyzed using the SPSS version 22 program. The frequency and percentage of responses were displayed using descriptive statistics and tables. Qualitative data obtained through the use of open-ended questions were limited.

4 Results and Discussion

4.1 The profile of ESP educators

As mentioned above, the study evolved around four thematic categories. The first was the profile of the ESP practitioners (first section of the questionnaire), the majority of whom had less than 20 years of teaching experience in ESP and a multifaceted role to play with a variety of duties. Many of the practitioners had received ESP training mainly from conferences, seminars, and lectures on ESP. The participants' demographic profile is presented in Table 1.1.

Table 1.1: ESP practitioners' demographic profile

	Percentage of ESP practitioners (N = 67)
Current position	
HE[a] Cyprus	35
VE[b] Cyprus	2.5
HE Greece	47.5
VE Greece	11.3
SE[c] Cyprus	1.3
SE Greece	2.5
Sex	
Female	86.6
Male	13.4
Age	
20–29	1.5
30–39	29.9

40–49	31.3
50–59	28.4
60 or more	9
Years of ESP experience	
1–5	10.4
6–10	26.9
11–15	16.4
16–20	14.9
Over 20	31.3
Duties	
Course design	19.2
Teaching	20.8
Materials selection	18.6
Materials development	18.9
Course evaluation	12.3
Research	10.4
Prior ESP teacher training as part of:	
Pre-service training	7.3
In-service training	13.1
BA	9.5
MA	21.2
PhD	5.8
Seminars, conferences, lectures on ESP	32.1
No ESP teacher training	10.9

[a] higher education, [b] vocational education, [c] secondary education.

Demographic information also included the different ESP disciplines that ESP practitioners taught. A total of 61 different disciplines were mentioned, with the most popular ones being English for Business, Mechanical Engineering, Computer Science, Electrical Engineering, Communication, and Civil Engineering.

Apart from stating the type of ESP TE they had received in the past (Table 1.1), the participants were asked to state how satisfied they were with each type of ESP TE they had received, i.e., as part of pre-service training, in-service training, BA, MA, PhD, seminars, conferences, and lectures on ESP, using a Likert scale from 1–5 (1 = unsatisfied and 5 = very satisfied). All of the responses for all these items were combined for presentation purposes, and a new scale was produced in which 1 represents the minimum level of satisfaction and 26 represents the maximum level of satisfaction (see Table 1.2).

Table 1.2: ESP TE satisfaction indicator

Level of satisfaction 0 = No ESP TE 1 = minimum level of satisfaction 26 = maximum level of satisfaction	Percentage of ESP practitioners, N = 67
.00	20.9
1.00	1.5
2.00	3.0
3.00	11.9
4.00	4.5
5.00	3.0
6.00	4.5
7.00	4.5
8.00	4.5
9.00	1.5
10.00	1.5
11.00	3.0
12.00	6.0
13.00	6.0
14.00	4.5
15.00	4.5
16.00	6.0
17.00	1.5
20.00	3.0
23.00	3.0
26.00	1.5
Total	100.0

Besides the fact that a percentage of the participants had received no ESP TE in the past (20.9%), the majority of responses were gathered in the middle of the scale, which means that the participants were moderately satisfied with the ESP TE they had received. This finding concurs with Feng's description of the status quo of ESP teachers and TE, which is in a "sink-or-swim" situation (2009, 195). Chostelidou, Griva, and Tsakiridou's study is also in accordance with the findings in Table 1.2 since participants in that research "declared dissatisfaction and insufficiency in regard to their pre-service preparation" in teaching ESP (2009, 140).

Despite the results, there were some aspects of ESP TE that they found useful, as the words of a participant show:

I was given the material (by colleagues) for the ESP courses I had to teach. My colleagues were always willing to help. Moreover, I learned a lot through discussions with colleagues and by setting up my own ESP courses.

Other participants, on the other hand, stressed the fact that they had to develop their own strategies and methods in order to cope with ESP teaching. One participant stated the following:

> *Never have I had the time and/or the luxury to undergo an ESP training. Because of my training in translation studies and comparative literature— and with the help of my students' comments—I was forced to develop methodologies for ESP students for non-English universities. These methodologies have been published in international publications.*

Another participant added:

> *I had acquired surface knowledge of the English that had to be taught.*

The questions that followed to establish the profile of the ESP practitioners that participated in the study concentrated on issues related to their teaching practices. Responses are summarized in Figure 1.1.

The ESP practitioners' responses indicated that the majority of the participants collaborated rarely or occasionally with subject specialists in the field, both for planning their ESP course and for delivering their course. The researchers' personal experience working in the field of ESP in the last twelve years can confirm that, in many cases, ESP courses were based on the instructors' own intellect instead of a systematic analysis of learners' needs or the views of subject specialists and professionals in the specific discipline. This is a fact that has been extensively recorded in the literature as an issue that needs to be addressed since constant collaboration with subject specialists is of vital importance in teaching LSP (Asolami 2014; Duyen 2014; Rajabi, Kiany, and Maftoon 2012).

As far as the use of technology is concerned, apparently both ESP practitioners and their students made use of technology in their ESP courses. However, the fact that more than half of the ESP practitioners (25.37% always and 47% very frequently) appear to request their students to use technology in their ESP courses might imply that the students use technology more than their instructors. This could also imply the lack of appropriate equipment in classrooms or ESP instructors' insufficient training in the use of technology, which is the case in many language-teaching contexts (Papadima-Sophocleous, Kakoulli Constantinou, and Giannikas 2014).

Regarding the material that ESP practitioners used, despite the fact that the majority of them made use of authentic material, they also preferred to rely on a coursebook for the delivery of their ESP course. Wright explained that, especially for newly qualified ESP educators, coursebooks "[o]ften set against the Common European Framework, offer course credibility and accountability as well as a certain degree of consistency and quality control" (2012, 2). They

e confidence in the ESP practitioner and serve as a guide that eases
f the instructor and ensures smooth classroom processes.

Figure 1.1: ESP practitioners' teaching practices

a) Do you collaborate with the subject
specialist(s) to plan your course?

b) Do you collaborate with the subject
specialist(s) to deliver your course?

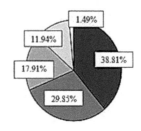

d) Do you use any technologies in
your courses?

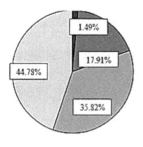

c) Do you ask your students to use
technologies in their ESP course?

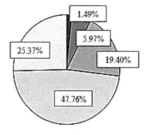

e) Do you use authentic material?

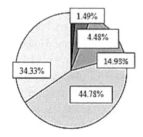

f) Do you use a coursebook?

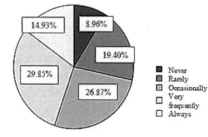

4.2 Participants' views on the role of the ESP educator

Apart from examining the profile of ESP practitioners in HE and VE in the
Republic of Cyprus and Greece, the research also aimed at finding the most
important qualities that an ESP educator should possess according to the
participants' views; this was attempted in the second section of the questionnaire.
Participants were given a list of qualities that they had to assess on the basis of
the Likert scale of importance (Table 1.3).

Table 1.3: The importance of different attributes that an ESP educator should possess

Attributes	Mean	Mode	Minimum	Maximum
Having specialized knowledge about the subject	3.7612	4.00	1.00	5.00
Collaborating with subject specialists	4.1940	5.00	2.00	5.00
Collaborating with colleagues / networking	4.2687	5.00	2.00	5.00
Being the source of knowledge	4.4179	4.00	1.00	5.00
Being a facilitator of learning	4.7313	5.00	3.00	5.00
Guiding students in their learning	4.7910	5.00	3.00	5.00
Identifying students' needs	4.8507	5.00	1.00	5.00
Defining the course objectives	4.8507	5.00	3.00	5.00
Designing the course syllabus/content	4.7761	5.00	3.00	5.00
Selecting materials/resources	4.7761	5.00	3.00	5.00
Designing materials	4.5373	5.00	3.00	5.00
Using authentic materials	4.6269	5.00	2.00	5.00
Using authentic tasks	4.6269	5.00	2.00	5.00
Using a coursebook	3.2388	3.00	1.00	5.00
Using technology	4.2985	5.00	2.00	5.00
Conducting research	3.9701	4.00	2.00	5.00
Evaluating the course	4.5522	5.00	2.00	5.00
Other qualities	.2985	.00	.00	5.00

1 = unimportant, 2 = little important, 3 = moderately important, 4 = important,
5 = very important.

Despite the fact that almost all of the attributes presented in the table above were considered important or very important, as the mean (average) shows, the participants characterized the ability of the ESP practitioner to analyze the needs of the learners, to define the course objectives, and to decide on the content of the course and the material to be used for the delivery of the course as the most important qualities for an ESP educator. Another interesting finding is the ESP practitioners' view that it is important for the ESP educator to adopt the role of a guide and a facilitator of the learning process. Other attributes that ESP practitioners should have, which were suggested by participants, are the following:

> To know how to handle terminology because ESP Greek university students are required to transmit the knowledge they acquire from the English bibliographical references to their parallel classes conducted in Greek.

> Bringing "situations" from the actual place of work into the classroom so that the students will be able to get some idea before finding a job or even specializing in one area of their science.

> Guiding students towards achieving their ultimate goal, which is passing the course.

The participants' responses and views appear to be in line with the qualities and the role of the ESP educator presented in the literature. Crocker characterizes the LSP teacher as a "learning facilitator" rather than as the only source of knowledge (1981, 13); the facilitator has the skills to work together with the learners during the learning process. Dudley-Evans and St John (1998) suggest that the ESP teacher has a multifaceted role that differs from that of the GE teacher, a view supported by others nowadays (Bojović 2006, Johns 2013, Bracaj 2014, Latha 2014). ESP teachers are required to perform many roles and hence do much more than simple teaching. On that account, Dudley-Evans and St John used the term "practitioner" rather than "teacher," supporting the view that the ESP practitioner has five key roles: that of the teacher, course designer and materials provider, collaborator, researcher, and finally evaluator (1998, 13).

4.3 The ESP practitioners' needs in terms of in-service professional education

Aside from establishing the profile of ESP practitioners and defining the most important attributes, they should retain, the questionnaire also focused on the ESP practitioners' needs in terms of TE. This was done in the third section of the questionnaire in which participants were requested to state whether they felt the need to receive ESP TE and also to designate the aspects of their ESP practices that needed improvement. ESP practitioners in the Republic of Cyprus and Greece, as in many other countries of the world, have a positive perception of ESP TE, and they generally have the view that it will help them develop in many aspects of their profession (Figure 1.2).

Figure 1.2: ESP practitioners' view of an ESP TE course

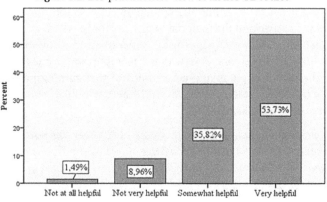

Table 1.4 outlines the reasons for which ESP practitioners would like to attend an ESP TE course, whereas Table 1.5 illustrates the aspects of their ESP teaching practices that need improvement. Participants' responses in both cases were gathered through multiple-response questions.

Table 1.4: Reasons for attending an ESP TE course

Reasons	Percentage of cases, N = 67
Develop professionally	74.2
Improve teaching methodology	71.2
Improve ESP syllabus design skills	65.2
Become a specialized ESP practitioner	36.4
Keep professionally abreast in the area of ESP	69.7
Increase self-confidence	27.3
Grow your network	45.5
Share ideas with other ESP educators	78.8
Satisfy your employer	10.6
Increase your income	10.6
Get promoted	10.6
Other reasons suggested by participants:	
Meet the needs of their students	1.5
Keep up with the developments of the sciences taught	1.5

Table 1.5: Aspects of ESP practices that need improvement

Aspects of ESP practices	Percentage of cases, N=67
Having specialized knowledge of the subject matter	35.8
Collaborating with subject specialists	58.2
Collaborating with colleagues/ networking	40.3
Identifying students' needs	31.3
Defining the course objectives	25.4
Lesson planning	23.9
Designing the course syllabus/content	29.9
Selecting materials/resources	34.3
Using authentic materials	25.4
Designing materials	23.9
Selecting activities/tasks	26.9
Designing activities/tasks	38.8
Teaching methodology	34.3
Developing learners' receptive skills (listening and reading)	31.3
Developing learners' productive skills (speaking and writing)	47.8
Developing learners' vocabulary	25.4
Developing learners' grammar	16.4
Using technology	34.3
Assessing students' performance	25.4
Evaluating the course	20.9
Managing the class	17.9
Providing feedback	20.9
Conducting research	31.3
Other aspects suggested by participants:	
Awareness of "inter-scientificity"	1.5
Training students on peer assessment	1.5

As the findings in both tables denote, ESP practitioners need TE for further professional development that centers around issues related predominantly to teaching methodology, including the use of technology and the development of a network with subject specialists as well as with colleagues in the field. This view is also expressed in literature in the area of ESP, in which research studies mainly focus on the needs of the learners as well as on the specialist discourse, in other words, on what to be taught in ESP programs rather than how such programs can be taught or implemented (Watson Todd 2003, Wu and Badger 2009, Basturkmen 2012). These findings imply that attention needs to turn to issues pertaining to the delivery of ESP courses instead of the design and content of such courses.

4.4 What an ESP TE program should include

In the last section of the questionnaire, participants were asked to state to which extent they agreed with the inclusion of certain components in a potential ESP TE course (Table 1.6) as well as potential modes of training (Table 1.7).

Table 1.6: ESP practitioners' views on the inclusion of certain components in ESP TE

Components to be included in ESP TE	Mean	Mode	Minimum	Maximum
Theories (on learning, ESP, etc.)	4.0896	4.00	2.00	5.00
Teaching methods (of EFL and ESP)	4.5224	5.00	3.00	5.00
Curriculum design (i.e., identify students' needs, define course aims and objectives, set the syllabus/content, select materials/resources, select tasks, etc.)	4.7015	5.00	4.00	5.00
Lesson planning	4.4179	5.00	2.00	5.00
Developing learners' receptive skills (listening and reading)	4.4627	5.00	3.00	5.00
Developing learners' productive skills (speaking and writing)	4.5373	5.00	3.00	5.00
Developing learners' language aspects such as vocabulary and grammar	4.2836	4.00	2.00	5.00
Ways of teaching with technology	4.3433	5.00	2.00	5.00
Ways to evaluate the course	4.4030	5.00	2.00	5.00
Ways to assess students' performance, provide feedback, keep scores, etc.	4.3134	5.00	2.00	5.00
Reflection on your teaching practices and on knowledge acquired from the course	4.5224	5.00	2.00	5.00
Feedback from the trainer	4.4627	5.00	2.00	5.00
Networking	4.1343	4.00	2.00	5.00

The findings show that the participants in the research study almost unanimously agreed that all of the components, as suggested by the researchers in the questionnaire, should be included in a potential ESP TE course. These findings are in accordance with those of other research in other contexts (Bezukladnikov and Kruze 2012). In other words, ESP practitioners in different teaching environments, including Cyprus and Greece, embrace the view that ESP TE should combine both a theoretical aspect of ESP and learning in general as well as a more practical, hands-on aspect, where issues of teaching methodology and curriculum design would be central.

The majority of the participants in the research study also stated that they wished to participate in a short program of two weeks (61.19%) instead of a program of four weeks (25.37%) or an MA in ESP teaching (7.46%). There were some other suggestions expressed by very few participants, which included one-day training and attending an ESP conference (5.97%). Evidently, ESP practitioners opted for quick and efficient forms of development that would not demand extensive commitment on their behalf.

Table 1.7: ESP practitioners' view on modes of teaching for ESP TE

Modes of teaching	Mean	Mode	Minimum	Maximum
Lectures, tutorials, seminars, workshops	4.5672	5.00	2.00	5.00
MOOCs	3.7164	3.00	2.00	5.00
Online courses	3.9552	4.00	2.00	5.00
Guided reading	3.4627	4.00	2.00	5.00
Case studies (trainees develop skills through analyzing case studies)	4.0448	4.00	2.00	5.00
Open learning (have access to learning materials at times convenient to yourself)	4.3881	5.00	3.00	5.00
Distance learning	3.8358	4.00	2.00	5.00
Collaborative learning (trainees work together to produce a learning product / to reach a goal)	4.1045	5.00	2.00	5.00
Cooperative learning (trainees are a team with each one working on their own part to reach a common goal)	4.0597	5.00	2.00	5.00
Forums / Class discussion	4.0000	4.00	2.00	5.00
Diaries/journals (trainees keep records and reflect on the learning process)	3.7761	4.00	2.00	5.00
Class observation	4.1045	4.00	1.00	5.00
Microteaching	3.8955	4.00	2.00	5.00
Practicing in authentic classrooms	4.3582	5.00	2.00	5.00

1 = very poor, 2 = poor, 3 = acceptable, 4 = good, 5 = very good

Participants were also requested to express their opinion concerning different modes of teaching that would be suitable for ESP TE (Table 1.7). Findings demonstrate that, apart from lectures, tutorials, seminars, and workshops, participants have a general preference and inclination toward modes of teaching that favor hands-on approaches and practical implementation of knowledge. This should be taken into account by anyone who attempts to design a TE course in the future.

   In general, the results of the present study led to the formation of certain parameters on which ESP TE programs could be founded; many of these parameters correspond to the findings of previous research studies conducted in the field. First of all, the results of the present research suggest that any future ESP TE endeavor should be based on the theoretical principles of ESP with the ideas of needs analysis (Dudley-Evans and St John 1998, Belcher 2009, Johns and Makalela 2011, Flowerdew 2013) and authenticity of materials and tasks (Breen 1985, Sifakis 2005, Shuang 2014) being at the nucleus of any TE program. Moreover, every ESP TE program needs to urge trainees to be engaged in continuous study of the professional cultures and language used by the particular discipline they are teaching, a view which concurs with Savaş' suggestions (2009), and to be in constant collaboration with content teachers, professionals, students, and other ESP educators (Rajabi, Kiany, and Maftoon 2012; Ur 1997). In addition, an ESP TE program needs to draw from the teachers' own teaching context and encourage teamworking, collaboration, and networking, inside and outside the immediate course context (Fortanet-Gomez and Räisänen 2008). Such a program needs to combine both academic study and the practical experience of teaching (Master 1997) and also embrace the multifaceted role of the ESP practitioners (teacher, course designer and materials provider, collaborator, researcher, and evaluator) (Dudley-Evans and St John 1998) as well as the integration of technology to meet pedagogical objectives in the classroom and for lesson preparation (Bloch 2013, Arnó-Macià 2014). Furthermore, it is also important to promote the incorporation of research (action research in particular) into the teaching practice, a view also expressed by Chen (2000) and Fortanet-Gomez and Räisänen (2008). Finally, ESP TE programs should be constructed on the most recent learning theories, such as social constructivism and connectivism, processes of continuous reflection, as Wallace (1991) and Farrell (2008) asserted in the past, and the idea of continuous professional development and lifelong learning.

Conclusion

Literature corroborates that issues pertaining to ESP TE have not been treated by research in detail yet, and there is still much to be investigated and much to be done on a worldwide scale. As a result, ESP practitioners are struggling to cope with their highly demanding role. The educational context in the Republic of Cyprus and Greece, as in many countries of the world, suffers from limited research in the area of ESP TE. ESP TE programs are almost nonexistent, and research concerning the analysis of ESP practitioners' needs in terms of TE is restricted. This research study has shed light on the profiles of ESP practitioners in higher education in Cyprus and Greece, analyzed their needs in terms of TE, and elicited their views on issues pertaining to ESP TE. Despite the fact that the sample was only from two countries (the Republic of Cyprus and Greece), the study has filled a gap in the literature regarding ESP TE in this part of the world and enhanced informed decisions concerning the design of future ESP TE programs in this and similar contexts.

In this era of connection and sharing, the present study embraces the view of a stronger ESP practitioners' community of practice where more experienced ESP educators can share their experiences with the new practitioners in the field. The use of new technologies can minimize distance and can make this task less challenging. More professional groups for ESP educators can be created on social media and online professional platforms. Additionally, more opportunities for professional communication could be generated through the establishment of ESP TE programs, preferably of a short duration of, for example, two weeks, the organization of conferences and symposia in the field, more publications in the field, staff exchange opportunities, internship opportunities, and opportunities for collaboration. Last but not least, there should be a stronger presence of a ESP practitioners' community of practice through the establishment of more professional organizations that operate in the field of ESP or the support and empowerment of the existing ones. In this respect, educators will have the opportunity to construct knowledge and keep abreast with the latest advancements in the field of ESP, which is continuously developing.

References

Abdulaziz, Maimoona, Sayed Kazim Shah, Rashid Mahmood, and Hafiz M. Fazal e Haq. 2012. "Change from a General English Teacher to an ESP Practitioner: Issues and Challenges in Pakistan." *Interdisciplinary Journal of Contemporary Research in Business* 4 (1): 434–65. https://journal-archieves18.webs.com/434-465.pdf.

Arnó-Macià, Elisabet. 2014. "Information Technology and Languages for Specific Purposes in the EHEA: Options and Challenges for the Knowledge Society." In *Languages for Specific Purposes in the Digital Era*, edited by Elena Bárcena, Read Timothy, and Jorge Arus, 3–25. Switzerland: Springer International Publishing.

Asolami, Eman. 2014. "Barriers to Teaching English for Specific Purpose among EGP Teachers in ELI." *English for Specific Purposes World* 15 (42).

Athanasiou, Androulla, Elis Kakoulli Constantinou, Maro Neophytou, Anna Nicolaou, Salomi Papadima-Sophocleous, and Christina Yerou. 2016. "Aligning ESP Courses with the Common European Framework of Reference for Languages." *Language Learning in Higher Education. Journal of the European*

Confederation of Language Centres in Higher Education (CercleS) 6 (2): 297–316. https://doi.org/10.1515/cercles-2016-0015.

Basturkmen, Helen. 2010. *Developing Courses in English for Specific Purposes.* London: Palgrave Macmillan.

Basturkmen, Helen. 2012. "Languages for Specific Purposes Curriculum Creation and Implementation in Australasia and Europe." *The Modern Language Journal* 96: 59–70. http://doi.wiley.com/10.1111/j.1540-4781.2012.01297.x.

Basturkmen, Helen. 2014. "LSP Teacher Education: Review of Literature and Suggestions for the Research Agenda." *Ibérica* 28: 17–34. https://dialnet.unirioja.es/servlet/articulo?codigo=5254138.

Belcher, Diane D. 2009. "What ESP Is and Can Be: An Introduction." In *English for Specific Purposes in Theory and Practice*, edited by Diane D. Belcher, 1–20. Michigan: University of Michigan Press.

Bezukladnikov, Konstantin, and Boris Kruze. 2012. "An Outline of an ESP Teacher Training Course." *World Applied Sciences Journal* 20: 103–6. https://doi.org/10.5829/idosi.wasj.2012.20.10020.

Bloch, Joel. 2013. "Technology and ESP." In *The Handbook of English for Specific Purposes*, edited by Brian Paltridge, and Sue Starfield, 385–401. Chichester: John Wiley & Sons, Inc.

Bocanegra-Valle, Ana, and Helen Basturkmen. 2019. "Investigating the Teacher Education Needs of Experienced ESP Teachers in Spanish Universities." *Ibérica* 2019 (38): 127–50.

Bojović, Milevica. 2006. "Teaching Foreign Language for Specific Purposes: Teacher Development." In *Co-operative Partnerships in Teacher Education Proceedings of the 31st Annual ATEE Conference*, Slovenia, edited by Mateja Brejc, 1–3. Ljubljana: National School for Leadership in Education.

Bracaj, Morena. 2014. "Teaching English for Specific Purposes and Teacher Training." *European Scientific Journal* 10 (2): 40–49.

Breen, Michael P. 1985. "Authenticity in the Language Classroom." *Applied Linguistics* 6 (1): 60–70.

Cabrita, Melo Eduarda, Isabel Ferro Mealha, and Rita Queiroz de Barros. 2014. "Challenges Facing Pre-service ESP Teacher Education: Legal and Medical English." In *English as a Foreign Language Teacher Education: Current Perspectives and Challenges*, edited by Juan de Dios Martínez Agudo, 339–57. Brill. https://doi.org/10.1163/9789401210485_019.

Chen, Tsai-Yu. 2000. "Self-Training for ESP through Action Research." *English for Specific Purposes* 19: 389–402. https://doi.org/10.1016/S0889-4906(00)00008-9.

Chen, Yinghuei. 2012. "ESP Development in Taiwan: An Overview." *ESP News, TESOL International Association.* Accessed December 22, 2020. http://news manager.commpartners.com/tesolespis/issues/2012-08-21/2.html.

Chostelidou, Dora, Eleni Griva, and Eleni Tsakiridou. 2009. "A Record of the Training Needs of ESP Practitioners in Vocational Education." In *Selected Papers from the 18th ISTAL*, edited by Anastasios Tsangalidis, 131–43. Thessaloniki: Aristotle University of Thessaloniki. http://www.enl.auth.gr/symposium18/papers/14_CHOSTELIDOU_GRIVA_TSAKIRIDOU.pdf.

Crocker, Tony 1981. "Scenes of Endless Science: ESP and Education. The ESP Teacher: Role, Development and Prospects." In *ELT Documents* 112, 7–15. London: British Council.

Dudley-Evans, Tony. 1997. "Five Questions for LSP Teacher Training." In *Teacher Education for LSP*, edited by Ron Howard and Gillian Brown, 58–67. Clevedon: Cambridge University Press.

Dudley-Evans, Tony, and Maggie Jo St John. 1998. *Developments in English for Specific Purposes: A Multi-disciplinary Approach*. Cambridge: Cambridge University Press.

Duyen, Le Thi Hong. 2014. "Learning to Teach ESP: Case Studies of Two Vietnamese General English Teachers." *Language Education in Asia* 5 (2): 228–37. http://dx.doi.org/10.5746/LEiA/14/V5/I2/A05/Duyen.

Farrell, Thomas S. C. 2008. "Brief Reflective Practice in the Professional Development of Teachers of Adult English Language Learners." *CAELA Network* 1–4. https://www.cal.org/caelanetwork/resources/reflectivepractice.html.

Feng, Julan. 2009. "A Study on ESP Teacher Education Models in Chinese Context." *The Asian ESP Journal*, Special Edition: The 1st Asian ESP Conference. Chonquing University: 192–205.

Flowerdew, Lynne. 2013. "Needs Analysis and Curriculum Development in ESP." In *The Handbook of English for Specific Purposes*, edited by Brian Paltridge and Sue Starfield, 325–46. Chichester: John Wiley & Sons, Inc.

Fortanet-Gomez, Inmaculada, and Christine A. Räisänen. 2008. "The State of ESP Teaching and Learning in Western European Higher Education after Bologna." In *ESP in European Higher Education: Integrating Language and Content*, edited by Inmaculada Fortanet-Gomez and Christine A. Räisänen, 11–50. Amsterdam: John Benjamins Publishing.

Gaye, Amina. 2020. "Implications of Current Research in ESP for ESL/ESP Teacher Training." In *English for Specific Purposes Instruction and Research: Current Practices, Challenges and Innovations*, edited by Nalan Kenny, Elvan Eda Işık-Taş, and Huang Jian, 203–25. Cham: Palgrave Macmillan. https://doi.org/10.1007/978-3-030-32914-3.

Harmer, Jeremy. 2001. *The Practice of English Language Teaching*. Third edition. Harlow: Pearson.

Hewings, Martin. 2002. "A History of ESP Through English for Specific Purposes." *English for Specific Purposes World* 3 (1). http://www.esp-world.info/Articles_3/Hewings_paper.htm.

Howard, Ron. 1997. "LSP in the UK." In *Teacher Education for LSP*, edited by Ron Howard and Gillian Brown, 41–57. Clevedon: Multilingual Matters.

Jackson, Jane. 1998. "Reality-Based Decision Cases in ESP Teacher Education: Windows on Practice." *English for Specific Purposes* 17 (2): 151–67. https://doi.org/10.1016/S0889-4906(97)00004-5.

Johns, Ann M., and Leketi Makalela. 2011. "Needs Analysis, Critical Ethnography, and Context: Perspectives from the Client—and the Consultant." In *New Directions in English for Specific Purposes Research*, edited by Diane D. Belcher, Ann M. Johns, and Brian Paltridge, 197–221. Michigan: University of Michigan Press.

Johns, Ann M. 2013. "The History of English for Specific Purposes Research." In *The Handbook of English for Specific Purposes*, edited by Brian Paltridge and Sue Starfield, 5–30. Chichester: Wiley Blackwell.

Johnstone, Richard. 1997. "LSP Teacher Education (Foreign Languages): Common and Specific Elements." In *Teacher Education for LSP*, edited by Ron Howard and Gillian Brown, 11–21. Clevedon: Multilingual Matters.

Kavanoz, Suzan. 2020. "Use of Action Research as a Viable Paradigm for the Professional Development of ESP Instructors." In *English for Specific Purposes Instruction and Research: Current Practices, Challenges and Innovations*, edited by Nalan Kenny, Elvan Eda Işık-Taş, and Huang Jian, 247–65. Cham: Palgrave Macmillan. https://link.springer.com/chapter/10.1007%2F978-3-030-32914-3_13.

Kennedy, Chris. 1983. "An ESP Approach to EFL/ESL Teacher Training." *ESP Journal* 2 (3): 73–85. https://www.sciencedirect.com/science/article/pii/027 2238083900240.

Kniazian, Marianna, and Olena Khromchenko. 2019. "The ESP Lecturers' Self-development Competence in Higher Educational Context." *Journal of Teaching English for Specific and Academic Purposes* 7 (3): 385. https://doi.org/10.22190/jtesap1903385k.

Latha, B. Madhavi. 2014. "Teacher Education and ESP." *IMPACT: International Journal of Research in Humanities, Arts and Literature* 2 (4): 73–82. http://oaji.net/articles/2014/488-1400577101.pdf.

Mahapatra, Santosh Kumar. 2011. "Teacher Training in ESP: A Historical Review." *English for Specific Purposes World* 11 (33): 1–15.

Master, Peter. 1997. "ESP Teacher Education in the USA." In *Teacher Education for LSP*, edited by Ron Howard and Gillian Brown, 22–40. Clevedon: Multilingual Matters.

Morgan, Brian. 2009. "Fostering Transformative Practitioners for Critical EAP: Possibilities and Challenges." *Journal of English for Academic Purposes* 8: 86–99. https://doi.org/10.1016/j.jeap.2008.09.001.

Munby, John. 1978. *A Communicative Syllabus Design*. Cambridge: Cambridge University Press.

Paltridge, Brian, and Sue Starfield, eds. 2013. *The Handbook of English for Specific Purposes*. Chichester: Wiley Blackwell.

Papadima-Sophocleous, Salomi, Elis Kakoulli Constantinou, and Christina Nicole Giannikas. 2014. "Teachers' Attitudes towards the Use of Technology in EFL within Public Junior Secondary Schools in Cyprus." In *Attitudes to Technology in EFL/ESL Pedagogy*, edited by Marina Dodigovic, 53–66. Dubai: TESOL Arabia.

Platt, Elizabeth. 1993. "Vocational/VESL Teacher Collaboration: Some Substantive Issues." *English for Specific Purposes* 12: 139–57. https://doi.org/10.1016/0889-4906(93)90015-G.

Rajabi, Peyman, Gholam Reza Kiany, and Parviz Maftoon. 2012. "ESP In-service Teacher Training Programs: Do They Change Iranian Teachers' Beliefs, Classroom Practices and Students' Achievements?" *Ibérica* 24 (2012): 261–82. https://www.redalyc.org/articulo.oa?id=287024476017.

Räsänen, Anne. 2008. "Tuning ESP/EAP for Mobility, Employability and Expertise: A Pedagogical Process of Change in Focus, Insight, and Practice." In *ESP in European Higher Education: Integrating Language and Content*, edited by Inmaculada Fortanet-Gomez and Christine A. Räisänen, 247–66. Amsterdam: John Benjamins Publishing.

Richards, Jack C. 2001. *Curriculum Development in Language Teaching.* Cambridge Language Education. Cambridge: Cambridge University Press.

Savaş, Bekir. 2009. "Role of Functional Academic Literacy in ESP Teaching: ESP Teacher Training in Turkey for Sustainable Development." *The Journal of International Social Research* 2 (9): 395–406. http://www.sosyalarastirmalar.com/cilt2/sayi9pdf/savas_bekir.pdf.

Shuang, Liang. 2014. "Authenticity in Language Teaching." *Applied Mechanics and Materials* 543–47: 4294–97. https://doi.org/10.4028/www.scientific.net/AMM.543-547.4294.

Sifakis, Nicos. 2005. "English for Specific and Academic Purposes—A Trendy Demand? Orientations in ESP/EAP Research, with a Critical Perspective on the Greek Situation." In *Teaching Foreign Languages for Specific Purposes: A Trend or a Demand? 1st ESP Conference in Kavala—Conference Proceedings,* edited by Fotini Perdiki, Evmorfia Panourgia, E Vergidou, and K. Samara, 17–30. Kavala, Greece: Technological Education Institute of Kavala.

Thaine, Craig. 2010. *Teacher Training Essentials: Workshops for Professional Development.* Cambridge: Cambridge University Press.

Ur, Penny. 1996. *A Course in Language Teaching.* Cambridge: Cambridge University Press.

Ur, Penny. 1997. "Teacher Training and Teacher Development: A Useful Dichotomy?" *The Language Teacher Online.* http://jalt-publications.org/old_tlt/files/97/oct/ur.html.

Wallace, Michael J. 1991. *Training Foreign Language Teachers: A Reflective Approach.* Cambridge: Cambridge University Press.

Watson Todd, Richard. 2003. "EAP or TEAP?" *Journal of English for Academic Purposes* 2 (2003): 147–56. http://linkinghub.elsevier.com/retrieve/pii/S1475158503000146.

Wright, Ros. 2012. "Throwing CELTA Grads an ESP Lifeline." *ESP News: The Newsletter of the English for Specific Purposes Interest Section,* December 2012. TESOL International Association. Accessed December 22, 2020. http://newsmanager.commpartners.com/tesolespis/issues/2012-12-18/8.html.

Wu, Hui Dan, and Richard G. Badger. 2009. "In a Strange and Uncharted Land: ESP Teachers' Strategies for Dealing with Unpredicted Problems in Subject Knowledge during Class." *English for Specific Purposes* 28: 19–32. https://doi.org/10.1016/j.esp.2008.09.003.

Yeught, Michel Van Der. 2018. "Introduction. Charting the Diachronic Dimension of Specialised Languages: Epistemological Challenges and Pedagogical Relevance." In *Languages for Specific Purposes in History,* edited by Nolwena Monnier, 1–15. Newcastle upon Tyne: Cambridge Scholars Publishing.

Zavasnik, Michaela. 2007. "ESP Teacher Training Needs: The Case of Slovenia." In *XVI European Symposium on Language for Special Purposes (LSP) Book of Abstracts: Specialised Language in Global Communication,* 97–98. Hamburg: University of Hamburg. https://nats-www.informatik.uni-hamburg.de/pub/LSP07/Section2Tue/Zavasnik.pdf.

CHAPTER 2

Investigating the teacher's role in ESP classrooms and its connection to professional identity based on a survey of higher-education institutions in Hungary

Klára Bereczky

Budapest Business School, University of Applied Sciences, Hungary

Abstract

The study reflects on the instructor's role in the ESP classroom as described in relevant literature and compares these descriptions to insider accounts gained from a survey on and interviews with ESP teachers working in higher education. Conclusions are drawn based on the importance of roles in the professional identity construction of ESP teachers. As ESP teachers' assigned and claimed identities do not seem to match, signs of a potential identity crisis are also identified.

Keywords: LSP, ESP, business English, teacher role, teachers' professional identity, identity crisis, assigned identity, claimed identity

***

Introduction

The teacher's roles in the ESP classroom have been described in numerous sources. Given the unique role of the teacher in the learning process, it is also relevant to look at whether ESP teachers identify with the roles attributed to them, how they see their own roles, and how they cope with these roles. Teachers' assigned roles through social discourse on teachers form their identity (Gu and Benson 2015, Korthagen 2004). ESP teachers' identity struggles have a direct effect on their teaching practices and, consequently, on students' learning (Tao and Gao 2018). Ultimately, teacher identity is the foundation that makes it possible to adapt to ever-changing educational contexts (Kubanyiova and Crookes 2016).

The aim of this study is to explore the changes in the role of ESP teachers through time and specialization. The roles identified by a content analysis of relevant literature will be compared to the results of a survey of 53 ESP teachers working in higher education (HE) in Hungary related to their professional identity and roles in the ESP classroom in order to reveal the extent to which they identify with the detected roles.

To gain generalizable data on the career paths and development processes of ESP teachers, an anonymous questionnaire (Appendix 2.1) was designed based on the data obtained from the relevant literature, previous ESP teacher and trainer interviews, as well as the researcher's personal business English (BE) teaching experience. The data were collected as part of a larger survey on ESP teacher identity; only the questions relevant to the present study are shown in the appendix. During the pilot, the teachers were asked to fill in the questionnaire while thinking aloud, and they were recorded with their prior consent. The pilot data were used to enhance the reliability and validity of the questionnaire; ambiguous and biased questions were reworded and repiloted, frequently occurring answers were included as options, the space available for answers was tested, the format was changed to one that was easier to analyze, etc. Finally, an online version of the questionnaire was prepared using the free online Kwik Surveys program (www.kwiksurveys.com), which was also piloted the same way with teachers of LSI, Budapest, a private adult education provider. The questionnaire contained 44 multiple-choice questions, out of which nine were completed by a comment line and 16 open-ended questions, out of which six required keying in only a few words, making 60 questions altogether. In order to avoid creating the impression that the participant is being tested, most biodata was collected at the end of the questionnaire. This also helped in treating the fatigue effect (Dörnyei, 2002), as filling in personal qualification data is a routine task for teachers. Since straining participants' memory by requesting data from their distant past might risk losing data by participants quickly deciding that they do not remember, the questions were ordered in a way that was hoped to refresh memories. After that, the questionnaire was sent to HE institutions offering business- and economics-related courses in Hungary. The questionnaire was prepared in English and Hungarian so that every participant could fill it in in his or her mother tongue. The collected data were analyzed with descriptive statistical methods. References to participants when quoting answers and comments are made by code numbers.

The participants were teaching at 20 state-funded and private Hungarian higher-education (HE) institutions. The questionnaire (Appendix 2.1) addressed educators of the following subjects: English for Economics, Finance, Trade, Foreign Trade, Banking, Stock Exchange, Management, Marketing, Insurance, Accounting, Auditing, Controlling, Taxation, Customs, Freight Forwarding, and Logistics. Selection criteria included that the educator had been teaching at least one of the above subjects at any time in the ten years preceding the time of the survey in HE, including Higher Level Vocational Training in Hungary. Altogether 53 academics aged 18–70 filled in the anonymous questionnaire, the majority of 35 teachers, i.e., 66.03%, being 31–60 years of age. No data on the participants' gender was collected in order to provide full anonymity as there are very few ESP practitioners in some institutions; thus, collecting such data might have threatened their anonymity. Thirty-six participants (67.92%) were non-native speakers of English, three participants (5.66%) were native speakers of English, twelve participants (22.64%) marked they were near-native speakers of English, i.e., had lived in an English-speaking country for an extended time, and one participant (1.88%) did not mark any category. As to qualification, thirty-six participants (67.92%) had an MA degree in English language and literature, six participants (11.32%) had a BEd or BA in English, twelve participants (22.64%) held an MSc in Economics, other teaching qualifications like DELTA and RSA were held by two participants (3.77% each), and CELTA and Trinity CertTESOL were held by one participant (1.88% each). The qualification data pointed out that many educators held more than one type of qualification, a teaching degree and a business degree, the majority holding an MA degree in English.

Among the 60 questions of the electronic survey, the following issues relevant to teachers' roles were covered: participating in an ESP training course; collaboration with subject teachers; working simultaneously in HE, secondary education, and in corporate or private courses; attitude to teaching Language for Specific Purposes (LSP); the difference between ESP and General English (GE) teachers; and notions on the ideal ESP educator. The comparison of the survey data and the views expressed in professional literature makes it possible to compare ESP educators' *assigned*, i.e., imposed by others (Buzzelli and Johnston 2002, 113), with claimed identities, i.e., taken on or *claimed* by the person (Buzzelli and Johnston 2002, 110).

1 The significance of the teacher

As a counterpoint to the widespread learner-centered language teaching, several authors have pointed out the significance of focusing on teachers in the educational process (Csizér and Kormos 2007, Kennedy 1983). At the time when scientific methods were given a more and more prominent role in second and foreign language teaching, the role of the individual teacher started to lose significance until the point when following a given method was much more important than the teacher (Woods 1996). In that tradition, even untrained or undertrained persons could function as teachers, which is economical for several interested parties in language teaching.

The teacher has been considered the main educational factor since the beginning of time (Mocanu 1996). One of the earliest examples of this approach comes from Diesterweg in 1865: "A school is worth as much as its teacher" (qtd.

in Tarrou 1996, 14). Freeman and Johnson go as far as calling teachers the "protagonists" of teaching (1998, 413). They outline a revised model of the knowledge-base of language teaching: the new knowledge-base must focus on the teacher. The new model gives a central role to the teacher in understanding and improving English language teaching. The central role of the teacher is also considered to be true in the ESP classroom. As Teemant, Varga, and Heltai put it, "[a]lthough vocational language learning requires a learner-centered approach, teachers will always remain the key figures in the classroom" (1993, 491). Richards also (1997) emphasizes the fact that an in-depth perspective on teachers' professional lives is essential for planning ESP teacher-education courses.

Since most students have acquired some general English by the end of primary or secondary education, ESP is a rapidly emerging area at the international level (Harding 2007, Nikolov 2007, Tao and Gao 2018). At the same time, LSP is a challenge for teachers to teach (Rachayon 2020, Szilágyi and Szőke 2007). The extent of the challenge ESP means for teachers can be illustrated by the expression used by perhaps the most well-known experts of the profession, Hutchinson and Waters, who term ESP "the Wild West of ELT" (1987, 158). For GE teachers, teaching ESP seems to be, in one word, problematic. Hutchinson and Waters (1987) even speak about fear and hostility towards the ESP subject matter, which has a negative effect on teaching. Several factors contribute to the above attitude. There seems to be a general agreement in international studies (Ghafournia and Sabet 2014; Hutchinson and Waters 1987; Kennedy and Bolitho 1984; Palmer and Posteguillo 1997; Teemant, Varga, and Heltai 1993) that GE teachers find it difficult to understand ESP subject matter probably due to their humanities-based education that provided very little or no education in science; they are not trained to teach ESP, find science and technology boring and incomprehensible, have little motivation to invest energy in ESP, prefer general language, and often fail to cope with the diversity of expectations in spite of in-service training or retraining courses. There is, though, one point of disagreement. The general attitude is "to expect teachers to conform to the requirements of the target situation," which is termed "unreasonable" by Hutchinson and Waters (1987, 163). However, they provide no alternative. More recent data also refer to GE teachers' attitude problems and their need for a "vocational consultant" to be able to teach ESP (Kurtán 2003, 260) and to the lack of proper training in TEFL degree courses in the case of teaching BE (Bereczky 2009, Donna 2000) and ESP (Mahendra 2020, Tao and Gao 2018).

Several studies found that most teachers had received no training in teaching LSP before they started to teach it (Fóris, Kováts, and Póla 2003; Mahendra 2020; Nikolov and Öveges 2009; Tao and Gao 2018). The 53 ESP practitioners working in HE in Hungary confirm this result; three-fourths of them started teaching ESP before receiving any training in how to teach it.

The hostile attitude towards teaching LSP was, however, not confirmed. Only 22.64% of the surveyed practitioners had found LSP frightening before they started teaching it, 9.43% had had no idea about it previously, 50.94% had found it interesting, and 22.64% gave no answer. At the time of the survey, 41.50% felt no preference for either GE or ESP, 3.77% did not teach GE anymore, and 35.84% preferred ESP. Nevertheless, the surveyed educators can be regarded as experienced teachers in ESP, with an average of 10.875 years of ESP teaching experience.

2 Role and identity

The roles enacted by teachers might be interpreted as reflections of their identity. Norton defines identity as "how people understand their relationship to the world, how that relationship is constructed across time and space, and how people understand their possibilities for the future" (1997, 410). Norton points out the connection between identity and desire: "the desire for recognition, the desire for affiliation, and the desire for security and safety" (1997, 410).

The most salient characteristic of identity is *affiliation* (Van Dijk 1998), i.e., belonging to a group or a category, be it gender-specific, professional, geographical, etc. In this respect, identity is partially built on others' view of the individual or group, i.e., *assigned* identity (Buzzelli and Johnston 2002, 113). When an individual engages in common experiences with a group, the individual and the group self-representations may blend to a certain extent, just like in the case of the ESP teachers in Mahendra's study (2020) who felt the need to become part of an ESP discussion forum and workshop during the process of constructing their ESP teacher identity. Therefore, teachers' professional self-representation or identity is closely related to the roles by which they are described (Korthagen 2004).

It is also possible to belong to a group and not to share their identity. In other words, dissociate from their identity and, presumably, from their ideology as well. This is common in the case of not only "inherent identity groups (young, old, men, women, blacks, whites, etc.)" (Van Dijk 1998, 119) but also professions. As to the ESP teaching profession, Tao and Gao (2018) found that some of their ESP teacher interviewees did not assume the identity of an ESP practitioner due to the low status of ESP among colleagues teaching literature and linguistics. Leaving a group might have serious consequences, which is also reflected in some of the expressions used to describe such "traitors" or "dissidents" (Van

Dijk 1998, 119). Not surprisingly, hearty identification will be appreciated. The strength of identification with a group depends on a comparison of the personal self and the social self. "If the membership criteria, activities, goals, norms, values, position or resources of the group are in line with (at least consistent with) those of the personal self-construct, identification may be more or less strong. If not, a process of dissociation may take place, including association with other groups" (Van Dijk 1998, 120). Dissenting is particularly problematic in cases when group ideologies are ingrained in one's everyday practices, e.g., professional practices. If one disagrees with professional practices, dissenting might have more serious consequences.

Another aspect of the relationship between roles and identity is described by Carver and Scheier (2017). They place job-related or professional roles among the core roles having a fundamental influence on identity. The consequences of not being able to meet the expectations related to professional roles are serious, such as feeling guilty.

Richards describes the factors that form identity in teaching as "personal biography, gender, culture, working conditions, age, and the school and classroom culture. The concept of identity thus reflects how individuals see themselves and how they enact their roles within different settings" (2008, 167). The context and how it shapes identity can be discovered by looking at case studies, lesson plans, personal journals, and teacher narratives (e.g., Chang 2017, Mahendra 2020, Tao and Gao 2018); these will show how teachers' professional identities have emerged. Such discourses also shape identities. The various references to ESP teachers reflect what is expected of them in terms of their roles and tasks. Studying these roles might provide insights into the assigned identity of ESP teachers. The investigation of the self-reference system of Hungarian ESP teachers aims to detect whether they take on any of these identities and how they see themselves as professionals.

3 The role of the teacher

3.1 General teacher's roles

ESP teachers are mostly described as differing from other teachers (Bell 2002, Kennedy and Bolitho 1984, Kurtán 2003). In order to appreciate the special features of ESP teachers, it is necessary to review the roles of teachers in general and those of language teachers first. Teachers' tasks are often described by their roles; however, roles might also refer to a certain expected behavior. Role "refers to the shared expectation of how an individual should behave (Dörnyei and Murphey 2003, 109). Following the expected pattern of behavior is connected to status. If a teacher does not behave in a way the interested parties, i.e., students, parents, or administrators, and ultimately the society, interpret as appropriate, the teacher might have to face a loss of status, i.e., their esteem, admiration, and approval. Some of the expectations remain unexpressed but still function as the basis for assessing a teacher's behavior and status of that teacher (Oxford et al. 1998). Almost all sources on ESP/BE teachers emphasize that the teacher's role in a specialized class is remarkably different from a GE teacher's role. For in-company ESP/BE teachers, it is vital to be aware of the behavior expected of them since their students often fill the role of clients to whom they provide a service and who decide on their employment. This section looks at the similarities and differences between GE and ESP educators' roles and highlights some of the trends observable in the descriptions of teacher roles, which are interpreted as reflections of ESP teachers' assigned identities.

The oldest and most widespread teacher model is the classical authoritarian transmitter of knowledge (Kraiciné Szokoly 2006). More recent models reflect several layers of responsibilities. For example, Zrinszky's model incorporates categories of traditional teacher roles, the pedagogue, the subject specialist, and the officer/administrator, with the modern roles of a colleague, education partner for parents and culture conveying institutions, and a person who appears before the public (1999, qtd. in Kraiciné Szokoly 2006, 65). These roles refer to teachers working in primary and secondary education and partly in tertiary education.

In the 20th century, a new concept of knowledge acquisition, lifelong learning, started to spread. By the second half of the 20th century, globalization and the development of information technology initiated the demand to reach a knowledge-based society. In such a society, the content of knowledge is different from knowledge in the traditional sense. Besides academic knowledge gained in school, everyday practical knowledge and competencies that are appreciated in the labor market become upgraded. The road to a knowledge-based society leads through lifelong learning, which has become an integrated part of the official educational policy of the European Union as it is reflected in its *Memorandum on Lifelong Learning* (2000, qtd. in Kraiciné Szokoly 2006, 11).

Lifelong learning involves adult education; therefore, it is vital to review adult educators' or andragogues' roles for the purpose of comparing them to LSP teachers' roles. Kraiciné Szokoly mentions following the andragogues' roles depending on the type of school they work in: subject specialist (lecturer/teacher), navigator (explainer, learning guide, intermediary), partner for cooperation (equal with student), learning scenario provider, officer/administrator, school organizer/leader and entrepreneur (in private schools), researcher and innovator, clinician/therapist (sympathizer, trouble shooter, and conflict manager), collaborator with colleagues, adult education methodologist, student activator and activity controller, culture transmitter, and model personality (2006, 74). The author notes that these roles refer to different tasks. Adult educator's roles are special in a sense that andragogues are able to change roles flexibly and quickly meeting the challenges posed by the swiftly changing world. Andragogues also focus on learners; the difference from pedagogues originates in the age-range of students, the transferred knowledge, and the organization of institutional education processes, such as the timing and control of learning processes, education starting and ending requirements, and evaluation (Kraiciné Szokoly 2006, 74). A feature that is important in comparison with LSP teachers is that andragogues are expected to collaborate closely with colleagues, whereas in traditional school education such cooperation is not typical. Also, adult educators treat students as equal partners, continuously cooperate with them, and define tasks and expected results meticulously. At the same time, the adult learner's perspective is one of the features that cause the largest number of difficulties for LSP teachers (Ewer 1983, Dudley-Evans 1997).

Kotschy (1996) identifies the causes in teachers' role changes in Central and Eastern Europe as social changes in the 1990s towards democracy and the communication revolution, especially the storage-capacity and information-organizing possibilities of personal computers. These have radically changed teachers' roles in storing and conveying knowledge. The most important change lies in changing from knowledge-centered education to practice- and student-centered education. The teacher in this new role is a facilitator capable of critical thinking and making individual professional decisions (Kotschy 1996). The emphasis has recently shifted from the teacher as master and a source of knowledge to teachers as guides. Teachers are not expected to dominate in all classroom activities anymore; their role is rather a guide or manager (Mocanu 1996).

3.2 Language teacher's roles

Looking at language teachers, their role descriptions are similar to those of teachers in general, with more emphasis on subject-related knowledge and skills, and less on the social role. In the communicative framework, the teacher wears several hats: facilitator of the communication process, independent participant in the group activities, researcher, needs analyst, counselor, and group process manager (Richards and Rodgers 1986, 77–79). Harmer (1991, 235–43) lists the following GE teacher roles: controller, assessor, organizer, prompter to encourage students to participate or suggest how to go on, participant in students' tasks, resource of help if needed, tutor or counselor in students' self-study and project work at higher levels of proficiency, investigator of new methods and professional development.

3.3 ESP teacher's roles

Several sources emphasize that teachers need to reconsider their roles in ESP and BE classrooms (Bell 2002, Kennedy and Bolitho 1984, Kurtán 2003). Even at first sight, the list of tasks is much longer than those of teachers in general and those of GE teachers. Kennedy and Bolitho (1984, 137–39) specify requirements for ESP teachers as follows: carry out and interpret a needs analysis, design a syllabus, be familiar with a lot of ESP materials and select from them, select texts and write tasks, write course reports, be ready to deal with both international and monolingual groups (sometimes even to deal with pastoral problems of students far away from home and friends), be ready to teach several branches of ESP, be ready to teach both in their own institution or in company settings, and tolerate that clients (in this case students or business organizations) expect from them not only instruction but also value for money.

Comparing the roles described above is not easy, as not all sources expressly name certain things that are obvious. For example, language teachers and GE teachers are undoubtedly expected to be subject specialists in their fields though this requirement is not stated. Other aspects appear under differing names, probably reflecting a difference in the extent to which that characteristic is expected. For instance, the pedagogue role refers to a more direct educator role, whereas the model personality in adult learning is similar though more indirect. Language teachers serve as models as well, which is not stated in the list. The reason for this is probably that only the most prominent roles are listed for language teachers, and those are already included in the teacher role in general.

Still, other roles look similar but are manifested in differing contexts. The partner role in primary and secondary education reflects a partnership with parents and cultural institutions, whereas for adults it is a learning partner equal to the student and reflects a more democratic role. As it can be seen, many roles that appear at first for adult educators reach teachers in general as well due to societal changes, e.g., the facilitator role, the learning therapist, or the mental health therapist role. The pastor or mental health therapist role is equally new to ESP teachers, teachers in general, and language teachers included though not expressly mentioned by authors. Probably, very few teachers are prepared for this role during their teacher training.

Comparing the ESP teacher's roles to the roles of other types of teachers, one can find several categories that are present under the ESP teacher heading in an extended form. The subject specialist role is the most outstanding as it contains expertise not only in one field but in several fields. This requirement seems to be a tall order in itself.

What emerges as a role present in all kinds of teachers is being an expert in the methodology relevant to their field. However, for ESP teachers, not only monolingual groups, like for EFL teachers, but also multilingual groups of learners are expected to be within competency limits. Teaching multilingual groups is not a typical element of TEFL courses; thus, it is expected that ESP teachers are probably not prepared for such a task. Curriculum design is mentioned as a new task for teachers; the same is true for ESP teachers. Task preparation is a familiar area for all language teachers, but a lot of authentic materials, which are indispensable for ESP, cause comprehension problems for ESP teachers preparing tasks from such materials (Ewer 1983, Mahendra 2020), which takes additional time and energy. This fact, together with the limited availability of authentic texts in certain fields, has identified the source of the increased preparation time of ESP teachers mentioned by Bell (1999). The extended preparation time issue is still true, as out of the 53 surveyed HE educators in Hungary, 37.73% reported that they needed much more preparation time than for GE lessons. In HE, an additional factor arose that increased the teacher's preparation time, namely the missing background knowledge of the students. Over 47% of the surveyed teachers complained that students were not familiar with economic concepts or processes while 41.50% said that students did not understand the course book content even in their mother tongue. This means that the missing knowledge needs to be provided by the language teacher who is not prepared to do that, which leads to a degradation and feeling of inadequacy referring to non-identification with the role of subject specialist. Exactly 56% of the surveyed educators felt the need for a second degree or at least an LSP teaching course when they started teaching ESP, which refers to feeling unprepared for LSP teaching after their TEFL course, which reinforces the literature.

Though it is not listed among the roles of andragogues, both adult educators and ESP teachers often provide instruction not only in their own institution but in corporate circumstances as well, just like the surveyed HE educators in Hungary. Leaving the safety of one's own classroom and entering the alien territory of a company probably represents a change of roles and loss of control, which might lead to a shocking experience. The expectation that an in-company ESP teacher should tolerate that clients want value for money means taking on the role of a businessperson or of a service provider (Kennedy and Bolitho 1984), which is not easy for teachers used to the role of a classroom authority and a respected source of knowledge. Teachers' beliefs are mostly shaped by their experiences during school years (Falus 2006) when most probably their teachers took on the traditional classroom-authority and knowledge-source roles. Even after years of orienting towards new roles, like the facilitator, the earlier ingrained roles still influence ESP teachers practicing nowadays. At the same time, ESP teachers might also be influenced by their notions of their expected roles, i.e., what they assume that their students expect from them. Trying to meet this assumed expectation (assigned identity) causes attitude problems and a sense of inadequacy for ESP teachers.

The comparison of teachers' roles in general, language teachers', and ESP teachers' roles has shown that most ESP teachers' roles are not new to teachers. At the same time, the roles are extended in the case of ESP teachers compared to both other types of teachers. Several of these extensions mean an increased demand on ESP teachers that not all teachers are ready to face.

3.4 Role diversification of ESP teachers

A closer look at the literature reveals an abundance of ESP teachers' roles reflected in the numerous terms used referring to the teacher and, in many cases, instead of the teacher as illustrated in Table 2.1 and 2.2 below. The tables contain sources that elaborate on the role of the ESP teacher; only the new roles are listed that arise besides language teaching. As some sources deal with only one type of ESP teachers, BE teachers exclusively, these sources appear in a separate table.

The first look at the references to the teacher in ESP literature shows that most sources use various alternative terms to refer to the person providing instruction; there are only six sources that confine to the word *teacher* (Ghafournia and Sabet 2014, Kennedy and Bolitho 1984, Bell 2002, Szilágyi and Szőke 2007, Sándor 2017, Rachayon 2020). The other denominations might refer to diverse points of view. Some authors wish to emphasize that the tasks of an ESP teacher are more numerous than those of a teacher. Dudley-Evans and St John claim that they "use the term 'practitioner' rather than 'teacher' to emphasize that ESP work involves much more than teaching. We see the ESP practitioner as having five key roles: teacher, course designer and materials provider, collaborator, researcher, evaluator" (1998, 13). Bell expresses a similar view: "[i]n ESP, much more than in EGP, the traditional roles of teachers and students are often changed, with teachers no longer being perceived as the undisputed holders of all the knowledge" (2002, 2). This determines the new role of the teacher as collaborator. Both these sources use the word teacher in its restricted meaning referring to a knowledge transmitter.

Table 2.1: Role diversification of ESP teachers

Year	Authors	Reference to LSP/ESP teacher	Role
1984	Kennedy and Bolitho	teacher	• service provider, counsellor, collaborator with subject specialist
1987	Hutchinson and Waters	ESP teacher, ESP practitioner	• materials writer, syllabus designer, analyst, collaborator, negotiator
1993	Teemant, Varga, and Heltai	language teacher, instructor	• facilitator, situation and needs analyst, materials writer, selector and adaptor, discourse analyst, syllabus designer
1997	Dudley-Evans	LSP/ESP teacher	• in learner- or learning-focused classes—same as in a GE class • in HE team-teaching—intermediary between students and subject teacher • in other subject-specific classes—source of information on language matters
1998	Dudley-Evans and St. John	ESP professionals (qualified) and EBP practitioners (not qualified)	• teacher, coach, consultant, advisor • provider of input and activities—facilitator, intermediary between student and subject specialist, collaborator with specialists, course designer, materials provider, researcher, evaluator
2002	Bell	teacher	• willing to show interest, collaborator with students
2003	Kurtán	language teacher also teaching LSP	• intermediary between education and the world of work, needs analyzer • transformer: transforms needs analysis results into learning processes, sets aims and requirements, selects content • course materials developer: regularly upgrades elements of LSP training process, monitors LSP developments • integrator: cooperates with stakeholders, integrates general vocational and LSP learning, e.g., through CLIL, motivating to learn the vocation through LSP training • motivates students to use the language • can analyze language use of specialists in professional situations • course progress evaluator
2004	Biri	ESP instructor, ESP practitioner	• refers to Dudley-Evans and St John's (1998) categories above
2007	Harding	ESP teacher, ESP practitioner	• language consultant • researcher: gathering and understanding ESP material • collaborator • evaluator: materials and course designer, test producer
2014	Ghafournia and Sabet	ESP teacher, ESP practitioner	• simultaneous teacher and counsellor, reinforces learners' inherent decision-making ability and autonomy • course designer, evaluator • adult educator, deals with learning problems, e.g., anxiety, embarrassment, lacking self-confidence • collaborator with content teachers to design syllabus • additional role: action-based researcher, theorizer
2020	Rachayon	teacher	• refers to Dudley-Evans and St John's (1998) ESP practitioner • additional role: discourse analyst

The variation in terminology may refer to the teacher's qualification; for instance, Dudley-Evans and St John (1998) refer to qualified teachers as *ESP professionals* and to unqualified teachers as *EBP practitioners*. The terminology may also refer to the teaching context; for instance; Teemant, Varga, and Heltai (1993) and Kurtán (2003) concentrate on secondary and tertiary education, i.e., school contexts, and use the terms *language teacher*, *teacher*, and *instructor*. In

BE, Ellis and Johnson (1994) opt for using the term *trainer* because training is used for what employees are provided within corporate contexts, and they want to avoid the term *teacher* with its negative connotations for businesspeople. They expressly take the view that a BE teacher is a company trainer and even add that BE teaching takes ideas from management training reflected in tasks involving problem solving, making decisions, and teambuilding. Nevertheless, they mention that English for General Business Purposes exists, and the learners often need to learn subject content together with language. A similar view regarding ESP appears on Mahendra's study (2020).

Donna (2000) uses the term *language trainer* synonymously and simultaneously with *language teachers, instructors,* and *consultants* reflecting the variation in the environment of BE instruction, which may be a company setting or a HE institution, or even private communication training. A similar differentiation is that of Frendo (2005). In his understanding, the term *teacher* refers to a person-oriented perspective; the teacher helps the student to learn a language for different purposes whereas the expressions *trainer, coach,* or *consultant* refer to job-oriented functions training students to behave linguistically and pragmatically in a specific way. It also seems relevant to mention Swales (1985, qtd. in Hutchinson and Waters 1987, 157) who refers to *ESP practitioners* rather than *ESP teachers*. This reference successfully combines the various context-specific terms above. Hutchinson and Waters (1978) and Harding (2007) use the terms ESP teacher and ESP practitioner simultaneously without the intention of differentiating contexts or other characteristics. Ghafournia and Sabet also use the terms ESP teacher and ESP practitioner simultaneously while pointing out that "ESP teachers have to take heavier responsibilities than EGP teachers" (2014, 7).

Table 2.2: Role diversification of BE teachers

1994	Ellis and Johnson	trainer	• skills developer mostly regarding language use, negotiator, provider of input and activities, facilitator, consultant, counsellor
2000	Donna	language trainer, language teachers, instructors, consultants	• in company teacher • teacher in HE institute • private communication training *call center/helpdesk* (not the author's term)
2004	Claypole et al.	contemporary BE teacher	• educator, entertainer, explainer
2005	Frendo	teacher, trainer coach, consultant	• person-oriented, helping learner to learn a language for different purposes, • job-oriented, training students to behave linguistically and pragmatically in a certain way
2007	Szilágyi and Szőke	teacher	• syllabus and materials writer, evaluator, learning partner
2017	Sándor	teacher	• language teacher, creates friendly classroom atmosphere, prepares for language exam

In most cases, however, the different terms reflect the different roles that teachers have to take on when dealing with ESP or BE. The basic roles of ESP teachers have been defined by Dudley-Evans and St John who differentiate *teacher as provider of input and activities* and *teacher as facilitator* (1998, 149). In the former role, the teacher provides information and controls the class and the activities. This role seems to match the traditional role of teachers and apparently most likely occurs in classes for pre-experience learners. The latter role, also called *teacher as consultant,* is somewhat more difficult to adopt for professionals used to the traditional function of teachers. In this scenario, the course content is a result of negotiation with the learners, and course materials are also often provided by them (Dudley-Evans and St John 1998). In some cases of this role, the teacher has comparatively little knowledge about the subject or content-related skills of the ESP course; rather the teacher organizes the information provided by the learners. In this role, the teacher, who might even work in a team with a subject specialist, serves as an intermediary between the learner and a specialist teacher. Ellis and Johnson (1994) take an analogous position when defining the roles of a BE trainer as skills developer mostly regarding language use, negotiator (with interested parties), provider of input and activities, facilitator, consultant, and counsellor.

The facilitator role also appears in Teemant, Varga, and Heltai (1993). Dudley-Evans and St John (1998) assert that the teacher as facilitator role is productive especially with learners with sophisticated and specified purposes, in other words, with job-experienced learners. As a conclusion, they advise that the teacher's approach should always be tailored to the learners' expectations as some learners might take to this approach whereas some might prefer the traditional teacher as input provider role. However, Bell (1999) does not seem to share the view that the teacher as facilitator role is practicable and claims that the need to use a dictionary to find the specific vocabulary puts the teacher into the same position as that of the students. There is a disagreement in the consulted sources as to how much background knowledge is expected from a BE teacher.

Dudley-Evans (1997) describes the roles of the LSP/ESP teacher in three situations that typically occur in HE. In learner- or learning-focused LSP classes where the class is like a GE class, the teacher's role is also the same as in a GE class. In HE team-teaching, a special learning situation where both a subject teacher and a language teacher are present, the language teacher works as an intermediary between the students and the subject teacher ensuring clarification of issues that might not have been comprehended and provides information on communication, academic lecture style, examination questions, etc. However, the author does not clarify how the two teachers collaborate in giving the class apart from stating that the subject teacher is present to provide information on subject-matter issues, which makes the LSP teacher's situation easier not having to deal with subject content issues. In other subject-specific classes, the language teacher acts as a source of information on language matters, like solving reading tasks, lexis, etc., whereas the students provide information on the subject content. In all three situations, what the language teacher needs is "a willingness to listen, to think on one's feet and an enjoyment of reacting quickly to problems as they emerge" (Dudley-Evans 1997, 61). These are summarized by the author as improvising skills. Nevertheless, there is no information regarding how to gain possession of these features. The latter two types of collaborative classes between subject and language teachers did not appear in the interview studies investigated.

When asked if they identify with the term BE teacher, 37.73% of the surveyed Hungarian HE educators agreed, 30.18% did not agree, 32.07% did not answer the question. Those who disagreed with the term indicated the following self-categorizations: most listed teacher or language teacher or English teacher giving their specializations; there was one mention of ESP teacher, one of a linguist, and one of freelancer intellectual, and those who had higher positions in the hierarchy listed them as, e.g., department head adding their subjects. It seems that broadly one-third of the surveyed teachers changed their claimed identity to BE teacher after years of teaching BE. At the same time, another third of the educators did not; they insisted on their initial GE teacher identity as the expression *teacher* is closely related to the learning facilitator role. This finding resembles Mahendra's study (2020) in which some of the interviewed ESP teaching staff retained their GE teacher identity, while one took on the role of materials designer and evaluator, thereby refraining from the teacher or ESP teacher identity. The remaining third was not clear about their identification with the given term; further investigation would be necessary to clarify the reasons.

Several studies also report that it is the learning facilitator role that emerges as the basis of HE ESP teachers' claimed identity (Bereczky 2009, Sándor 2017, Tao and Gao 2018), which is a basic language teacher's role. There are, however, signs that the identities assigned to teachers and the ones claimed by them are not in harmony. In Sándor's study, the interviewed teachers express that they feel a discrepancy between their claimed role as learning facilitators and the role assigned to them by students as providers of language-exam preparation. Similarly, Tao and Gao's interviewees found themselves fallen between two stools when facing the contradicting obligations of doing research on a topic imposed by their affiliated linguistics department on topics unrelated to the ESP course that they were teaching (2018). The 53 ESP educators surveyed in Hungary also expressed the cognitive dissonance they perceive in their professional roles, especially when they are obliged to carry out administrative tasks that they feel are out of the scope of language teachers, such as scrivener at dissertation defenses or evaluating students' descriptions of their placement in companies.

To sum up, most authors list similar functions: counsellor, collaborator, coach, consultant, facilitator, activity provider, needs analyst, course materials, and syllabus developer and selector. New roles also appear. For example, Claypole et al. (2004) refer to teachers as contemporary BE teachers who have three impressive functions: educator, entertainer, and explainer. Donna (2000) does not expressly use the all-embracing term *call center* or *helpdesk*, but implies a similar function when mentioning that students appreciate if teachers can easily be contacted and addressed with questions and problems at all times. The call center role also appeared in an interview with an ESP teacher working in HE (Bereczky 2009). The interviewed teacher called this role *the think tank of the school* since students approached him in connection with all kinds of issues from university Math to visa or personal issues, expecting him to be able to answer all questions. A similar role called *problem solver* is reported by Chang (2017, 84) who followed the identity-transition process of an EAP teacher to ESP teacher.

3.5 Changes in roles

While studying the roles that the references to ESP/BE teachers have conveyed in the past 34 years together with the roles identified in descriptions of ESP/BE teachers in 3.3 and 3.4, a tendency of diversification can be observed. On the one hand, there is a tendency to assign more and more roles to ESP/BE teachers. On the other hand, the assigned roles themselves diversify. The diversification can be illustrated in the following three areas.

In the area of planning, teachers are expected to write tasks first, then writing course materials, followed by syllabus design, discourse analysis, needs analysis, evaluation of materials, evaluation and selection of teaching methodology. In the end, this planning role turns into a researcher role where the teacher constantly keeps up to date with development in his or her specialization field, analyzes authentic materials, and even gains a second degree in the specialism.

A relevant aspect of planning is the time spent on it. Hutchinson and Waters (1987) point out an extension of the materials writer role. They state that, unlike in GE teaching, much of the ESP teacher's time is occupied by materials writing. This is the result of three scenarios. The first is when the institution wants to provide teaching materials to fit students' specific subject area, and such materials are not available commercially. The second is when buying available materials is not viable due to currency or import restrictions. The third scenario has to do with marketing rather than education; the aim is to enhance the reputation of the institution. Based on experience, two additions could be made to the list. Recently, writing electronic teaching materials has become widespread either with or without technical help from the institution, and the last case is when neither the institution nor the students wish to spend on course materials, thereby hindering the teachers' work. Teachers then feel compelled to solve the problem on their own. Hutchinson and Waters (1987) regard the above situations as an abuse of teachers as few teachers have had any training in the skills and techniques of materials writing. They say that it is unreasonable to imply that if one can teach, one is also able to produce course materials. They end their reasoning with these words: "How many actors are expected to write their own plays …" (Hutchinson and Waters 1987, 106).

The collaborator role also becomes increasingly extended. It is not only the students who ESP/BE teachers need to cooperate with as learning partners but with all interested parties, like department heads, sponsors, language school or public education staff and leaders, as well as subject specialists, ESP or BE colleagues in departments, ESP/BE teachers and other subject teachers in various forms of team-teaching, materials providers such as publishers, subject teachers to provide relevant authentic materials for secondary or tertiary students, and company staff or chambers of commerce or industry to obtain relevant authentic corporate documents. In addition, the student takes on a new role to collaborate with—the source of knowledge. All these roles reflect the fact that the ESP/BE educator is in a heavily dependent situation. The utmost extension of the collaborator role is the call center or problem solver role when the teacher can be addressed at any time regarding any issue. At the same time, the collaborator role with corporate students is controversial. Harding (2007) relates a story when his students were reluctant to share virtually any information about their jobs or specialisms.

Several authors propagate collaboration with a subject specialist or at least consulting one. Dudley-Evans and St John (1998) describe the learning situation in which the language teacher works in a team with a subject specialist as an intermediary between the students and the subject content; however, it is not clear which teacher gives the class or whether they give the class together. The intermediary role suggests that it is the subject teacher who gives the class, and the language teacher is present to give help if needed. In this situation, however, it is not clear what happens in the language teacher's classes or how the team-taught classes can be recorded for workload-assessment purposes. In the public education field, collaboration is suggested by Kurtán (2003) on the grounds that the teacher with a humanities-based qualification needs a consultant. She also notes that collaboration for the subject specialist at the university level might mean a better sense of language use. An additional advantage of close collaboration with HE subject teachers is mentioned by Bell

(2002). He states that it decreases the intimidation that subject teachers feel lest ESP teachers trespass on their territory. In such cases the choice of specialist is critical since the available or most knowledgeable specialist may not be as useful as a sympathetic one. Ideally, the cooperation should be a two-way process: the specialist helps the teacher in learning more about the learners' target situation whereas the ESP teacher can make the subject specialist more aware of the language problems students and ESP teachers encounter. Out of the 53 surveyed ESP educators in Hungary, 68% clearly stated that they rarely or never had an opportunity to collaborate with subject teachers because subject teachers were not willing to take part in collaboration. The personal comments about what to change regarding cooperation with subject teachers show that ESP teachers are open to consulting subject teachers; 92.85% wished they had at least some contact with the vocational teachers. The comments on the above question in the survey make it clear that the relationship is bad. "Language teachers are 'second class citizens' in a business college ..." (1769863) or "They [subject teachers] should first get off their high horses and begin treating their colleagues in ESP departments with some respect" (2741971). A similarly low status of ESP teachers was reported by Tao and Gao (2018) in the Chinese HE context. The situation has not improved much over more than thirty years compared to the lack of contact between language and vocational teachers reported by Johns in 1981.

The requirement to possess more and more professional or business skills can also be deduced from the descriptions. Being able to tolerate the fact that the teacher is a service provider also takes a skill, but negotiating is definitely a business skill that appears from the earliest descriptions on. Various areas of skill development are added to the list through the years: presentations, meetings, negotiations, business writing skills, interpersonal skills, communication and intercultural communication skills. Finally, especially for BE teachers, the list of requirements is extended to becoming a businessperson who has an overview of business processes, understanding of the business environment and multinational corporate culture, business-like attitude, business-like appearance, flexibility, and even business experience. This person is not a teacher anymore but a consultant or a coach.

3.6 Niche in role descriptions

Authors agree (Hutchinson and Waters 1987, Kurtán 2004, Szilágyi and Szőke 2007) that a distinctive characteristic of ESP is the sensitivity to the target situation which is connected to learners' job-related tasks. Additionally, Harding (2007, 6) underlines the fact that this practical application prevails over other aspects of language learning. Dudley-Evans (1997) also notes that ESP is often constrained by time limits and is meant for adult learners. This latter characteristic leads to the problem that ESP taught in secondary or tertiary education does not fit the adult learning category although the age of the students would indicate adult education methods at least to some extent. Also, Teaching English as a Foreign Language (TEFL) training does not usually contain adult learning considerations; thus, teachers might not be aware of the methodology of adult education. In fact, the differing age of ESP learners compared to GE learners is listed as one of the main difficulties facing ESP teacher trainees by Ewer (1983).

Although all the consulted sources differentiate between or refer to English for General Business Purposes (EGBP) and English for Specific Business Purposes (ESBP) learners and mention that ESBP learners come to the classroom with specific and explicit expectations as to the content and outcome of the ESP course and, sometimes, even as to the methodology applied; only three sources use the term "adult learners" (Dudley-Evans 1997, Dudley-Evans and St John 1998, Donna 2000). Writers on BE emphasize that the aims of the BE course *always* relate to students' work. BE students' language needs are often immediate and urgent, and they even present tasks meant for adult learners. Still, a similarly explicit treatment of adult teaching methods is missing. While GE teaching acknowledges that adult learners are a distinct group, ESP teaching does not treat adults separately from other age groups (Sifakis 2003). It is only in the mid-2010s that references to the adult learning context start to appear in ESP research and methodology (e.g., Ghafournia and Sabet 2014).

There are two consequences of this niche. The first is that GE teachers approaching ESP and preparing from the above sources are not made aware of the fact that many features they face and fear in ESP education (such as losing control, accountability, the cost effectiveness orientation, having to meet urgent practical needs, the learning partner, call center and counsellor roles, etc.) are simply consequences of dealing with adult learners. In fact, these factors are known as elements of the adult educator role (Kraiciné Szokoly 2006). As andragogy is not a typical part of TEFL training, GE teachers cannot be expected to recognize or tackle the above factors.

Sifakis (2003) suggests that on the basis of common characteristics of adult and pre-adult learners, an integrative model should be adopted for ESP curriculum design by making the ESP learner an active participant in decision-making based on their experience regarding learning, defining aims, syllabus, and lesson planning especially for Computer-Assisted Language Learning (CALL) programs. In this framework, the students function as learners/participants and the teacher takes on the additional role of studying methods counsellor.

Another consequence is that the differences between adult and pre-adult learners, i.e., job-experienced learners and students in tertiary education, not to mention secondary education, are not usually treated within the same source. Authors usually concentrate on one type of learner, possibly mention that there exist other types of learners but often fail to emphasize that the teacher's roles, the tasks, and preparation suggestions they mention apply only to one type of learner or situation, the one they had in mind when writing their book or article. In many cases, readers are not informed about to which learner type or teaching context the author refers. Sources for BE teachers tend to focus on in-company settings. A teacher who prepared from such sources will be surprised to find markedly different expectations manifested by HE students as to the role of the teacher in the classroom tending perhaps towards the more traditional source of knowledge and attitude. Similarly, a teacher who encountered a source describing the HE scenario only might be surprised to find no subject-specialist advice available when working for a language school, though that was recommended as a necessary element of ESP teacher preparation for classes. There seems to be an obvious need for clarifying the teacher's role towards the different types of learners in terms of age, vocational knowledge, and work experience as well as outlining strategies for the teacher to handle the frequent changes between contexts if the same practitioner teaches pre-experience and job-experienced learners.

Conclusion

To sum up, investigation into the assigned identity of ESP teachers found that most sources use the word *teacher* when referring to ESP/BE education in a school context, especially the HE context. The only exception seems to be Bell (1999) who uses *EAP teacher, EAP trainer,* and *EAP instructor* without differentiating them. The sources that use differing terms intend to refer to the different contexts teachers work in or their differing expertise in teaching skills or subject content. The terms similar to the ones used by professionals in a given field to denote people providing instruction for job-experienced learners (for example *trainer, coach,* or *consultant*) reflect the wish of integration into that profession. Comparing the roles of ESP/BE teachers over the past 34 years, it can be seen that both qualitative and quantitative changes have occurred. More and more roles must be assumed by ESP teachers, and the roles also diversify. The diversification of roles is the most salient in three areas: planning, collaboration, and professional or business skills. The fact that sources about ESP teachers' preparation do not usually clarify whether they focus on corporate or tertiary education students only escalates the possibility of teachers facing complicated and unexpected teaching scenarios, thus contributing to their feeling of inadequacy. Also, the perspective of adult education is, to a large extent, missing from ESP professional literature though it could significantly contribute to making ESP classes more manageable.

Regarding educators' claimed identities, the variety of role descriptions in the literature reflects a similar variability in the surveyed HE ESP teachers' role identification. Identification with the term BE teacher was found in one-third of the cases whereas another third kept their GE teacher identity. Also, one-third of the educators was not able to verbalize their claimed identity apart from not agreeing with the term BE teacher. Whether this non-identification with the BE teacher role is a consequence of retaining the GE teacher identity or dissenting from the BE teacher role or of other factors is the subject of further research.

The transition process from the GE teacher to the ESP teacher raises the question of identity crisis as well. Many GE teachers believe that they are unprepared to tackle technical texts. Still, most of the sources of literature contemporaneously deny the need for deep professional knowledge or extra science degrees for ESP/BE teachers. In this case, ESP/BE teachers' claimed and assigned identities seem to be clashing, which gives grounds for hypothesizing that an identity crisis or at least identity reorganization might occur when a GE teacher specializes in teaching LSP similarly to the one found by Chang (2017). The survey results point to an emerging cognitive dissonance between the assigned and claimed identities of teachers in the field of ESP. The difference between ESP teachers' assigned identity, which appears in the literature in the form of various other terms used instead of the teacher, like trainer, consultant, etc., and the identity claimed by teachers themselves, i.e., the learning facilitator, is a sign of the cognitive dissonance that ESP practitioners experience. Another sign of the crisis is the discrepancy in teacher versus exam preparation roles seen by the teachers in Sándor's study (2019) and between the roles of educator versus administrator perceived by the surveyed HE educators in Hungary. It seems that the difficulty to cope with the diversity of expectations as to ESP teachers' roles mentioned in the literature in Section 1 above has been confirmed by empirical studies (see, e.g., Tao and Gao 2018).

Certainly, more investigations are needed to map the claimed identities of ESP educators in HE so as to get a comprehensive picture of language teaching and learning. For investigating the professional identity, the analysis of teachers' narratives (Chang 2017) appears to be a method that potentially provides ample information on the contexts for ESP teachers' work as well as one that discloses their professional "private universe" through reflecting on their experiences.

References

Bell, Doug. 2002. "Help! I've Been Asked to Teach a Class on ESP." *IATEFL Issues* 169. http://www.esp-world.info/!encyclopaedia/IATEFL%20Issues%20169%20-%20Help!%20I've%20been%20asked%20to%20teach%20a%20class%20on%20ESP.htm.

Bell, Timothy. 1999. "Do EAP Teachers Require Knowledge of Their Students' Specialist Academic Subjects?" *Internet TESL Journal* 5 (10). http://iteslj.org/Articles/Bell-EAPRequireKnowledge.html.

Bereczky, Klára. 2009. "The Identity of the Business English Teacher." In *University of Pécs Roundtable 2008, Empirical Studies in English Applied Linguistics*, edited by Marianne Nikolov and József Horváth, 83–98. Pécs: Lingua Franca Csoport.

Biri, Andrew G. 2004. "The Challenges of Eurospeak in ESP." In *Angol szaknyelv a felsőoktatásban* [ESP in Higher Education], edited by Katalin Vargáné Kiss, 33–38. Győr: Széchenyi István Egyetem, Gazdság-és Társadalomtudományi Intézet.

Buzzelli, Cary A., and Bill Johnston. 2002. *The Moral Dimensions of Teaching: Language, Power, and Culture in Classroom Interaction*. New York: Routledge Falmer.

Carver, Charles S., and Michael F. Scheier. 2017. *Perspectives on Personality*. Eighth edition. New York: Pearson Education Limited.

Chang, Karen Ch. 2017. "From EAP to ESP: A Teacher's Identity Development." *Taiwan Journal of TESOL*, 14 (2):71–100. https://eric.ed.gov/?id=EJ1171158.

Claypole, Maurice, Ann Claypole, Cornelia Kreis-Meyer, and Karen Richardson. 2004. "HalPet—What Makes a Contemporary Business English Teacher?" *IATEFL/BESIG Business Issues* 2: 18–19.

Csizér, Kata, and Judit Kormos. 2007. "Az angol nyelvtanulási motiváció alakulása Budapesten tanuló egyetemisták és főiskolások körében [Language Learning Motivation among Students in Tertiary Education in Budapest]." *Magyar Pedagógia* 107 (1): 29–43.

Donna, S. 2000. *Teach Business English*. Cambridge: Cambridge University Press.

Dörnyei, Zoltán. 2002. *Questionnaires in Second Language Research*. Hillsdale, N. J.: Lawrence Erlbaum.

Dörnyei, Zoltán, and Tim Murphey. 2003. *Group Dynamics in the Language Classroom*. Cambridge: Cambridge University Press.

Dudley-Evans, Tony. 1997. "Five Questions for LSP Teacher Training". In *Teacher Education for Languages for Specific Purposes*, edited by Ron Howard and Gillian Brown, 58–67. Clevedon: Multilingual Matters.

Dudley-Evans, Tony, and Maggie J. St John. 1998. *Developments in ESP*. Cambridge: Cambridge University Press.

Ellis, Mark, and Christine Johnson. 1994. *Teaching Business English*. Oxford: Oxford University Press.

Ewer, J. R. 1983. "Teacher training for EST: Problems and methods," *The ESP Journal* 2 (1): 9–31. https://doi.org/10.1016/0272-2380(83)90007-0.

Falus, Iván. 2006. *A tanári tevékenység és a pedagógusképzés új útjai* [New Ways of Teacher Activity and Teacher Education]. Budapest: Gondolat Kiadó.

Fóris, Ágota, Anna Kováts, and Péter Póla. 2003. "Nyelvi és szaknyelvi oktatás egy felmérés tükrében [Language Teaching for General and Specific Purposes Reflected in a Survey]." In *Nyelvek és kultúrák találkozása* [The Juncture of Languages and Cultures], edited by Szergej Tóth, 161–66. Szeged: Szegedi Tudományegyetem Juhász Gyula Tanárképző Főiskolai Kar Alkalmazott Nyelvészeti Tanszék.

Freeman, Donald, and Karen E. Johnson. 1998. "Reconceptualising the Knowledge-Base of Language Teacher Education." *TESOL Quarterly* 32: 397–417. https://www.jstor.org/stable/3588114.

Frendo, Evan. 2008. *How to Teach Business English.* Fourth edition. Harlow: Pearson Education.

Ghafournia, Narjes, and Shokoofeh Ahmadian Sabet. 2014. "The Most Prominent Roles of an ESP Teacher." *International Education Studies* 7 (11): 1–9.

Gu, Mingyue, and Phil Benson. 2015. "The Formation of English Teacher Identities: A Cross-cultural Investigation." *Language Teaching Research* 9 (2): 187–206.

Harding, Keith. 2007. *English for Specific Purposes.* Oxford: Oxford University Press.

Harmer, Jeremy. 1991. *The Practice of English Language Teaching.* Harlow: Pearson Education.

Hutchinson, Tom, and Allan Waters. 1987. *English for Specific Purposes.* Cambridge: Cambridge University Press.

Johns, Tim. 1981. "Some Problems of a World-Wide Profession." *ELT documents: The ESP Teacher, Role, Development and Prospects* 112: 16–22.

Kennedy, Chris. 1983. "ESP Approach to EFL/ESL Teacher Training." *ESP Journal* 2:73–85.

Kennedy, Chris, and Rod Bolitho. 1984. *English for Specific Purposes.* London: Macmillan Press.

Korthagen, Fred A. J. 2004. "In Search of the Essence of a Good Teacher: Towards a More Holistic Approach in Teacher Education." *Teaching and Teacher Education* 20: 77–97. https://doi.org/10.1016/j.tate.2003.10.002.

Kotschy, Beáta, ed. 1996. *A tanár szerepe és a tanárképzés: Közép-kelet-európai áttekintés* [The Role of the Teacher and Teacher Education: Central and Eastern European Review]. Budapest: Eötvös Loránd Tudományegyetem, Neveléstudományi Intézet.

Kraiciné Szokoly, Mária. 2006. *Pedagógus-andragógus szerepek és kompetenciák az ezredfordulón* [Educator-Andragogue Roles and Competences at the Turn of the Millennium]. Budapest: ELTE Eötvös Kiadó.

Kubanyiova, Magdalena, and Graham Crookes. 2016. "Re-visioning the Roles, Tasks, and Contribution of Language Teachers in the Multilingual Era of Language Education Research and Practice." *The Modern Language Journal* 100: 117–18.

Kurtán, Zsuzsa. 2003. *Szakmai nyelvhasználat* [Language Use for Specific Purposes]. Budapest: Nemzeti Tankönyvkiadó.

Kurtán, Zsuzsa. 2004. "Cultural Aspects of Professional Language Competence." In *Angol szaknyelv a felsőoktatásban* [English for Specific Purposes in Higher Education], edited by Katalin Vargáné Kiss, 9–20. Győr: Széchenyi István Egyetem, Gazdaság-és Társadalomtudományi Intézet.

Mahendra, Aloisius Wisnu. 2020. "Constructing Identity: Experiences of Indonesian ESP Teachers in a Language Institute." *English Language Teaching Educational Journal* 3 (3): 229–40.

Mocanu, Mihaela. 1996. "Conference Contribution on Changing Teacher Roles." In *A tanár szerepe és a tanárképzés: Közép-kelet-európai áttekintés* [The Role of the Teacher and Teacher Education: Central and Eastern European Review], edited by Beáta Kotschy, 29–31. Budapest: Eötvös Loránd Tudományegyetem, Neveléstudományi Intézet.

Nikolov, Marianne. 2007. "A magyarországi nyelvoktatás-fejlesztési politika— nyelvoktatásunk a nemzetközi trendek tükrében [The Language Teaching Development Policy—Hungarian Language Education Reflected in International Trends]." In *Fókuszban a nyelvtanulás* [Language Learning in Focus], edited by Irén Vágó. Budapest: Oktatáskutató és Fejlesztő Intézet. https://ofi.oh.gov. hu/tudastar/fokuszban-nyelvtanulas/nikolov-marianne.

Nikolov, Marianne, and Enikő Öveges. 2009. "An Exploratory Study of Vocational Schools' Self-Assessment." In *UPRT 2008: Empirical Studies in English Applied Linguistics,* edited by Réka Lugossy, József Horváth, and Marianne Nikolov, 13–28. Pécs: Lingua Franca Csoport.

Norton, Bonny 1997. "Language, Identity and the Ownership of English." *TESOL Quarterly* 31 (3): 409–428.

Oxford, Rebecca L., Stephen Tomlinson, Ana Barcelos, Cassandra Harrington, Roberta Z. Lavine, Amany Saleh, and Ana Longhini. 1998. "Clashing Metaphors about Classroom Teachers: Toward a Systematic Typology for the Language Teaching Field." *System* 26: 3–50.

Palmer, Juan C., and Santiago Posteguillo. 1997. "A Teacher Training Approach to a Degree in English Philology: Implementing TESP." In *Teacher Education for Languages for Specific Purposes,* edited by Ron Howard and Gillian Brown, 202–09. Clevedon: Multilingual Matters.

Rachayon, Suphatha. 2020. "A Language Teacher in the ESP Classroom: Can We be a Successful Dweller in This Strange and Uncharted Land?" *English Language Teaching* 13 (9): 119–124. https://doi.org/10.5539/elt.v13n9p119.

Richards, Jack C. 2008. "Second Language Teacher Education Today." *Regional Language Centre Journal* 39 (2): 158–177. https://doi.org/10.1177/003368820 8092182.

Richards, Jack C., and Theodore. S. Rodgers. 1986. *Approaches and Methods in Language Teaching.* Cambridge: Cambridge University Press.

Richards, Keith. 1997. "Teachers for Specific Purposes." In *Teacher Education for Languages for Specific Purposes,* edited by Ron Howard and Gillian Brown, 115–126. Clevedon: Multilingual Matters.

Sándor, Eszter. 2017. "Business English Teachers' Perceptions of Their Professional Role in a Hungarian Business School." *Working Papers in Language Pedagogy* 11: 1–20.

Sifakis, Nicos C. 2003. "Applying the Adult Education Framework to ESP Curriculum Development: An Integrative Model." *English for Specific Purposes* 22: 195–211.

Szilágyi, Anikó, and Andrea Szőke. 2007. *1 tanár + 1 diák: 1 könyv azoknak, akik üzleti nyelvet tanítanak magánúton* [1 Teacher + 1 Student: 1 Book for Those who Teach Languages for Business Purposes to Private Students]. Budapest: Nemzeti Tankönyvkiadó.

Tao, Jian, and Xuesong Gao. 2018. "Identity Constructions of ESP Teachers in a Chinese University." *English for Specific Purposes* 49: 1–13.

Tarrou, Anne-Lise H. 1996. "Introductory Conference Presentation." In *A tanár szerepe és a tanárképzés: Közép-kelet-európai áttekintés* [The Role of the Teacher and Teacher Education: Central and Eastern European review], edited by Beáta Kotschy, 11–16. Budapest: Eötvös Loránd Tudományegyetem, Neveléstudományi Intézet.

Teemant, Annela, Zsófia Varga, and Pál Heltai. 1993. *Hungary's Nationwide Needs Analysis of Vocationally-Oriented Foreign Language Learning: Student, Teacher, and Business Community Perspectives.* Budapest: Hungarian Ministry of Culture and Education, Hungarian Ministry of Labour, United States Information Agency, Council of Europe Modern Languages Project Group.

Van Dijk, Teun A. 1998. *Ideology: A Multidisciplinary Approach.* London: Sage Publications.

Woods, Devon. 1996. *Teacher Cognition in Language Teaching: Beliefs, Decision-Making and Classroom Practice.* Cambridge: Cambridge University Press.

Appendix 2.1

QUESTIONNAIRE FOR TEACHERS OF ENGLISH FOR BUSINESS/ECONOMICS IN HIGHER EDUCATION

Text version of the online questionnaire; only the questions relevant for this study are shown.

I. Basic data (12 questions)

1. Your age
    - 18–30 years
    - 31–40 years
    - 41–50 years
    - 51–60 years
    - 61–70 years
    - 71–80 years

2. Are you a native, non-native, or a near native teacher?
    - native teacher
    - non-native teacher
    - near native teacher (lived in an English-speaking country for a long time)

3. How many years teaching experience do you have? (Any subject, maternity leave excluded.)
    - 1–2 years
    - 3–5 years
    - 5–10 years
    - more than 10 years

4. Please select from the list the ESP field(s) that you have taught any time in the past ten years and write in the number of years that you taught the subject. If you have taught other business-related ESP fields, please write down the name of the field as well.

	YEARS
English for Accounting	
English for Auditing	
English for Banking	
English for Business	
English for Controlling	
English for Customs	
English for Economics	
English for Finance	
English for Foreign Trade	
English for Freightforwarding	

English for Insurance	
English for Logistics	
English for Management	
English for Marketing	
English for the Stock Exchange	
English for Taxation	
English for Trade	
Presentation Skills	
Other:	

5. If you have taught other subjects than business English (i.e., the subjects listed above), please write here the subject(s). If you have taught other subjects, in what language(s) have you taught them?

6. Do you have any work experience other than teaching ESP including teaching other subjects or various fields of economics and management? If so, in which field(s)? (You may mark several options.)
    - I do not have any other work experience.
    - sole proprietorship
    - member of partnership or ltd
    - accounting
    - banking office work
    - secretarial activities
    - multi-level marketing (MLM) / network marketing
    - translating
    - interpreting
    - teaching other subjects / other (please specify)

7. Please mark the types of school or course where you teach. (You may mark several options.)
    - university/college
    - secondary school
    - language school
    - private classes
    - other (please specify)

8. Where do you teach or have you taught business English? (You may mark several options; Higher Level Vocational Training is included in higher education.)
    - higher education
    - secondary education
    - language school
    - private classes
    - other (please specify)

9. Is your relationship with your business English students the same as your relationship with your students learning general English?
    - Yes
    - No
    If not, can you describe the difference?

10. What kind of relationship do you have with vocational subject teachers, for example with teachers of Economics, Finance, etc. in your school?
    - Good. We have regular consultations I feel free to contact them regarding my queries.
    - Average. We have consultations sometimes; they are not too happy if I ask professional questions.
    - Not very good. We rarely have consultations; I would rather not ask them professional questions.
    - I have no contact with them.
    If you want to change the relationship, what would you change in it?

11. What is your perceived status in your school compared to subject teachers?
    - better
    - the same
    - worse
    How do you relate to this situation?

12. Have you ever had the feeling that at the university or college where you teach or have taught, business English classes are at a disadvantage compared to other subjects? For instance, they are scheduled at a less advantageous time slot than other subjects such as Friday afternoon, last class of the day, blocks of classes, etc.
    - Yes
    - No
    - No answer
    How do you relate to this situation?

II. Positive and negative aspects of teaching business English (9 questions)

III. How did you start teaching business English? (12 questions)

22. When you started teaching business English, did you have work experience from any other field (including teaching other subjects and various fields of economy/business)? If so, in which field(s)? You may mark several options.
    - I did not have any other work experience.
    - sole proprietorship / self-employed
    - member of partnership or ltd
    - accounting
    - banking

- secretarial activities
- multi-level marketing (MLM) network marketing
- translation
- interpreting
- teaching general English
- other (please specify)

25. What ideas did you have about teaching business English before starting to teach it?
    - It seemed interesting.
    - It seemed frightening.
    - I had no idea.
    - other (please specify)

26. Have you ever felt isolated as a business English teacher? If so, what were the reasons for that? (You may mark several options.)
    - I have never felt isolated.
    - As a part-time teacher I do not / did not know the other teachers.
    - Language teachers are/were not regarded as subject teachers here.
    - I am/was the only language teacher in the institution.

27. Have you ever felt that you would need another degree/qualification to teach business English? If so, what course would you benefit / would you have benefited from?
    - I have never felt so.
    - testing
    - business correspondence
    - presentation skills
    - economics or finance
    - teaching English
    - teaching English for specific purposes
    - other (please specify)

28. What other help would you have needed when you started teaching business English?

29. What sources have you used for self-development for business English teaching purposes? (You may mark several options.)
    - professional books / higher education coursebooks related to the field in English
    - professional books / higher education coursebooks related to the field in Hungarian
    - secondary school coursebooks related to the field in English
    - secondary school coursebooks related to the field in Hungarian
    - printed general dictionaries
    - printed professional dictionaries

- business/economic magazines
- articles on teaching business English
- professional books on teaching business English
- further training on teaching business English
- Internet-based forums on teaching business English
- Internet-based general dictionaries and/or encyclopedias, e.g., Wikipedia
- Internet-based professional dictionaries
- consulting with language teaching colleagues
- consulting with colleagues teaching vocational subjects
- consulting with business experts
- consulting with my students who work in business
- further training in the field, e.g., marketing
- working for a company

30. Which source from the ones marked above for question 29 did you find the most useful? Please mark only one.

31. How did you feel in the first business English class you taught? What made you feel so?

32. Could you describe your memories about the first business English course you taught?
    - Was it a company, higher education, secondary education, or private class?
    - What level was the group?
    - Was it a positive or a negative experience? What made you feel so?

33a. Did you feel unsure about anything when you taught your first business English classes?

33b. If so, what were you unsure about?

33c. Have you become more self-confident since then?

33d. How long did you need to teach with more self-confidence after the first business English class you taught?

IV. The process of becoming a business English teacher (10 questions)

V. Courses and qualifications (17 questions)

44a. Please mark your qualifications (language, teaching, and economic/business or any other as well). (You may mark several options.)
    - BEd or BA in teaching English
    - MA in English Language and Literature
    - Trinity College London's CertTESOL
    - CELTA

- DELTA
- RSA
- Postgraduate Certificate in Education (PGCE) in EFL
- BSc or MSc in Economics
- MSc in Economics with a specialization in teaching Economics
- I have no degree yet.
- other (please specify)

45. Have you attended any courses related to English for business or teaching English for business?
    - Yes, as part of my higher education studies.
    - Yes, as further training after my higher education studies.
    - I have not attended such a course.

46a. Please mark the further education courses that you have participated in and the main contents as far as you can recall.

A Certificate in Teaching English for business (LCCI CerTEB)	
B (Mérei Ferenc) Pedagogical Institute, Budapest – Business English and Communication	
C (Mérei Ferenc) Pedagogical Institute, Budapest – Advanced Business English and Communication	
D translation and interpretation course	
E teaching economic vocational subjects in English	
F teaching ESP – specialization for university graduates with economic degrees within the university	
G other 1	
H other 2	
I other 3	

I have participated.		psychology	
testing and evaluation		selecting coursebooks	
sample tasks		vocabulary	
preparing/writing tasks		curriculum design	
Internet-based sources		negotiation skills	
methodology		solving and practicing business English tasks	
language practice		business English task types	
Pedagogy		business English topics	
presentation		differentiating and defining general and business English business approach	

46b. If there was anything else you learned at the courses marked above and is missing in the list, please write it here giving the letter of the course.

46c. Please write here how many lessons the courses you marked above at
      question 46a involved.

a	b	c	d	e	f	g	h	i

46d. Please write here the letters of the above courses that were intensive
      courses.

46e. Please mark how useful the courses you marked above at question 46a
      were for you (1= useless, 5= very useful).
      • 1—2—3—4—5

47.   What were the most important positive aspects of the above courses
      (question 46a) for you? (To ease filling in you can find the same list here).

A Certificate in Teaching English for business (LCCI CerTEB)	
B (Mérei Ferenc) Pedagogical Institute, Budapest – Business English and Communication	
C (Mérei Ferenc) Pedagogical Institute, Budapest – Advanced Business English and Communication	
D translation and interpretation course	
E teaching economic vocational subjects in English	
F teaching ESP – specialization for university graduates with economic degrees within the university	
G other 1	
H other 2	
I other 3	

general orientation in the field of business English		dealing with unknown words and areas	
building confidence		involving students in interpreting professional content	
familiarizing with business topics		other (please specify	

48.   If you attended a course on teaching business English, was the course
      before you first started teaching business English? Please mark only
      one option.
      • First, I attended a course on teaching business English and
        started teaching business English only after the course.
      • First, I started teaching business English and attended a course
        on teaching business English only after that.
      • I attended a course on teaching business English and started
        teaching business English at the same time.
      • I have not attended a course on teaching business English.

59.   Do you consider yourself a business English teacher?
- Yes
- No

If not, how would you define your profession?

60.   Anything else you would like to say about the topic or this questionnaire?

CHAPTER 3

Being a legal alien: Inspecting the (in)accessibility of specific professional communities to LSP teachers

Martina Vránová

Brno University of Technology, Czech Republic

Abstract

Languages for specific purposes as a discipline has been defined by its purposes and goals as student-centered, communication-oriented, task-based and multidisciplinary. What is usually left out is the agents who initiate and carry out all these characteristics to a successful goal—the LSP teachers. In order to be effective agents of language teaching, LSP teachers have to have thorough knowledge of and familiarity with the target-language community. Nevertheless, specific professional communities are exclusive and deny or at least complicate entrance to outsiders. This paper inspects the hard times LSP teachers may have fully participating in the academic community of their university, as their academic identity is compromised by not doing strategic research and teaching a tool not content, and also the superhuman efforts they have to make to get in touch with the target community of professionals whose language they teach. LSP teachers thus resemble legal aliens whose sense of not belonging where they should complicates their roles as academics, authoritative experts, cooperators, researchers, ethnographers, and materials providers, among others.

Keywords: LSP teachers' identity, LSP teachers' roles, LSP teacher training, specific language communities, needs analysis

***

Introduction

Languages for specific purposes (LSP) as a discipline has correctly been defined by its purposes and goals as student-centered, communication-oriented, task-based, and multidisciplinary (see e.g., Belcher, Johns, and Paltridge 2011; Paltridge and Starfield 2013; Colpaert, Aerts, and Oberhofer 2015; Tual, Geslin, and Rinder 2016). What this characterization implies, but is very frequently left unmentioned, is that all these purposes and goals are reached only if the proper agents take them up and carry them out to successful fulfillment. These agents being, of course, LSP teachers.

Some effort to draft the LSP/ESP teacher's roles was undertaken quite early by now traditional studies. Notoriously well-known is that by Dudley-Evans and St John (1998), who distinguish the role of those who teach LSP/ESP into teacher, course designer and materials provider, collaborator, researcher, and evaluator, showing that the role is, indeed, multifaceted. On top of that, they also propose the term LSP/ESP "practitioner" rather than "teacher" "to emphasize that ESP work involves much more than teaching" (1998, 13). What I intend to show in this paper is that I find this naming rather confusing, as it is exactly the "practice" to which LSP teachers have the least and the most difficult access. It seems more logical, in my view, to use the term LSP practitioner for the person who uses a second language for communication in his or her professional life.

In order to be effective agents, LSP teachers have to have a thorough knowledge of and familiarity with the target-language community for which they prepare their students. Nevertheless, it is exactly these specific professional communities that are exclusive, even secretive, and that inherently deny or at least complicate access to outsiders. Informed by my long-term experience with teaching ESP at several higher-education (HE) institutions in the Czech Republic, I will inspect the hard times LSP teachers may have fully participating in the academic community of their university, as their academic identity is compromised by not doing strategic research and teaching a tool (language) not content (subject matter), and also the superhuman efforts they have to make to get in touch with the target community of professionals whose language they teach. The outcome is that LSP teachers may be compared to legal aliens: they exist on the outer brink of their university's academic community. Such a position necessarily complicates the LSP teachers' roles as academics, authoritative experts, cooperators, researchers, ethnographers, and materials providers, among others.

1 Incomplete pre-service education

Even though I was not an English teaching major, I took a teacher-training course during my university studies (around the turn of the millennium) which, nevertheless, never even mentioned the concept of ESP. The focus was methodology of general English. Later the English program I had originally attended[1] got extended to include a separate English methodology option, but the general language focus stayed the same as the primary goal was preparation for secondary-school teaching. My personal narrative has remained a standard situation. In the Czech Republic, there is no specialized pre-service study program of ESP or LSP. The result is not only the unpreparedness of future LSP teachers but also the undermining of LSP as an independent discipline. LSP teachers are left on their own to become experts in an area they cannot study. They are, first of all, denied a contact with other LSP teachers in pre-service study which hinders their further development.

As Dressen-Hammouda correctly notes, the rise of LSP is concurrent with the social turn "in language and literacy studies, which considers that language use cannot be properly described and understood outside its context of social use" (2013, 501). Language has been studied in close connection to the situations in which it manifests itself, to communities where it is used, to social values and cultural artifacts which it transmits and constructs. Speaking a language, not talking about teaching it, means an immersion into the target-language community and culture. By a lack of specific pre-service training, students of LSP are denied a natural entrance into their own professional community, easy group assimilation, sharing the same language (learning the language of LSP which is also specific in its purpose), and the necessary university networking that commonly establishes lifelong relationships. The inexperience with one's own professional community may result in a long search for one's own identity as a professional.

Yet the lack of LSP training has further, more serious consequences. By not understanding what teaching LSP really involves, it usually gets reduced to the question of vocabulary and content. Helen Basturkmen in her overview of the topic finds that "[a]lthough the literature on teacher education in LSP is not extensive, a number of themes can be identified. There has been discussion of the role of specialized knowledge in LSP teacher education […] and strategies teachers can use to compensate for gaps in their subject knowledge" (2014, 21). My experience confirms the fact that general language teachers, students, and also the general public, usually think that LSP only requires specialist vocabulary. Dang, Webb, and Coxhead confirm that "[t]here are a small number of high-frequency words (around 2,000 items) (e.g. *think, alright, important*) that cover from 70% to 90% of the words in different kinds of texts (e.g. newspapers, general conversation, TV programs, and academic texts)" (2022, 618). This small number of high-frequency words give rise to either

---

[1] English Language and Literature program at Faculty of Arts, Masaryk University, Brno, Czech Republic.

underestimation or overestimation of the role of specialized vocabulary in LSP. On the one hand, some general language methodology students rush into teaching LSP without any warning of what it involves as they assume they will only memorize a few new words and rely for the rest on their general language studies as most vocabulary is that of the high-frequency kind. On the other hand, LSP is feared by lots of others who assume that one has to be a subject-matter expert to teach the language required for it. Both extreme views are also probably caused by the fact that LSP serves an infinite number of disciplines. This could be amended by introducing LSP as a true discipline with a pre-service study apparatus and clear community infrastructure.

2 Compromised academic identity

The primary position of the university as a center of pure research has been changing for at least the last 50 years. Where post-World-War-II universities could have been boasting of academic excellence, raising specialists, and leadership in pure research, many HE institutions nowadays concentrate on carrying out strategic research demanded by the industry and educating professionals who will never have anything to do with research as such. The split between strictly academic goals, on the one hand, and business-like or national economic interests, on the other, has a serious impact on the self-perception of academics and the academia itself. The ongoing fragmentation of university purposes, goals, and services breaks down the once so solid image of an academic as a subject expert who educated future subject experts and was involved in research (Briggs 2005, 258). This fragmentation is reflected in an ever-increasing number of roles the HE teacher should assume.

The university environment has been changing to catch up with the demands of national, European, or even global economic policies and to cope with reduced public funding. The once independent institution, sometimes perceived as self-enclosed in its own pure research and education of subject experts continuing this highly esteemed academic endeavor, has become preoccupied with the generation of income (Henkel 2005, 159). Starting in Western Europe in the late 1970s but not missing the former Eastern Bloc by the turn of the millennium, the trend of adopting managerial structures and mechanisms has caught up with most HE institutions—rationalization, performance, priority setting, and strategic research being the catchphrases (Henkel 2005, 159). Facing the challenge of academic independence, universities have become increasingly dependent on cooperation with and thus sponsorship from the industry and on educating higher numbers of non-specialist students primarily in bachelor studies. The stress on meeting demands—may they be political, economic, industrial, or public—has had a negative effect on academic autonomy and on the stable academic identity which HE institutions once offered their faculty (Henkel 2005, 155). Should academics be primarily researchers, publishing authors, industry consultants, information and human resources managers, teachers of the masses, or educators of specialists?

Elkington and Lawrence resonate with this situation in their apt observation that academics nowadays are required to teach beyond their skills and knowledge: "they teach subjects and genres different from those subjects in which they have expertise or which relate to their research" (2012, 52). The authors' study also reveals that true academics should be both subject specialists, having subject-matter knowledge, and teaching specialists, having teaching experience and mastering the methodology of their subject (Elkington and Lawrence 2012, 54). Such an ideal is rather infrequent. Due to the increasing attempts to attract wider studentship which will bring the necessary income, many HE teachers find themselves teaching subjects on which they are not experts. This decentralization of expert knowledge in practical academic life causes both intra-personal and inter-personal tensions: "Our findings not only suggest that HE teachers derive their sense of identity as academics firstly from the subject they teach, but the added expectation of teaching unfamiliar subjects often leads to feelings of uncertainty. Teaching unfamiliar subjects was also often perceived negatively in terms of professional identity" (Elkington and Lawrence 2012, 56). Those who teach what they know are necessarily perceived as more valuable than others.

If subject specialists are insecure about themselves as academics since their subject matter is the foundation stone of their identity, what should be said of LSP teachers as academics? Language teachers starting their employment at a university feel anxiety on the doorstep. They do have a methodological background and pedagogical knowledge, which is in the Czech Republic not required of subject specialists, but their subject matter expertise seems compromised right from the beginning. LSP teachers do not teach science as such; they do not teach linguistics or cultural studies. They teach an instrument which, when mastered, only mediates the real science. Such a view of language teaching in HE is acknowledged by Tual, Geslin, and Rinder when they say that LSP "has long been perceived as an 'add-on' [...], therefore relegating it to an anecdotal position" (2016, n.p.). Additionally, the instrument has to be practiced on a subject matter in which the LSP teachers are not only non-specialists but utter amateurs. If an academic's identity is firmly grounded in the knowledge of his or her discipline, then an LSP teacher's academic identity is shaken in its foundations.

The contemporary university, as Henkel asserts (2005, 163), is a complex organizational structure reaching out into external cooperation, thus creating an ambiguous network of relationships, which leads to increasingly fragmented views of what it is to be an academic. Yet it is curious how the fragmentation of roles diminishing the once central role of the seat of knowledge production makes the universities of today react in such a way as to accentuate the lack of the role which is being taken away from them. Logic dictates that those academics bringing the most financial resources to departments will be the most valued ones. Of course, such money usually comes from strategic research (winning grants or being commissioned by industry). This is also reflected in the evaluation of academic staff and researchers where pure research or teaching are the most neglected items. In Brno University of Technology's system of internal evaluation in the area of educational and research activities, the lowest score (0) is given to unscheduled classes, the next lowest score to scheduled seminars (2), and the highest score (80) to a patent or development of tested technology, both financially profitable items (2022).[2]

What profitable activities can an LSP teacher or a university language department engage in? It is not totally unfeasible to do research in LSP, as the current publication proves, yet the volume of research is rather limited, most of it being of practical nature informing the teaching practice itself. The probability of strategic research is next to zero. It is teaching that LSP departments excel in including thorough methodological grounding.

The question of undervalued teaching or how to balance teaching and research has been bothering many HE teachers. As Elkington and Lawrence elicited from their academic interviewees, "[t]here's a dichotomy in the department [...] there's research active people and non-research active people, and if you're seen to be research-active then by extension you are more specialist in your teaching. But that is an ideal few achieve because as a department so few of us now have the opportunity to do any meaningful research" (2012, 57). If this is the concern of a marketing specialist, the LSP teacher should start panicking. Being seen as primarily teaching practitioners lowers their status as academics. Can LSP teachers ever become full-fledged members of academia?

3 Shattered expert authority

"The ESP teacher, for the most part, does not in any straightforward sense conform to the image of a knower," wrote Early in the early days of studying LSP (qtd. in Basturkmen 2014, 22). The status of being "only teachers," not subject-matter specialists and researchers, diminishes the LSP teachers' authority in the eyes of both their expert colleagues from other university departments and their students. Luo and Garner acknowledge the perceived

---

[2] The necessity to introduce this internal evaluation was given by the Czech Higher Education Act (2021). The actual form of evaluation is, however, developed by each university.

lower academic status by saying that for some subject teachers "English language teaching is not a discipline" and also provide observations from other studies in which English teachers "expressed their concern about losing their disciplinary identity [and] frequently find themselves in a subservient relationship" (2017, 83). LSP teachers' identity as academics is threatened not only in relation to the university as an institution but also in relationships with human subjects constituting the academic community. Johns examines academia as an example of high culture and states that "cultural membership requires a long and often arduous initiation. A person cannot become a member of a university faculty without completing the necessary rites and rituals required. Professionals must not only be educated (correctly!), but they must serve long internships within their professions. Thus [...] community membership is exclusive and restricted" (1994, 4–5). The hardships connected with teaching a tool, not content, are evident: LSP teachers do not fit into the university or faculty community primarily because they did not undergo the arduous education and professional practice that science or technology subject teachers and students do.

The question of how much subject-matter knowledge the LSP teacher should possess has been an everlasting topic of discussion. Unarguably, an LSP teacher educated both in language and the target discipline is a great advantage. Yet such an ideal, balancing both the subject and the language tool, is hard to find. An interesting view, and a very relevant one, of the discipline-connected knowledge was adopted by Ferguson in distinguishing specialized knowledge from specialist knowledge which "is usually taken to refer to knowledge of the content of the student's discipline or subject" (1997, 84). Specialized knowledge, on the other hand, involves a knowledge of disciplinary cultures and values, of the epistemological basis of various disciplines and of genre and discourse typical for those disciplines (Ferguson 1997, 85). Genre analysis and discourse studies are definitely part of linguistic education, theories of knowledge production should be the basis of any education in humanities, and the sociological focus on a particular disciplinary culture could be, at least partially, provided by the LSP teachers' participation in the academic community. Even though not without its problems, as I intend to show further on, it is this specialized knowledge that LSP teachers should possess, rather than thorough specialist knowledge.

Even though the LSP teacher assumes "the role of a 'consultant,' not a 'font of all wisdom'" (Dudley-Evans and St John 1998, 189), the issue of specialist knowledge persists. Let us leave the question of "how much" aside and rather consider the question of "how to get it" when needed. Notoriously well-known is the recommendation to consult subject specialists and also use them in teaching in the three forms of cooperation, collaboration, and team-teaching

(Dudley-Evans and St John 1998, 42–48). Cooperation in the form of asking for advice is hardly ever a problem, but when it comes to collaboration on course design, not much collaboration can be expected from subject specialists unless they share the stakes involved. Why waste knowledge and resources on something that will not be profitable to myself or will not advance my academic carrier? On top of that, the low reputation of teaching, as opposed to the research mentioned above, hinders this kind of collaboration, making the subject specialists often deny help so that they can concentrate on their own valuable strategic research. Team-teaching may be effective only on condition that all teachers are interested in the common project. One of the most important advantages of team-teaching is that students "become aware of the direct relationship that English has for their subjects of study" and that they develop higher order skills (Barron 1992, 8). On the other hand, team-teaching is also "time consuming and very demanding on organisational or management skills" and it "can be particularly disastrous if one member of the team has an agenda that differs from the goals the team has determined" (Barron 1992, 9).

What to do when collaboration or team-teaching are not an option? The specific community to turn to are the students themselves. The imperative is that the LSP teacher "must acknowledge and use the learners' greater knowledge of the carrier content" (Dudley-Evans and St John 1998, 189). The incorporation of student-generated content definitely empowers students, as it gives them an active role in shaping their own knowledge. It "allows teachers to bring student experiences and voices into the centre of the community of practice [...] and acknowledges the importance of their prior experience" (Snowball and McKenna 2017, 605). Yet it is exactly the level of learners' greater knowledge and the quality of student-generated content that presents a variable worth considering.

Students with more expert knowledge, such as master-degree students or doctoral candidates, have thorough grounding in their field and their own resources (laboratory reports, bachelor and master theses, presentations, etc.) to offer for language classes. Hloušková, in her report on innovative approaches adopted at the University of Pardubice, Czech Republic, advocates for simulated student conferences and poster sessions (2014). Also, with more expertise comes more understanding of the fact that their language teacher's knowledge lies somewhere else. Thus, students are more open to cooperation to achieve a shared goal, e.g., producing a research paper in English. Such a cooperation is, indeed, based on a working partnership of two groups of experts exchanging information on an equal level.

Nevertheless, the situation may be quite different with pre-service students who may have very limited specialist knowledge. First-year bachelor-degree students bring their secondary-school attitudes into the class, which is not surprising as they are only entering the academic community and learning the different styles of conduct and relationships. They have a prominent tendency to view the teacher as an authority on the content (just like their secondary-school general language teachers were authorities on the culture of the foreign language countries) and may be disappointed with the sudden lack of teacher-to-student knowledge transmission. With such pre-service students, establishing the rapport of cooperation is a real challenge for the LSP teacher. Nevertheless, the rise of Web 2.0 has enabled LSP teachers to incorporate student blogs, wikis, or podcasts in the learning process (Wheeler, Yeomans, and Wheeler 2008). Starting on the level of popular science, students may produce short input into a particular topic (presentations, wordlists, written explanations, commentaries on visual material, etc.) which can then be collaboratively expanded either in class or through wiki or forum modules. Shifting the responsibility for content to students may help them adopt new roles as producers, commentators, and classifiers (Wheeler, Yeomans, and Wheeler 2008, 988), thus partake in the university's essential function—critical knowledge creation (Snowball and McKenna 2017, 608). Yet this effort also brings tangible rewards and immense satisfaction to the LSP teacher as it is the students, the ones with whom the teacher is in the most frequent contact, that let him or her into the community of their discipline much more easily, probably because they are also only entering it. Students may become the ushers. And for the sake of getting more knowledge, LSP teachers should not be afraid of admitting their ignorance and losing a little authority in order to gain it somewhere else.

4 Desperate ethnographer

Undervaluing real-life communication in a specific professional community does not pay, which is a fact of which LSP teachers and theoreticians are well aware. As Huckin and Olsen note if, for example, "technical people cannot communicate to others what they are doing and why it is important, it is they and their excellent *technical* skills that will be superfluous. From this perspective, communication skills are not just handy; they are critical tools for success, even survival, in 'real-world' environments" (1991, 3). For this reason, studying and subsequently teaching the nature of communication specific to a particular language community has become one of the primary concerns in LSP. Inspecting *New Directions in English for Specific Purposes Research* yields a realization that the majority of current research is concerned with materials development, corpus studies, genre analysis, and discourse analysis (Belcher, Johns, and Paltridge 2011). This gigantic endeavor is, of course, motivated by an honest attempt to teach those communication skills the students will actually need and use.

In some areas of LSP, e.g., business, academic, or medical English, the teachers' situation is easier than in others as there is an enormous variety of textbooks from which they can choose; yet "they can rarely base an entire course on them as is sometimes possible in general language teaching" (Basturkmen 2014, 19). This is, indeed, true in my own practice where courses developed by me, two on technical writing and three on academic English for mechanical engineers, are a compilation of materials from an immense number of sources put together in order to suit just those mechanical engineering students that I teach. The question of why LSP is so demanding in course design can be answered by emphasizing its local character. As Belcher states, "unlike many other educational practices, ESP assumes that the problems are unique to specific learners in specific contexts and thus can be carefully delineated and addressed with tailored-to-fit instruction" (2006, 135). This focus on the specific, particular, and local language context makes course design and materials development rather problematic.

This is, however, not to say that attempts to come up with a solidification and focus on the global character of a specific discipline are not worth pursuing or inspecting. The current Global Engineers Language Skills (GELS) project is grounded in arguing that in the globalized world, working environments "transcend national, cultural, and linguistic borders" (Rinder, Geslin, and Tual 2016, n.p.). The GELS team's goal is to identify the "most useful communication skills used required by engineers working in industry" all over the world, to map "these requirements against the skills and proficiency levels (A1–C1) of the Council of Europe's CEFR" from which a specific GELS framework will be formed, and finally to provide "a bank of progressive teaching and learning resources that prepare students for the particular demands of working in the field of engineering" (Rinder, Geslin, and Tual 2016, n.p.). Another project, completed and ready to use, is the Global Scale of English (GSE) which also extends the CEFR into language-level descriptions for professional communication purposes. GSE provides Job Profiles "created using job descriptions from the O*NET database compiled by the United States Bureau of Labor Statistics [...]. Each task in a job description was mapped to the Global Scale of English Learning Objectives for Professional Learners to identify the linguistic skills that someone would need to master in order to carry out that task in English" (*Global Scale of English Learning Objectives for Professional English* 2018, 7). Together with a teacher toolkit, this is definitely a great resource but still a resource open for selection (unless the teacher simply settles for Pearson textbooks informed by this project). A responsible ESP teacher will still use these resources selectively, choosing those learning objectives and activities that he or she considers really specific for his or her students of a particular discipline in a particular country. Even though our world is getting more and more globalized, it does not get unified. Globalization is necessarily accompanied by localization. Where some ends meet in a single one, others particularize and disperse to suit just one linguistic task and one cultural context.

Determining specific language needs of their particular group of students is an everyday, mundane research activity for all LSP teachers. Thus the first step is usually the needs analysis which is defined by Brown as the "systematic collection and analysis of all subjective and objective information necessary to define and validate defensible curriculum purposes that satisfy the language learning requirements of students within the context of particular institutions" (1995, 36). In a later publication, Brown elaborates on his definition so as to include three vital concepts: (1) stakeholders (e.g., teachers, students, administrators); (2) a defensible curriculum that "satisfies most of the language learning and teaching requirements of the students and teachers within the context of the particular institution(s) in such a way that it can be successfully defended to and accepted by all stakeholder groups"; (3) necessary information including "all types of quantitative and qualitative information from all relevant stakeholder groups" (2016, 4). Understandingly, one starts with identifying the stakeholders who will work as primary informants for the needs analysis, which was also the course of action I took for my own short research survey in order to get more information to design, expand, and ameliorate English courses at the Faculty of Mechanical Engineering, Brno University of Technology. The primary group of stakeholders was the students themselves, particularly those in bachelor and master programs who train for "real-world" professional careers in industry (disregarding doctoral students mostly pursuing academic careers for now) and the Faculty's graduates' most important employers. In the spring semester of 2019, both of these groups were given questionnaires. A total of 100 Czech and Slovak students completed an online version of the questionnaire.[3] All years in both bachelor's and master's degrees were represented. I used a yearly job fair to personally circulate a questionnaire to HR representatives of 62 employers. This job fair is frequented by both national and international companies with branches in the Czech and Slovak Republic (for composition of survey participants, see Figure 3.1).

---

[3] The questionnaire was in the Czech language, which means that only Czech and Slovak students (who study in Czech) could fill it out.

Figure 3.1: Composition of BUT mechanical engineering students
and employers taking part in the survey

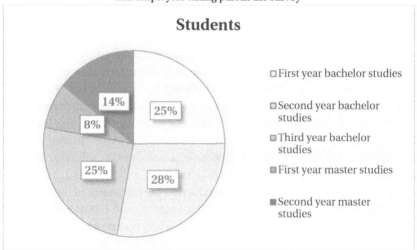

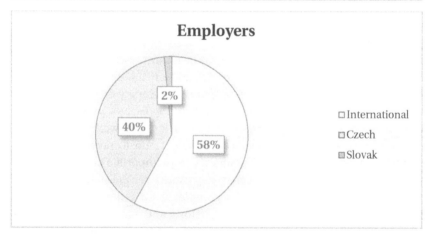

This survey has revealed four very significant realizations. Results for students raise an important question of motivation to learn languages—89% consider language learning an important part of their university education. Nevertheless, 73% study languages to increase their employability, and 86% study languages to have better opportunities in their future lives in general (such as better traveling opportunities and watching films in the vernacular). Thus, teaching LSP must be supplemented with teaching general language, which is in agreement with the Faculty's Institute of Foreign Languages' policy to teach languages for both specific and general purposes. Balancing technical and general language skills was reflected in the fact that 58% of employers require knowledge of technical language at job interviews but 42% do not. This rather leveled ratio may mean that employers consider knowledge of general language primary and technical language a kind of superstructure supported by the general language. The significance of both general and technical language is supported by 68% of employers who provide further language education in both areas of skills.

Figure 3.2: A comparison of students' predictions and information from employers about the range of communicative activities at work in a foreign language

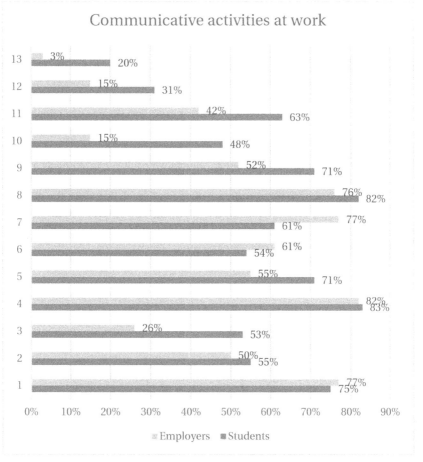

Activities: 1 making phone calls, 2 meeting participation, 3 presenting, 4 writing informal emails, 5 writing formal correspondence, 6 giving or following instructions, 7 reading general language texts, 8 reading short technical reports, 9 reading long technical documentation, 10 reading research papers, 11 writing short technical reports, 12 writing long technical documentation, 13 writing research papers.

The second realization is that LSP should not only concentrate on communication as such but specifically on immediate dialogic forms of communication. In skills, students primarily felt they needed more extensive practice in listening and speaking. When predicting foreign language activities in their future jobs (Figure 3.2), they thought these would mainly be composed of telephone conversations, both informal and formal correspondence (e-mails), and reading short technical texts (each getting more than 70%). Students were also aware of the fact that they would communicate in a foreign language with other business stakeholders—in their view, mostly with suppliers and customers (Figure 3.3). According to their open comments, they missed "conversation-targeted" courses or opportunities to speak with a native speaker. The employer survey (Figure 3.3) showed that students were correct that they would mostly communicate with suppliers and customers but underestimated the international team environment, as employers also said that over 70% of communication would be among colleagues. The most frequent communication activities, according to employers, are telephoning, informal e-mail writing, reading technical documentation (regardless of length) and, interestingly, reading research papers (Figure 3.2). They also commented on the need to equip graduates with a level of language suitable for everyday communication, to teach students not to be afraid to speak and make mistakes, and to focus more on conversation. This proves the necessity to master dialogic communication with an immediate purpose both in formal and informal registers.

Figure 3.3: A comparison of students' predictions and information from employers about who employees communicate with in a foreign language

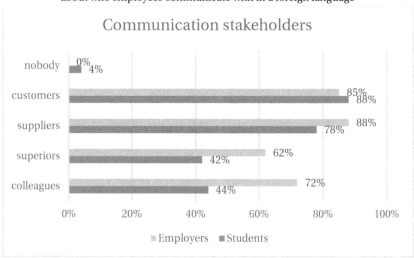

Another outcome of the survey throws light on the current state of needs analysis in the Czech HE. What is worth pondering upon is the significant discrepancies between students' predictions and information from employers. Where students accentuated the skill of delivering presentations (53%), employers rated this activity much lower (26%). Conversely, students' predictions about writing texts in their future jobs were quite low, unlike the information from employers (Figure 3.2). This contrast may be caused by the usual practice in university LSP classes. When the professional aspect of language is concentrated on, students are required to give presentations on their research areas or interests. This by itself is an appropriate way to activate students and involve them in the learning activity (see discussion above). Nevertheless, it may also give them the not quite correct impression that presenting (prepared frontal activity) will also be one of the major activities in their jobs. For this reason, any presentation by students must also involve well-thought-out follow-up activities, such as discussions, group tasks, or collecting wordlists, to shift the focus from the monologic presentation to dialogic communication. Practicing writing skills is a notorious weak spot at Czech universities. Even though there are seminars for writing bachelor's and master's theses, their level and content differ greatly. They are also organized by the specific departments' academic staff, not language teachers, thus focusing more on conducting research than writing about it. In language courses, writing activities are usually considered an "adjunct" and assigned as homework, as they are rather time consuming. The results of my survey, however, call for a radical reassessment of students' needs so as to include reporting as a major skill to be trained in LSP courses.

My last realization does not concern the results or content of the survey but rather the form. In comments from students, there were none involving the meaning of questions asked, no expressions of uncertainty about whether the students chose the proper item or suggestions about what else should be included in the questionnaire. When circulating the questionnaire to HR specialists personally, however, I was asked lots of questions and received various comments. The HR people expressed, for example, the variability of jobs where B1 English is sufficient for a designer, but a project engineer needs a B2 level. They also reflected on changes in the work environment where a replacement in leadership (from a Czech team leader to a foreign one) may totally change the list of language skills and their proportions from one day to another. One HR specialist was unable to answer the question about communication with business stakeholders and composition of language activities and skills in a technician's job as she admitted she did not have access to the actual practice; she was only involved in hiring and administrative personnel procedures. The reason for such a discrepancy between the informant groups may be twofold. First, it can be assumed that I know my faculty's students much better than employers, as I have everyday contact with them. I am familiar with their reasoning, student life, and study problems, which is also the reason why I was able to construct more appropriate or fitting questions. The other reason for the high number of questions and comments from employer representatives is the personal contact while administering the questionnaire. The HR specialists simply used the opportunity of me being present and asked, commented, and expressed concerns. Both of these explanations, however, illustrate the necessity of an LSP teacher's inclusion into the target-language community and the importance of ethnographic research.

Naturally, a needs analysis cannot be equaled with a simple questionnaire. Necessary information "should be gathered using a variety of complementary methods (e.g., interviews, surveys, document analysis, focus groups). Underlying this information-gathering process is the need for the results to be valid and representative of the actual needs" (Trace, Hudson, and Brown 2015, 8). The necessity of applying a whole range of complementary methods which will yield a holistic picture of a particular discourse community is another reason for ethnographic, or rather ethnography-inspired research (not to pretend that LSP teachers can master full-blown ethnographies). Conducting ethnography-inspired research in the actual industry would provide invaluable information to be incorporated into LSP teaching practice at the university level. Doubly so, as the results would not only be linguistic skills, a collection of relevant texts, and a creation of discipline-specific corpus, but also realizations of "unspoken assumptions of social life" in a particular professional community (Davies 2001, 135). These unspoken assumptions or "generalised behaviour patterns, constructed through a cognitive network of norms, beliefs, and events" are what make up a culture of a particular discourse community (Boswood and Marriott 1994, 6). A discourse community is described by Swales as having "common goals, participatory mechanisms, information exchange, community specific genres, a highly specialized terminology and a high level of expertise" (1990, 29). Also, Boswood and Marriott stress that the LSP teacher "must be confident of mediating to learners the culture of the target community" (1994, 7). Where else should one gain such confidence than in actual knowledge of the target-language community? A particular engineering company culture would be a good example (or even a case study) of a discourse community culture.

The problem of conducting such ethnography-inspired research is at least twofold. The first concerns methodology. Hardly any LSP teacher is educated to convey such research. LSP teachers view themselves as mostly practitioners who want to teach; their focus is pedagogical. Even if some are interested in linguistic research, in their pre-service education they were not prepared for the fact that they will have to be experts in applied linguistic research methods or ethnography as such. The other problem is the one dealt with on various levels in this chapter. It is the target-language community admission. Being exclusive, the target-language community will typically view an LSP researcher as an outsider. Moreover, nowadays engineering (and other industrial branches too) focuses on protecting their industrial and intellectual property. Non-disclosure agreements and the GDPR policy have become a necessary pre-requisite to any negotiation. In theory, contacting a company and asking to do interviews with some of their employees can be done, but being present at meetings or video conferences with the head office representatives, reading e-mails to suppliers, recording negotiations with customers, or observing a discussion over a technological issue are out of the question. Ethnographers distinguish an etic (outsider) view of a community and an emic (insider) view. Under the above-mentioned conditions, not even the etic approach is feasible. There could be a chance of getting a second-hand emic perspective, even though not without its problems. In the fall of 2018, my colleagues and I intended to compile an English corpus for engineering. The primary problem to solve was how to get the texts. The technical documentation freely available is of an outdated kind, norms and standards can be requested only personally from a national agency, and academic databases have safeguards preventing bulk downloads. There were only two options left. One was to deal only with papers from open-access academic journals, which was only one area we wanted to cover, disregarding the fact that the reputation of such journals would have to be thoroughly checked. The other was to identify a company willing to cooperate on text collection, which could be done with the help of the public relations and industry cooperation departments of the university. However, then a company's employee responsible for choosing such materials would have to be appointed (question remaining by whom). This individual would have to be instructed on what kind of texts the research team finds relevant and would, of course, select those not transgressing any intellectual property or delete the restricted information. This step in itself calls the validity of such research into question. Moreover, this person would have to be motivated to cooperate, ideally by a financial incentive.

A way out?

The purpose of this chapter has not been to paint a gloomy picture and spread despair among LSP teachers. Rather, it has been to address some obstacles they will face in their professional lives. They will find themselves in a complicated position when accessing various professional communities. There is no avoiding it for, as Trace notes, in "most LSP contexts, the culture of the community seems almost as important to learn as the linguistic content itself" (2015, 276). They will have to overcome their insecurity about being true academics and disregard their limited ability to contribute to the university's income maximization. They will have to invest an immense effort in their work in order to elevate the widely perceived subservient position of LSP to other university disciplines in order to prove they are authorities on what they teach. They will have to be aware of the fact that the uneasy access to target-language communities may have other negative impacts on their work than only those mentioned above. Materials adaptation will be tedious as the collected texts will not always be relevant and very often content overloaded. Assessment criteria will have to be reevaluated in order to be "indigenous" (Jacoby and McNamara 1999, 214) and test tasks will have to be authentic so that they ensure "the interaction between language knowledge and specific purpose content knowledge" (Douglas 2000, 2). To extend my analogy in the title, Superman was also a legal alien. It is time now LSP teachers transformed themselves from the asocial Clark Kent to the omnipotent Superman who can still stumble when the kryptonite of entering target-language communities gets into view. There are, however, ways to fight the numbing effects of this kryptonite. The easiest access to target-language communities is provided by LSP teachers' own students. Establishing a relationship of cooperation will definitely prove invaluable. The other option is networking within the LSP community. Probably as the lack of pre-service training is painfully felt by LSP teachers, there are numerous opportunities of further development in forms of national and international associations, conferences, training sessions, and publications, which are places and events for sharing experience, strategies, and resources.

References

Barron, Colin. 1992. "Cultural Syntonicity: Co-operative Relationships between the ESP Unit and Other Departments." *Hong Kong Papers in Linguistics and Language Teaching* 15: 1–14.

Basturkmen, Helen. 2014. "LSP Teacher Education: Review of Literature and Suggestions for the Research Agenda." *Ibérica* 28: 17–34.

Belcher, Diane Dewhurst. 2006. "English for Specific Purposes: Teaching to the Perceived Needs and Imagined Futures in Worlds of Work, Study and Everyday Life." *TESOL Quarterly* 40: 133–56.

Belcher, Diane Dewhurst, Ann M. Johns, and Brian Paltridge (eds.). 2011. *New Directions in English for Specific Purposes Research*. Ann Arbor: University of Michigan Press.

Boswood, Tim, and Alison Marriott. 1994. "Ethnography for Specific Purposes: Teaching and Training in Parallel." *English for Specific Purposes* 13 (1): 3–21.

Briggs, Senga. 2005. "Changing Roles and Competencies of Academics." *Active Learning in Higher Education* 6 (3): 256–68.

Brno University of Technology. 2022. "Metodika hodnocení—SHAP 2022 [Instructions for Evaluation—Internal Evaluation of Academic Staff and Researchers]". https://www.vut.cz/intra/hodnoceni/metodika-hodnoceni/125.

Brown, James Dean. 1995. *The Elements of Language Curriculum: A Systematic Approach to Program Development*. New York: Heinle & Heinle.

Brown, James Dean. 2016. *Introducing Needs Analysis and English for Specific Purposes*. New York: Routledge.

Colpaert, Jozef, Ann Aerts, and Margret Oberhofer (eds.). 2015. *Task Design & CALL: Proceedings*. Seventh International CALL Conference, Tarragona, Spain, July 6–8, 2015. Antwerpen: Universiteit Antwerpen.

Dang, Thi Ngoc Yen, Stuart Webb, and Averil Coxhead. 2022. "Evaluating Lists of High-Frequency Words: Teachers' and Learners' Perspectives." *Language Teaching Research* 26 (4): 617–41. https://doi.org/10.1177/1362168820911189.

Davies, Alan. 2001. "The Logic of Testing Languages for Specific Purposes." *Language Testing* 18 (2): 133–47.

Douglas, Dan. 2000. *Assessing Languages for Specific Purposes*. Cambridge: Cambridge University Press.

Dressen-Hammouda, Dacia. 2013. "Ethnographic Approaches to ESP Research." In *The Handbook of English for Specific Purposes*, edited by Brian Paltridge and Sue Starfield, 501–17. Madden: Wiley Blackwell.

Dudley-Evans, Tony, and Maggie Jo St John. 1998. *Developments in English for Specific Purposes: A Multi-disciplinary Approach*. Cambridge: Cambridge University Press.

Elkington, Sam, and Lesley Lawrence. 2012. "Non-specialism and Shifting Academic Identities: A Sign of the Times?" *Innovations in Education and Teaching International* 49 (1): 51–61.

Ferguson, Gibson. 1997. "Teacher Education and LSP: The Role of Specialised Knowledge." In *Teacher Education for Languages for Specific Purposes*, edited by Ron Howard and Gillian Brown, 80–89. Clevedon: Multilingual Matters.

Global Scale of English Learning Objectives for Professional English. 2018. Pearson. Accessed September 1, 2020. https://online.flippingbook.com/view/272343/55/#zoom=z.

Henkel, Mary. 2005. "Academic Identity and Autonomy in a Changing Policy Environment." *Higher Education* 49: 155–76.

Hloušková, Jitka. 2014. "Innovations in LSP/LAP Courses in Postgraduate Programmes at the University of Pardubice." *UNICOM 2014*: 44–47. Conference UNICOM 2014, Pardubice, Czech Republic, June 9–11, 2014. https://jc.upce.cz/sites/default/binary_www_old/jc/unicom/metodika/tvorba-jaz-k/jaz-kur.pdf.

Huckin, Thomas N., and Leslie A. Olsen. 1991. *Technical Writing and Professional Communication: For Nonnative Speakers of English*. Second Revised Edition. New York: McGraw-Hill.

Jacoby, Sally, and Tim McNamara. 1999. "Locating Competence." *English for Specific Purposes* 18 (3): 213–41.

Johns, Ann M. 1994. "LSP and Culture: A Special Relationship." *ASp* 5–6: 1–10. https://doi.org/10.4000/asp.4002.

Luo, Jing, and Mark Garner. 2017. "The Challenges and Opportunities for English Teachers in Teaching ESP in China." *Journal of Language Teaching and Research* 8 (1): 81–86.

Paltridge, Brian, and Sue Starfield (eds.). 2013. *The Handbook of English for Specific Purposes*. Madden: Wiley Blackwell.

Rinder, Jamie, Teresa Sweeney Geslin, and David Tual. 2016. "A Framework for Language and Communication in the CDIO Syllabus." *Proceedings of the 12th International CDIO Conference*, Turku, Finland, June 12–16. http://cdio.org/node/5995.

Snowball, Jen D., and Sioux McKenna. 2017. "Student-Generated Content: An Approach to Harnessing the Power of Diversity in Higher Education." *Teaching in Higher Education* 22 (5): 604–18. https://doi.org/10.1080/13562517.2016.1273205.

Swales, John M. 1990. *Genre Analysis: English in Academic and Research Settings*. Cambridge: Cambridge University Press.

Trace, Jonathan. 2015. "Looking Ahead in Language for Specific Purposes." In *Developing Courses in Languages for Specific Purposes*, edited by Jonathan Trace, Thom Hudson, and James Dean Brown, 270–85. Honolulu: University of Hawaii. http://hdl.handle.net/10125/14573.

Trace, Jonathan, Thom Hudson, and James Dean Brown. 2015. "An Overview of Language for Specific Purposes." In *Developing Courses in Languages for Specific Purposes*, edited by Jonathan Trace, Thom Hudson, and James Dean Brown, 1–22. Honolulu: University of Hawaii. http://hdl.handle.net/10125/14573.

Tual, David, Teresa Geslin, and Jamie Rinder. 2016. "A Case for LSP." Paper presented at New Trends in Foreign Language Teaching, the PETALL International Conference, Granada, Spain, April 28–29.

Wheeler, Steve, Peter Yeomans, and Dawn Wheeler. 2008. "The Good, the Bad and the Wiki: Evaluating Student-Generated Content for Collaborative Learning." *British Journal of Educational Technology* 39 (6): 987–95. https://doi.org/10.1111/j.1467-8535.2007.00799.x.

CHAPTER 4

The role of LSP in demotivation and remotivation: The instructors' perspective

Viktória Lázár

Budapest Business School, University of Applied Sciences, Hungary

Abstract

The research conducted among language learners over the years has proved that the very nature of language learning motivation is unstable: motivation can easily turn to demotivation. However, not only learners but also teachers can provide valuable insights into language learners' motivation. The primary aim of this qualitative research was to present a group of LSP practitioners' views on the nature of their students' motivation. The secondary aim was to understand how teachers interpret the role of LSP in the motivation process. The research was conducted among 22 LSP practitioners of five languages (English, German, French, Italian, and Spanish), working at the same department responsible for teaching LSP and other language-related skills at a business university (Hungary). Semi-structured interviews were conducted, the responses were recorded, transcribed, and then coded with the RQDA software. The findings showed the curve of LSP students' motivation can turn from the initial motivation to demotivation, or from demotivation to remotivation. The responses also shed light on two important pedagogical situations LSP practitioners face: students start learning LSP without any discipline-specific knowledge, and if they do, then they are selective in doing classroom tasks. The research highlights the unique role LSP plays in students' remotivation by making students love their professions first.

Keywords: demotivaton, LSP needs, instrumental motivation, teacher identity, tertiary education

***

Introduction

This study presents the findings of the research conducted among Language for Specific Purposes (LSP) teachers in a Hungarian business university. The focus of this study is to add some useful insights into exploring the reasons why students lose their motivation by as early as the second year (Fűköh 2018). The research, however logical it may have been, was not conducted among the students but among the teachers.

The findings reveal that LSP practitioners[1] are aware of the processes of demotivation and remotivation among their students, but their interpretations and reactions are different. Motivating students is regarded by some practitioners as an integral part of their professional identity, but an impossible, Sisyphean task by others.

This study focuses on the different student motivational patterns LSP teachers identified during the interviews, on the roles teachers attributed to LSP in motivation, demotivation, and remotivation, and finally on how the practitioners see their own roles as motivators.

1 Literature review

1.1 Demotivation

Demotivation, the process when—partly or completely—individuals lose their interest in an already-started or still-planned activity due to external forces (Dörnyei and Ushioda 2011) is a common feature among language learners. There is a theoretical consideration whether demotivation is a completely distinctive construct or merely a decrease in motivational intensity (Kim and Kim 2013).

There are several causes of losing motivation in learning a foreign language. Research findings invariably name teachers who play a crucial role in students' demotivation in the following areas: teacher-student relationships (Oxford 1998, Dörnyei 1998), teaching methods (Ushioda 1998), especially the grammar translation method (Kikuchi 2009; Falout, Elwood, and Hood 2009), classroom activities (Ushioda 1998, Oxford 1998), boring classes (Jung 2011), or difficult requirements (Cheng and Lee 2018). The learning context, e.g., too big groups or frequent changes of teachers, can also lead to demotivation (Dörnyei 1998); furthermore, the overall workload of students and their busy schedules (Cheng and Lee 2018) may make them lose their motivation.

Language learners, however, attribute their state of demotivation to personal reasons as well. The most salient one is reduced self-confidence (Falout, Elwood, and Hood 2009; Dörnyei 1998) and self-regulatory factors, like a lack of will to learn (Jung 2011) and a lack of self-determination (Kim 2015).

---

[1] The terms "teacher" and "practitioner" will be used interchangeably throughout the paper.

Negative attitude to the language or the course material (Dörnyei 1998) and the difficulty of the language are also believed to make learners demotivated. A lack of achievement, like low scores on tests (Jung 2011), and not experiencing improvement or success (Kim 2015) can lead to a loss of motivation as well.

The lack of meaningful purpose (Kim 2015), i.e., questioning the very reason for learning a foreign language, has the most devastating effect on motivation. In other words, the inability to see the instrumental value of learning LSP for the job (Jung 2011) undermines effort, desire, and the positive attitude to learning, i.e., the tripod of motivation (Gardner 2001). This leaves learners vulnerable to fatigue, which can easily lead to amotivation, the state of complete loss of motivation (Deci and Ryan 1985). Amotivated students start missing classes, then whole courses, and eventually drop out.

Remotivation is different from motivation from a sequential point of view: initial motivation can easily turn to demotivation, which, in a way, is a natural process. The phase of demotivation can be transformed into remotivation when one finds the drive that has been lost. This process is neither natural nor spontaneous. Being remotivated is more valuable than being motivated because it is a consciously built structure, more resilient to demotivating factors. Remotivation is the seasoned counterpart of motivation. If learners are able to identify what made them lose their motivation in the first place, they are more likely to find coping strategies to get remotivated later when their motivation wanes again.

Getting remotivated requires learners to make a conscious effort to regain the motivation lost. When analyzing language learners' strategies, we find a remarkable difference between the strategies applied by high- and low-achieving students (Falout 2012). In a large-scale survey, where 900 university students were asked about their motivation, Falout, Elwood, and Hood (2009) found that more proficient learners were able to regulate their learning by finding alternative ways of learning which were more enjoyable than the learning taking place in the classroom. Furthermore, these students could improve their self-confidence as well, whereas less proficient learners experienced self-denigration.

In the research aimed at analyzing the difference between high- and low-achieving language learners in a Lithuanian university environment (Navickiene, Kavaliauskienė, and Pevcevičiūtė 2015), the results showed that students with a high or a very good command of a language are less prone to demotivation: they enjoy learning, making effort, and do not mind the intense work. However, low-level students tend to miss more classes, have an overall negative attitude to the language due to their disappointment. Although low-achieving students are just as aware of the importance of learning ESP as the high-achievers, they are less resourceful when facing demotivation.

In some cases, though, the remotivating process can happen through the context of learning. In his research conducted among Korean university students, Jung (2011) found that high test scores, a new learning environment, the use of various media for improving their language skills, or the mere situation of being able to use English, and a newly found positive attitude to the culture and the teacher can rekindle motivation. However powerful context-dependent motivation is, the self-induced kind of motivation is stronger.

The strongest remotivating force lies within the L2-self system (Dörnyei 2009). The *ideal L2-self* comprises the deepest ambitions of an individual regarding their endeavor to learn a foreign language. The *ought to L2-self* refers to those ambitions that are shaped by external factors, like society or people with influential roles (parents, teachers) in a language learner's life. The third construct, the *learning experience*, involves the actual learning situations that somehow influence a language learner's motivation.

In Kim's research (2015), those university students who had strong ideal L2-selves were able to set personal goals and got engaged in meaningful activities after experiencing demotivation. Similar results were found in the survey conducted among Korean university students, who got remotivated when they became aware of the instrumental value of English for their future jobs (Jung 2011).

In conclusion, being able to see learning a foreign language, especially LSP, as an organic part of the ideal L2-self facilitates remotivation. In a similar vein, the strongest demotive is the lack of vision, the inability to see the usefulness of LSP, whereas the presence of this vision, understanding the purpose of learning LSP, is the most powerful motivator.

Finally, we should consider the teachers' perspective. Logically, nearly all motivation research examined motivation from the language learners' perspective. However, the other stakeholders, the teachers, are rarely asked about their students' motivation. One example is a qualitative study conducted among EFL teachers asking about their definitions of motivation and the strategies they employ (Cowie and Sakui 2011). However, seeing that a large body of research has found that language learners attributed their demotivation mostly to their teachers, it seemed logical to conduct research and ask the teachers how they see their students' motivation, what reasons they can identify behind demotivation or remotivation, and how they see their own roles in motivating their students.

1.2 Teacher's roles and identities

In order to understand the significance of the roles teachers undertake or refuse to undertake, we should have a look at how roles are manifested as identities. Although teachers' identities are always "in flux or development" (Pennington 2015, 35), my research is able to provide a cross-sectional, nevertheless meaningful, view of these identities.

In a framework of teacher's identities, Pennington identified five practice-centered frames: instructional, disciplinary, professional, vocational, and economic; and three contextual frames: global, local, and sociocultural (2015).

The instructional identity comprises teachers' classroom personas, the roles they undertake while teaching, e.g., a facilitator or a subject-matter expert, and the relationship they build with their students. At the same time, being a TESOL teacher means using specific techniques, methods typical of the larger TESOL community. However, when another orientation, e.g. ESP, gets into the picture, it may influence language teachers' practices, therefore the instructional identities will transform as ESP teachers learn new contents, methods, curriculum content, etc. (Pennington 2015). Although the role of motivating language learners is only implied in Pennington's model, in other, more motivationally orientated models, it is an unquestionable responsibility of language teachers: "teacher skills in motivating learners need to be seen as central to teaching effectiveness" (Dörnyei 2013, 523).

The disciplinary identity bridges a teacher to a specific field and its connected research, e.g., psychology, linguistics. It also relates to academic ambitions, e.g., obtaining a PhD degree. The disciplinary identity connects colleagues of the same department, even across the faculties of the university. The final component is doing research within the field of TESOL and disseminating the findings.

The professional identity is the unique blend of teacher characteristics that have developed under the influence of the disciplinary knowledge, expectations, and practices of the field. This identity is highly informed by the educational experience, and more than any other identities it is prone to evolve, e.g., when teachers formulate their ideal teacher-selves.

Vocational identity is defined as the altruistic aspect of teacher identity; it focuses on giving and serving others. When teachers say that teaching is rewarding, they do not mean it financially but emotionally. "A large component of enjoyment of the teaching job for many people is helping students achieve their goals" (Pennington 2015, 43).

The fifth, economic identity refers to the financial reward teachers receive and the "academic capital" that is manifested in articles and books published. This latter can contribute to teachers' well-being and self-image.

In Pennington's model, the outer frames (global, local, and sociocultural) harmoniously integrate the five identities in concentric circles, but the research conducted among Chinese university ESP teachers proved that societal changes, like higher expectations posed on teachers, can make identity formation difficult (Tao and Gao 2018). If the university requires teachers to pursue academic ambitions and get published in high-ranking journals and at the same time does not reduce their workload, the professional and disciplinary identities will be negatively influenced. Similarly, if the atmosphere does not support ESP teachers, and they are downgraded to "mere" language teachers next to their colleagues who teach content subjects, ESP teachers cannot find a community to form their identities, which also prevents them from having valuable insights into the profession. Therefore, based on their research findings, Tao and Gao (2018) modified Pennington's model (2015) by indicating how socio-economic factors influence the ESP teacher's identities directly, and institutional factors do so indirectly. Their modified model includes two more frames, professional development and work experience, both of which have direct effects on the ESP teacher's identities.

Based on actual research findings, anecdotal evidence—that far too many students lose their language-learning motivation during their studies at the abovementioned business university in Budapest—and regarding the substantial body of literature stating that there is a very strong relationship between student demotivation and teachers' practices, the following three research questions were formulated:

- What motivational patterns can LSP teachers identify among their students?
- What role does LSP play in motivation, if any?
- How do teachers see their roles in motivating their students?

2 Language requirements and choices at a business school in Hungary

There is no doubt that learning English or other foreign languages is inevitably useful when one is preparing for a career in business or tourism. The students of a prestigious business university in Budapest, the capital of Hungary, seem to be surrounded by helpful, professional teachers, and well-defined requirements on the university's part. Still, the majority of students get demotivated by the end of their language studies, which is typically their third term.

In order to get their BSc degree, they are required to have a B2 level Language Certificate for Business if they study Commerce and Marketing (Business) and two B2 Language Certificates for Tourism if they study Tourism and Catering. Students who already have a C1 level (general) language certificate can be exempted from taking a B2 language exam. These certificates can be obtained at the language exam center of the university or at any out-of-the house state-accredited language centers entitled to organize language exams and issue accredited certificates.

In order to promote learning LSP, the university offers language courses for the students. The courses last three terms, are built in the timetable, and worth three credits, which is the regular value of a seminar. Before starting the course, students take a placement test, and then they are allocated to a group suitable for their actual level. Typically, there are 20–25 students in English and German groups, but French, Spanish, and Italian language groups have 8–12 members.

There are two 90-minute-long classes a week. A set course book is used. The language course ends with an exam, which has a written and an oral part. The written part consists of three tasks: a vocabulary test, reading comprehension, and a writing task. The oral part also has three parts: general questions about studies, work, career plans, then students are given visual information (a graph, a diagram etc.) which they have to analyze, describe, and explain, and in the third part they have to talk about a specific topic using the prompts given. Even if students take ESP courses in two languages, which is obligatory for Tourism students, they have to take one exam. Tourism students are offered six terms for language learning, which can be divided into 2 + 4 or 3 + 3 terms between the two languages depending on personal preferences (see Table 4.1 below).

Table 4.1: LSP courses and requirements

	Terms	**1**	**2**	**3**	**Exam**	**4**	**5**	**6**	**7**	**BSc exit requirements**	
Majors	Tourism	LSP courses: language 1			+	LSP courses: language 2			-	B2 LSP certificate #1 **or** C1 general language certificate	B2 LSP certificate #2
	Business	LSP courses: language 1			+	-	-	-	-	B2 LSP certificate **or** C1 general language certificate	-

The majority of students choose learning ESP, although about three-quarters of the students already have general B2 language certificates, which enables them to deal with business situations. Their choice to learn the specific vocabulary and business-related skills suggests that students either perceive English as the primary language of business (Räisänen and Fortanet-Gómez 2008), or that they want to channel their energies to more demanding subjects.

The second most popular LSP is German, which is explained by the fact that in Hungary this is the second most widely taught foreign language at the secondary level. French, Spanish, and Italian are mostly learned by students of Tourism as a second LSP or less typically by students already having a C1 level language certificate in English or German. Russian is also taught but it is invariably a complete beginner's course which starts with mastering the Cyrillic alphabet. By the end of the third term, students' proficiency is a little above A2, which is not suitable for learning LSP. Therefore, Russian was excluded from the research.

3 Methods

3.1 Participants

The research was conducted among the members of the Language Department of a prestigious business university in Budapest (Hungary). The Language Department is responsible for organizing Business and Tourism LSP courses and offering classes of presentation skills, study skills, and cultural and career studies in the target languages.

The staff consists of 34 full-time practitioners (apart from part-time and visiting teachers). The criteria of selection for the interviews were the following: (a) being a full-time teacher at the institution, (b) at least one teacher should be interviewed per language (English, German, French, Italian, Spanish). There was a teacher of English and Russian, who was enlisted among her English-teaching colleagues not only because she dominantly taught English but also because Russian is taught for generic and not specific purposes. Table 4.2 below presents the distribution of language teachers according to languages, the total number of staff, and how many of them were interviewed.

Table 4.2: The distribution of language teachers

Languages taught	Full-time employees	Interviewees
English	19	16
German	11	3
French	2	1
Italian	2	1
Spanish	4	1
Total	38	22

Out of the 22 interviewees, there were 16 female and 6 male teachers. All teachers held MA degrees in English and 14 of them had doctorate degrees as well (see Table 4.3). The Head of the Department and the Head of the Language Institution were also interviewed among the interviewees. The interviewees took part in the research on a voluntary basis and the interviews were conducted in their native language (Hungarian). One interviewee was a native English speaker; therefore, his interview was conducted in English.

Table 4.3: The interviewees

Interviewee identification number	Gender	Language taught	Employment at the university (yrs.)	Qualification
01	male	English	5	MA, PhD
02	female	English	6	MA and vocational training in tourism, PhD
03	female	English	3	MA, CELTA
04	female	English	25	MA, BSc in Business
05	male	English, native	20	BSc in Business
06	female	Spanish	12	MA
07	female	French	13	MA, PhD
08	female	English	20	MA, PhD
09	female	Italian	25	MA, PhD
10	female	English, Russian	29	MA, BSc in Business
11	male	English	5	MA
12	female	English	28	MA, PhD
13	female	English	25	MA, PhD
14	male	English	8	MA, PhD
15	female	English	17	MA, PhD, BSc in Business
16	female	English	21	MA
17	female	English	28	MA, BSc in Business
18	male	English	23	MA, PhD
19	female	German	22	MA, PhD
20	female	German	10	MA, PhD
21	female	German	3	MA, PhD
22	male	English	7	MA, PhD

3.2 Research tool

The interview aimed to explore the teachers' views, opinions, and feelings about their students' motivation. There were 21 questions divided into three parts: professional experience, students, and LSP education.

In order to answer the original research questions, the following areas were covered. As language teachers' lack of subject-specific knowledge is a recurrent issue in ESP, there were questions aiming at the relevant qualifications or experience in business or tourism.

As for motivation, the teachers were asked about how they see their students' attitudes, goals, learning strategies, and motivation changing. As for the role of LSP, the teachers were asked to define LSP and its focal points in their teaching practice. Finally, the teachers were asked about their roles as motivators. They were to reflect on their teaching (goals and problems) at a task level, a course level, an institutional level, and at epistemological level.

The first version of the interview protocol was piloted with an experienced ESP teacher outside the institution. The piloted interview questions yielded rich and meaningful data; however, some questions were reworded and the sequence was altered to fine-tune the instrument. The final version consisted of 21 questions.

The semi-structured interviews were audio-recorded with the consent of the respondents, then typed verbatim, and analyzed using the constant comparison method (Maykut and Morehouse 1994) with the help of the RQDA software (Huang 2016). The total word count was: 31,574.

4 Findings

4.1 Motivational patterns and the role of LSP

When discussing the results of the research I merely focus on the motivation-related themes that emerged from the interviews; therefore some valuable but unrelated issues will not be discussed here. Based on the teachers' perceptions, students' motivational patterns fall into four main categories: consistently high motivation, consistently low motivation, motivation found, and motivation lost.

These patterns reflect the two dimensions by which teachers define student motivation. One is a perceived level of motivation, the presence or the absence of motivation at its extremes. The other is the temporal dimension denoting the trajectory of motivation, i.e., how certain students are perceived on the scale of being motivated and amotivated. Below are the categories and subcategories of the motivational patterns:

1. Consistently high motivation: students whose motivation does not seem to fluctuate during their studies.

2. Consistently low motivation: students not being motivated to learn LSP in the first place, and unwilling to change;

    (a) misplaced students: students landing in the university either as a safe school or because their parents expected them to study there.

    (b) mission accomplished: students who feel that they have already completed the requirements by passing a general B2 level language exam, and they do not feel motivated to learn LSP.

    (c) degree paid: students seeing their university degrees as mere documents, and the only price they are willing to pay for their degree is the tuition fee.

3. Motivation found: students who are originally not motivated, but during their university studies they come to see the purpose of learning LSP.

4. Motivation lost: students losing their motivation by as early as their third term due different causes;

    (a) initial motivation: students starting their university studies enthusiastically but losing the momentum over the time.

    (b) quitters: students who feel helpless and give up on their LSP studies.

    (c) high achievers: students already having a high command of language, not finding the level of instruction of LSP challenging enough.

4.2 Teachers' identities influenced by LSP

Motivation is an organic part of teachers' professional identities (Pennington 2015) and, as pointed out earlier, teachers do play a crucial role in motivating and demotivating their students. The interviews revealed the extent individual teachers see themselves as active agents in motivating their students, and what specific tasks they are willing to do to see their students succeed. Analyzing the texts of the interviews, the following themes emerged:

1. Motivators

    (a) Responsibility

    (b) Motivational strategies

2. Tasks

    (a) Adapting materials

    (b) Teaching the basics of the profession

5 Discussion

5.1 Motivational patterns and the role of LSP

Consistently high motivation

The most successful language learners in a business university are those with instrumental motivation. Students whose choice of university was a deliberate one find learning LSP highly instrumental to their future profession. They are aware that their career ambitions cannot be reached without language skills. These students are quite well-informed about the requirements of their future jobs; some students come from families running a hotel, a restaurant, or a business enterprise. Having such solid professional and/or family background keeps motivation alive and serves as a springboard to future careers as well.

> Interview 15 [5890: 6112] *But the motivated and more enthusiastic students nearly always have some background that makes [learning LSP] important. They're either working, or have worked, and are getting very good professional support, which makes them understand that they have a future here.*

However, there is a cohort of motivated, self-regulated students being autonomous and having an overall positive attitude to learning. Unfortunately, the interviewees could not give further information about the source of their motivation.

> Interview 08 [3003: 3156] *I don't think it depends on LSP how much they are motivated. LSP or not, motivation doesn't depend on it.*

Consistently low motivation

This category comprises students whose lack of motivation does not seem to change for the better throughout their studies. They do not have an initial motivation either; they have simply landed at the university because they could not find anything better to do. For many students it is a transitory phase; they might be studying for a future entrance exam at another university or simply passing the time.

> Interview 05 [3464:3693] *There isn't much interest in business outside the classroom. Nobody or very few people say, "Hey, I've read that in a newspaper, what do you think?" There is really just what we learn from the book, what I teach them at class ...*

    (a) Misplaced students: There are several, seemingly ideal students, with true intrinsic motivation to learn a foreign language. They love the language, the culture, traveling, but not the profession (i.e., Business or Tourism). They truly love all the intricacies of the language; however, when it comes to learning LSP, they get bored and complain that during a business English course they are talking too much about money (Interviewee 14). These students are usually highly cultured individuals who would do much better at an English Studies BA course.

> Interview 01 [5798:6202] *I quite often feel that when I teach the business topics, I cannot motivate twenty percent of students who are more sensitive and interested in literature. During the classes, when they ask off-topic questions, I give a short answer, then we move on to the original topic. It is very difficult to motivate them.*

(b) Mission accomplished: Some students feel that their foreign language education is complete when they obtain a general B2 level language certificate. Their language skills are often quite basic and functional. The fact that they can chat and buy things online lulls them into the false belief that this level will be enough when working in their profession. They are irritated by the university requirements, the LSP courses; they do not want to learn more.

> Interview 22 [3980:4523] *I consider those students unsuccessful, and there are plenty of them who think they know enough. There are many students, mainly those who learn English, already having some sort of language certificates, they sort of watch films in English, or they have an English-speaking friend, or they use the language in their jobs, let's say, at a level of a receptionist. And they think that's enough, they can get by, and really cannot understand why they should learn it any further.*

(c) Degree paid: None of the above is as detrimental to motivation as the attitude labeled as "degree paid." Students of this category feel that by having paid the tuition fee, they have done their part in learning; the rest is the teachers' or the institution's duty. They behave like a customer who has paid for a service and now is waiting to be served. Most practitioners found this attitude irritating and unacceptable, an insult to their professional identity and voiced their opinions rather resentfully.

> Interview 02 [2425: 2803] *[The students think if] they take part in a show, or what, say this and that, they'll be rolling in money. This is a general lack of motivation: daddy will buy it, or I've paid the fee, so I'll get the document, the document, as they say. [=degree]*

The next two categories will shed light on the unpredictable roles LSP can play in the lives of unmotivated students: it can remotivate them but at the same time, as the interviewees saw, irritate students and bring language learning into a deadlock. Seemingly, the effect depends on the students' attitude to their future profession. As soon as their professional goals are set, learning LSP seems a useful subject.

Motivation found

For some students, this university is not a conscious choice; they study Tourism or Business because both qualifications guarantee lucrative opportunities in the labor market. Having a BSc degree in business can be a pass to many multinational companies. However, during their internship or a visit to a hotel or traveling abroad, these students somehow realize that what so far only seemed a mere academic subject can be a true profession. As a result, they start to learn the content subjects more consciously and get motivated to learn LSP because now it is seen as a tool to achieve their career goals.

> Interview 15 [6520:6821] *And there is the type who gets such a big push while visiting a hotel [...] that you wouldn't believe. And this will ripple on in language classes as well, and they will manage.*

There is a subgroup here, typically made up of learners of English. These students have been learning English for 8–10 years (in primary and secondary school) and still cannot get higher than a B1 level. They have reached a plateau and are quite bored with general English-speaking topics. The very reason they do not quit learning is LSP. The new, practical skills acquired during LSP classes can be put into immediate practice at the workplace, which motivates students. Furthermore, those who have difficulties learning a foreign language do not find ESP as difficult as general English. As ESP is a rather vocabulary-focused subject, with less emphasis on grammar, students find it much easier to improve their knowledge and become successful communicators.

> Interview 10 [4682: 4830] *I think LSP can be interesting. They have been singing the same old song "My family ..." From a certain point of view, LSP does good to some [students].*

> Interview 07 [1848:2066] [...] *for them LSP may mean a lifebuoy because learning words is easier than learning grammar rules.*

Motivation lost

To the question why some students lose their general (or LSP-specific) motivation by the end of their studies or, in the worst case, by the second year when they still have a long way to go, the interviewees gave several answers.

The first was time, a phenomenon turning novelty into routine, excitement into boredom. As some respondents (e.g., Interviewee 1) concluded that interest could not be maintained for three terms with the same teacher and the same group. Another reason was perfectionism on the teachers' part which made students desperate, as they felt they could never be perfect or do enough (Interviewee 3). The third reason named was students having too much workload (Interviewee 7 and 15) apart from their language studies, which is a recurring theme in studies about motivation. Finally, administrative problems were mentioned as a reason for losing general motivation to learn. As an example, one instructor (Interviewee 14) recalled the situation when the university failed to communicate the requirements clearly, and some students could not start their courses.

(a) Initial motivation: Many students start the university with enthusiasm and optimism. However, this initial motivation can easily wane. In this case, LSP has nothing to do with the loss of motivation; it is a natural process. As soon as an activity—in our case university life—loses its initial attraction, self-regulation and self-discipline should take over in order to persevere.

> Interview 22 [2652: 3015] *They are in survival mode. As freshmen they're motivated by learning, taking part in seminars and the university life, but when they are in the second or third year somehow this enthusiasm dies out. They may start working or get interested in other things, so their main goal is to get the right grade or pass the course.*

(b) Quitters: The category of quitters consists of low-achieving students not making effort, not asking for help, and failing eventually. Actually, they should not have given up, and if they had wanted, they could have easily got help from their teachers. The fundamental problem with these low-achieving students is not that they do not reach a certain level but the fact that they do not seek help (Falout, Elwood, and Hood 2009; Navickiene, Kavaliauskienė, and Pevcevičiūtė 2015). Some fail, some nearly fail.

> Interview 18 [9751:10010] *I think students are unsuccessful when they give it up—and we see many of them, especially in lower-level groups. They say that this language [English] cannot be learned, and they don't even try to take the language exam, or when they do, they somehow pass it and eventually get a degree.*

(c) High achievers: This group forms a market niche at the university. The high-achievers who have already met the exit requirements of the university (i.e., having a C1 level language certificate) cannot find the classes challenging enough. Their linguistic needs remain unmet; they feel that their knowledge deteriorates by the end of their studies. They are dissatisfied with the opportunities the university can offer them. The problem is that most teachers see them as nuisances because these students cannot be motivated by classes focusing on exam preparation. They demand more, but the LSP teachers bound by the requirements of the university cannot or will not give them more. These students can easily fulfill, or have already fulfilled, all the requirements set for them, and they become bored and disappointed.

> Interview 03 [4282: 4501] *We can see that many students lose their motivation during the three terms. I'm not sure we can give them appropriate education. It is especially true for those first-year students who already speak a high level of the language.*

> Interview 14 [2198: 2690] *Those who read subjects in English want to improve or at least keep their knowledge at a good level. But as undergraduates they feel that they know less than they did when they started the university. [...] I don't think that it is an unjustifiable demand that they want to improve their language skills during their studies.*

5.2 Teachers' roles in motivation

5.2.1 Motivators

Responsibility

The instructional identity includes the teacher's task to motivate students. However, not all teachers necessarily act upon this role. The findings of the research reveal that some practitioners accept this assigned role, and they feel responsible for their students' motivation.

> Interview 16 [2258: 2336] *[Question: What motivates students to learn LSP?]*
> *The teacher. (laughing)*

Some instructors, however, do not think it is their responsibility to motivate their unmotivated students.

Interview 22 [4590: 4803] *Actually, there isn't much I can do, maybe others are better at it, but I can't awake motivation in those who have come here not seeing it important [to learn] in the first place.*

Interview 01 [5798:6202] *I quite often feel that when I teach the business topics, I cannot motivate twenty percent of students who are more sensitive and interested in literature. During the classes they ask questions off topic, I give a short answer, then we move on to the original topic. It is very difficult to motivate them.*

Motivational strategies

For most respondents, motivating students is an organic part of their identities, and they use a wide array of tools for that:

(a) They tell stories of successful businesspeople whose success was attributed to their foreign language skills.

> Interview 21 [4935: 5300] *I tell them stories of people who spoke a language well and got a really good job [...] and they knew as well that languages give them opportunities, jobs. And it seems to inspire them.*

Non-native teachers can motivate their students by their own examples, sharing their own language-learning experience.

> Interview 21 [4935: 5300] *[...] I tell them how I have learned languages: I was watching TV, videos, browsing the internet.*

(b) Reasoning is another motivational method mainly used by male teachers. They either tell their students how fierce the competition in the labor market is, or they appeal to their students' common sense, highlighting the financial benefits of learning "here and now."

> Interview 18 [11741:12362] *It's a waste of money. Why aren't they making use of this opportunity to learn languages at the university? It's more sensible to make use of it while they have nothing else to do but learn than later pay through the nose [for a language course].*

(c) The respondents' most common motivating technique is showcasing their own motivation. They consider their own enthusiasm to be the most effective motivational tool. All the interviewed teachers believed that motivation breeds motivation. In addition, their use of language reflects the different measures they have for their students and for themselves; "motivation" was used when referring to their students but "enthusiasm" when referring to themselves.

> Interview 14 [19416:20173] *I believe I can inspire them a lot. But it is viral. If the students see their teachers being interested in their job, they will do the tasks more willingly.*

> Interview 10 [10101:10342] *I would like to pass on my enthusiasm. Knowledge is joy, having a language certificate or an LSP certificate is joy. There is more to joy than finding a better job. If they go beyond a certain level, they will understand it. And there are some who do.*

(d) Possibly the most effective motivational tool is to help students set language-learning goals. Interestingly, out of all respondents only two mentioned it.

> Interview 14 [19416:20173] *[...] I can motivate them, set them goals the language brings with itself, mainly that they should find joy in learning a language. Speaking a language is a good thing, and it's important to accept it.*

> Interview 20 [1237:1393] *My goal is that they can reflect on themselves. When they are defining their goals, setting language-learning goals, they need my support. If there are language-learning goals.*

(e) Those teachers who reportedly motivate their students also facilitate their learning by teaching them learning strategies.

> Interview 13 [9858:10014] *I can give them practical methods, even unorthodox ones, which may not be found in methodology textbooks, but they work.*

(f) Bringing authentic and interesting materials to classes.

> Interview 05 [9287: 9734] *General business knowledge, very up-to-date news items, current news items they might be interested in, mobile phones, Apple, Samsung, what's happening in the business world, are there any threats to the companies they are coming from. Also, getting them to think about how they buy their phones, do they buy them in Hungary or abroad, why is a phone cheaper in other countries, in America, trying to get them think about not just an abstract idea what business is.*

5.2.2 Tasks

Adapting materials

This activity cannot be considered a mere motivational strategy because it often involves conscious choices, even sacrifices on teachers' part. They decide to teach a certain material because this way they could meet their students' anticipatory needs (Wade 1989), those reflecting their future career needs. In some cases, it is not a burden and seems to be an integral part of the professional teacher identity.

> Interview 11 [7430: 7633] *[...] I try to keep pace with them [the students] so that I could bring materials to class that interest them.*

> Interview 12 [2273: 2526] *They are really happy when we give them more information about their profession. I'm not criticizing teachers of content subjects but emphasizing our responsibility because they [the students] take us seriously, they acknowledge that LSP exists.*

However, the responses reveal that LSP teachers do better if they can leave behind the avid language teacher and put on a new LSP practitioner identity prioritizing professional needs over linguistic needs. Turning to be an LSP teacher is a new identity (Pennington 2015). Fulfilling the university requirements, most students want to get their language certificates as soon as possible. They become extremely pragmatic when it comes to language courses; some of them refuse to do a task if they cannot see its immediate relevance to the language exam.

> Interview 04 [2090: 2358] *We should explain in more detail why we are doing a certain task. Those old tasks meant to improve their language skills are not necessarily working. [...] They are unwilling to do them.*

Most LSP teachers are aware of the students' urgent need to get a language certificate so they themselves adapt their teaching, which in some cases is done with bitterness, with a feeling of mutilating other aspects of their professional identities.

> Interview 13 [1934:2158] *I've not been teaching the language for some 15 years. Yeah, the language as it is. I truly miss it. I improve exam skills, teach them with exam vocabulary extensively, test them on exam vocabulary, if I can.*

Teaching the basics of the profession

Teaching LSP begins in the first term at the university. Most students have neither professional experience nor theoretical knowledge about the disciplines they are studying. It means that LSP practitioners have to teach the basic concepts of the profession. When presenting a new technical term, teachers have to explain the context and provide background knowledge because they cannot rely on existing professional knowledge. In a way, LSP courses function as induction programs.

> Interview 18 [3541: 3910] *Ideally, they should have been learning their profession for one or two years before they could start learning LSP. But the reality is that they start LSP right after finishing the secondary school. When I was 18, I couldn't tell the difference between a bond and a share either. [...] We are trying to build walls without solid foundations. They learn the basics of business and tourism in our classes.*

This task can be really daunting and intimidating. Some teachers complained that they had never worked in business or tourism and that they did not feel qualified for this task, which is not a rare complaint (Hutchinson and Waters 1987). The teachers interviewed basically took two routes: they either educated themselves in business and/or tourism, asked experts, and then took on the responsibility to pass on professional knowledge, or they insisted on being language teachers and expected their students to provide or acquire the necessary professional expertise.

> Interview 19 [10802:11027] *I don't know if it's fortunate or not, but they need a theoretical background. And from the language-teaching point of view it is counterproductive [because I do frontal teaching], but I find it necessary because we have very short time to cover everything.*

> Interview 20 [431: 528] *Well, I don't think I'm qualified. They must have the professional knowledge.*

Conclusion

The findings suggest that LSP teachers can perceive several types of motivation among their students. Regarding the presence or absence and the temporal dimension of motivation, these follow four main patterns: consistently high, consistently low, motivation found, motivation lost. Within these, several other patterns can be identified.

As for what can make students find or lose their motivation, LSP can play a crucial role. LSP can cure overlearning or give a more practical—at least in the students' eyes—knowledge to its learners or can make a good introductory course to the students' profession (business and tourism).

Considering the perceived roles teachers play in student motivation, authenticity seems to have the highest value for teachers, i.e., motivating with their own motivation. However, teacher motivation is susceptible to student attitudes and motivation, and some teachers do not see it their responsibility to motivate students. Furthermore, conflicting goals between teachers and students, e.g., studying the language versus preparing for the language exam, can result in losing motivation on either or on both sides.

It seems that the surest and strongest way to be a motivated LSP learner is having a positive attitude towards one's future profession. If this is missing, nothing can motivate students to learn LSP. As soon as true intrinsic motivation for the profession emerges from internship or any work experience, a very strong instrumental motivation to learn LSP emerges as well. When students can set their professional goals, the usefulness of LSP is not questionable any longer.

Turning the disadvantageous timing of LSP classes, i.e., being one of the first courses, to their advantage, teachers can encourage their students to set professional goals by introducing practical and attractive aspects of their future profession. Furthermore, by selecting relevant materials and simulations, language teachers can strengthen the instrumentality of LSP.

The research has certain limitations. First, some more teachers could have been interviewed. Second, the university where the interviews were conducted has two more faculties with independent language departments. Interviewing teachers working there would also provide deeper insights into teachers' perspectives of students' motivational patterns.

As for further research directions, students will have to be asked about their views on motivation and demotivation. When the results of the two studies are compared and contrasted, action plans could be made to help those students who cannot set professional goals and fall behind in their studies. An effective plan based on these research findings could improve general motivation and reduce the drop-out rate radically.

References

Council of Europe. 2001. *Common European Framework of Reference for Languages: Learning, Teaching, Assessment.* Cambridge: Press Syndicate of the University of Cambridge.

Cheng, Adrienne, and Cynthia Lee. 2018. "Factors Affecting Tertiary English Learners' Persistence in the Self-directed Language Learning Journey." *System* 76 (4): 170–82.

Cowie, Neil, and Keiko Sakui. 2011. "Crucial but Neglected: English as a Foreign Language Teachers' Perspectives on Learner Motivation." In *Identity, Motivation and Autonomy in Language Learning,* edited by Garold Murray, Xuesong Gao, and Terry Lamb, 212–28. Bristol: Multilingual Matters.

Deci, Edward L., and Richard M. Ryan. 1985. *Intrinsic Motivation and Self-determination in Human Behavior.* New York: Plenum.

Dörnyei, Zoltán. 1998. "Demotivation in Foreign Language Learning." Paper presented at the TESOL 32nd Annual Convention, Seattle, Washington, USA, 17–21 March.

Dörnyei, Zoltán. 2009. "The L2 Motivational Self System." In *Motivation, Language Identity and the L2 Self,* edited by Zoltán Dörnyei and Ema Ushioda, 9–42. Bristol: Multilingual Matters.

Dörnyei, Zoltán. 2013. "Motivation and Second Language Learning." In *Teaching English as a Second or Foreign Language,* edited by Marianne Celce-Murcia, Donna M. Brinton, and Marguerite Ann Snow, 518–31. Boston: Cengage Learning.

Dörnyei, Zoltán, and Ema Ushioda. 2011. *Teaching and Researching Motivation.* Second Edition. Harlow: Pearson Education.

Falout, Joseph. 2012. "Coping with Demotivation: EFL Learners' Remotivation Processes." *TESL-EJ* 16 (3): 1–29.

Falout, Joseph, James A. Elwood, and Michael Hood. 2009. "Demotivation: Affective States and Learning Outcomes." *System* 37 (3): 403–17.

Fűköh, Borbála. 2018. "Language Learning Gains and Motivation of L2 and L3 Learners of ESP." In *UPRT 2017: Empirical Studies in English Applied Linguistics,* edited by Magdolna Lehmann, Réka Lugossy, Marianne Nikolov, and Gábor Szabó. Pécs: Lingua Franca Csoport.

Gardner, Robert C. 2001. "Language Learning Motivation: The Student, the Teacher, and the Researcher." *Texas Papers in Foreign Language Education* 6 (1): 1–18.

Huang, Ronggui. 2016. *RQDA: R-Based Qualitative Data Analysis.* R Package Version 0.2-8. http://rqda.r-forge.r-project.org.

Hutchinson, Tom, and Alan Waters. 1987. *English for Specific Purposes: A Learning-Centered Approach.* Cambridge: Cambridge University Press.

Jung, Sook Kyung. 2011. "Demotivating and Remotivating Factors in Learning English: A Case of Low Level College Students." *English Teaching* 66 (2): 47–72.

Kikuchi, Keita. 2009. "Listening to our Learners' Voices: What Demotivates Japanese High School Students?" *Language Teaching Research* 13 (4): 453–71.

Kim, Shinhye. 2015. "Demotivation and L2 Motivational Self of Korean College Students." *English Teaching,* 70 (1): 29–55.

Kim, Yoon-Kyoung, and Tae-Young Kim. 2013. "English Learning Demotivation Studies in the EFL Contexts: State of the Art." *Modern English Education* 14 (1): 77–102.

Maykut, Pamela, and Richard Morehouse. 1994. *Beginning Qualitative Research.* London: Falmer Press.

Navickienė, Violeta, Dalia Kavaliauskienė, and Sigita Pevcevičiūtė. 2015. "Aspects of ESP Learning Motivation in Tertiary Education." *TILTAI* (2): 97–108.

Oxford, Rebecca. 1998. "The Unraveling Tapestry: Teacher and Course Characteristics Associated with Demotivation in the Language Classroom." Paper presented at the TESOL 32nd Annual Convention, Seattle, Washington, USA, 17–21 March.

Pennington, Martha C. 2015. "Teacher Identity in TESOL: A Frames Perspective." In *Advances and Current Trends in Language Teacher Identity Research,* edited by Yin Ling Cheung, Selim Ben Said and Kwanghyun Park, 16–30. Abington: Routledge.

Räisänen, Christine, Inmaculata Fortanet-Gómez. 2008. "The State of ESP Teaching and Learning in Western European Higher Education after Bologna." In *ESP in European Higher Education: Integrating Language and Content,* edited by Christine Räisänen and Inmaculada Fortanet-Gómez, 11–51. Amsterdam: John Benjamins.

Tao, Jian, and Xuesong Gao. 2018. "Identity Constructions of ESP Teachers in a Chinese University." *English for Specific Purposes* 49, 1–13.

Ushioda, Ema. 1998. "Effective Motivational Thinking: A Cognitive Theoretical Approach to the Study of Language Learning Motivation." In *Current Issues in English Language Methodology,* edited by Eva Alcón Soler and Victória Codina Espurz, 77–89. Castello de la Plana: Universitat Jaume I.

Wade, Jerry L. 1989. "Felt Needs and Anticipatory Needs: Reformulation of a Basic Community Development Principle." *Journal of the Community Development Society* 20 (1): 116–23.

CHAPTER 5

Developing a language curriculum in a business institution

Christian Rubio

Bentley University, MA, USA

Abstract

Bentley University is a business institution located in the Greater Boston Area, and although it strives to integrate the arts and sciences and business, its curriculum contains several restrictions. Because of this, one must be creative when designing a new program. In effect, despite those limitations, there is a certain freedom that enables faculty to create majors and minors. In this article, I specifically describe the process of building a Spanish for Business minor that addresses business practices in Hispanic cultures, highlights the cultural differences, and explores ethical practices in Spanish-speaking countries. One of the aforementioned restrictions is the number of courses to complete a minor; as a result, I had to be selective not only in the content of the selected courses, but also the methods in those classes. Therefore, I detail some of the activities of these courses, including vocabulary games, launching marketing campaigns, and a service-learning component, to name a few. This article also calls for future collaboration between language teachers and researchers in order to maintain languages as an important component in an ever-changing higher-education landscape.

Keywords: curriculum development, Spanish for business, languages for the professions, student activities

***

Introduction

Language for the Professions (LP) is a field that remains overlooked by many graduate degree foreign language programs. Despite that several universities in the United States now offer some certificates and even LP undergraduate degrees, the instructors of these programs come from traditional graduate programs centered around literature, cultures, and to a certain extent, Second

Language Acquisition. As a result, these instructors often find themselves struggling to find materials when they are assigned to teach LP courses. This issue becomes even more critical when developing a curriculum that is centered around this new, but important, field. This article precisely addresses some of the shortcomings of this reality and offers some examples.

1 Background information

Bentley University, located in the city of Waltham, Massachusetts, USA, is a business institution founded as an accounting school in 1917. As a higher-education (HE) institution, Bentley is a unique place because it does not follow the regular pattern of most universities. For example, though the university has a Dean of Arts and Sciences and a Dean of Business, there are no separate colleges, and every student is considered an undecided business major on their first day on campus. Currently, Bentley offers thirteen majors in business and twelve in the arts and sciences. Additionally, Bentley is one of three universities in the United States that has been accredited by EQUIS, which is the European Foundation for Management Development (EFMD) Quality Improvement System. According to its website, it is a global, non-profit, membership-driven organization dedicated to management development, recognized globally as an accreditation body for business schools, business school programs, and corporate universities (EFMD Global 2022).

Throughout the years, Bentley has evolved into a business institution with a mission to change "the world with a transformative business education, integrated with arts and sciences, that inspires and prepares ethical leaders who will confront the challenges of today and shape the opportunities of tomorrow" (2022).[1] Within this mission, the Modern Languages (ML) Department has played a significant role in the growth of the institution. Currently, it offers classes in four languages: Chinese, French, Italian, and Spanish. All have offered minors since its initiation; and in the fall of 2012, the ML Department officially launched a Hispanic Studies major.

It is worth noting that Bentley boasts an excellent reputation in terms of job placement. According to the University, 99% of the 2018 graduating class is currently employed or attending graduate schools (Henrichs 2019). Furthermore, Princeton Review has recently ranked Bentley University career service department as number one in "The 386 Best Colleges 2021 Edition." More recently, the Center on Education and the Workforce from Georgetown University placed

---

[1] Bentley University revised its mission in May 2019. It is important to note that the prior mission was "to educate creative, ethical, and socially responsible organizational leaders by creating and disseminating impactful knowledge within and across business and the arts and sciences" (2017, 4).

Bentley as number 8 offering the best return on investment (Henrichs 2022). As a result of its reputation and success in job placement as well as in internship opportunities, Bentley attracts students that, for the most part, know they want to major in a business discipline before even stepping foot on campus. In fact, almost 90% of the 2018 graduating class majored in business, receiving a Bachelor of Science degree. These students also have the option to minor in various disciplines.[2] Additionally, they can opt for a second concentration, the Liberal Studies major, which has several specializations, such as Quantitative Perspectives, Media Arts and Society, Global Perspectives, and Health Studies, among others. As part of the undergraduate curriculum, students have two distinct sets of core classes. On the one hand, they have their General Education requirements, comprised of several courses in the Arts and Sciences, including Calculus, History, Science, Literature, Micro, and Macroeconomics. On the other hand, students must take eight General Business (GB) courses. Among the topics in this GB core are ethics and law, statistics, basic courses in finance, and accounting.

Despite the fact that Bentley strives to become attractive for global partners, language is not a requirement for those graduating with a Bachelor of Science. However, the number of students taking language classes continues to exceed expectations. Thus, the ML Department enjoys a robust number of students taking their classes and is one of the top minors chosen by the students. As is the case with most HE institutions in the United States (MLA, n.d.), Spanish is the language of preference among the students. Furthermore, and as one would expect based on the type of institution Bentley is, the most popular class offered by the ML Department is Spanish for Business (MLSP302). This class has always received the maximum number of students, with an average of 20 each time it was offered. (Language classes at Bentley are always capped at 20.) This demand for language for specific purposes reflects the need to study a foreign language in the twenty-first century due to "the rise in globalization of business and commerce, health and security matters that require international cooperation" (Cammarata, Tedick, and Osborn 2014, 1).

2 Needs and demand

As previously stated, in 2012 the ML Department began offering, in addition to its language minor, the option to major in Spanish. As part of the design of the program, several classes were created, including writing, literature, and culture

---

[2] In the United States higher education system, students have the flexibility to choose a program study, usually composed of eight to twelve courses of the same discipline. This is typically called major. A student can also choose a sub-concentration, which is typically composed of half of the courses required for a major. This is known as a minor.

courses. Despite this increase in options, MLSP302 remained the number one choice for students. This highlighted the need to fulfill a demand for LP courses. However, as various studies have highlighted, foreign language teachers face difficulties when trying to design content-based courses that are unfamiliar to them (Cummings and Lister 2014, 79). Despite these challenges, the ML Department proposed the creation of a Spanish for Business certificate, but Bentley University's soon to be old curriculum[3] has faced recent scrutiny and has gone through a major revision. This curriculum offered very little room for creativity. It is mainly for that reason that it has recently been overhauled and though the new Core offers some flexibility, the main issues the Department faced when creating the minor will continue because of the high number of prescribed credits.

In effect, whereas most American institutions of higher education where students take General Education requirements (roughly about one third of the students' courses) comprise mostly of Humanities, Arts and Sciences courses, at Bentley all students, even those not majoring in a business discipline, must also take a set of Business courses under both the previous and the new core curriculum. To put this in a greater context, a traditional American university has various colleges within its system; they can be College of Arts and Sciences, College of Education, College of Business, among others. A student entering those universities must take a set of foundational courses in the aforementioned disciplines. Once a student selects a major, he or she can simply declare it or in some cases, he or she must apply, as is the case in most Health and Sciences fields. Once they go through this process, they belong to the college in which their major is housed.

As previously mentioned, most students who choose Bentley have already decided to major in business. Therefore, it is assumed that they will have to be exposed to a General Education as well as the Business Core courses. In effect, the core curriculum comprises 60% of all students' coursework. It is for this reason that minors are comprised of only four courses. This particular restriction will continue even with the new Bentley Undergraduate Core.

3 The design of the Spanish for Business minor

Even though Bentley University has a somewhat cumbersome process to approve new programs, there are no specific guidelines for designing a minor. This meant I enjoyed certain curricular freedom within the minor. More

---

[3] At the time of writing and the soon to be old Bentley undergraduate curriculum has a total of 74 prescribed credit hours (47 credits of General Education and 27 of the aforementioned Business Core) plus 27–30 credit hours to fulfill any major, leaving roughly 18–21 credit hours of electives (Bentley University 2021).

specifically, the courses required to fulfill the minor could follow a certain pattern as long as they met the goals and objectives of the minor. Before outlining some specifics, I took into consideration various factors that would help me shape the curriculum, such as the research background faculty had in the Department, some of the newly created courses, and my knowledge, or lack thereof, in business practices. These factors allowed me to develop a curriculum that would highlight the different idiosyncrasies that influence the Hispanic world, including the United States.

Compared to other American institutions, the Spanish for Business minor at Bentley had to be limited to four courses—most minors in the United States require six—yet it also follows a similar path as other universities. For example, Kutztown University (Pennsylvania) and the College of Charleston (South Carolina) require writing courses, translation, and LSP classes. Because of Bentley's reputation as an institution with high rates of job placement after graduation, I included topics within the courses required for the minor that may be relevant to students' desire to attain jobs in a Spanish-speaking country or, if in the United States, where they could engage with a Spanish-speaking population.

On the other hand, to address the little knowledge I possessed in best business practices, I recognized that I needed flexibility in the courses. This would enable me to research this crucial topic, while at the same time I knew that my students would contribute to the class because of their strong business education. Once I considered all these components, I incorporated two existing classes, created a new one, and included a fourth from a list of Spanish courses. The overarching goal was to include several options that would meet the learning goals of the minor. These goals are to appreciate business practices in Spanish cultures, to understand cultural differences using their business acumen, and to gain new knowledge of ethical practices in Spanish-speaking countries. To this end, I designed the Spanish for Business minor with the following required courses:

- MLSP302 Spanish for Business I,
- MLSP312 Spanish for Business II,
- MLSP203 Advanced Grammar and Composition or MLSP305 Spanish Translation,
- one elective course.[4]

---

[4] An extensive list comprised of ML courses, as well as some from other disciplines, is available on Bentley University's Undergraduate Catalogue 2021–2022.

As previously noted, I created a second course (MLSP312) to fulfill the minor. Since foreign language education "has the potential to play a key role in stimulating interdisciplinary and transdisciplinary exploration" (Cammarata, Tedick, and Osborn 2014, 5), my intention was to provide a two-sequence course that could expand the business knowledge our students have while adding cultural content related to best business practices in Spanish-speaking countries.

4 Three courses: An attempt at an interdisciplinary approach

The two Spanish for Business courses I chose for the minor differ in their methods of delivery: one is theoretical in nature (MLSP302), while the other (MLSP312) is designed to be practical. The third required course focuses on either writing or translation.

4.1 Spanish for Business I (MLSP302)

Despite my objective to be innovative and because the amount of material available (mostly online resources) was underwhelming, I felt I needed a textbook to guide me through the unchartered waters of teaching LSP to business students. It is for this reason that I decided to keep the textbook Bentley had used for years, *Éxito Comercial* (by Michael Scott Doyle and T. Bruce Fryer). In the United States, this is currently one of the most popular textbooks in this field. The book is divided thematically into 14 chapters, including Globalization, Human Resources, Marketing, Banking, and the Office, to name a few. The book introduces a great deal of vocabulary words in each chapter, which can be daunting to non-business students, and includes some updated information about Spanish-speaking countries and Brazil. However, this cultural material can rapidly change as new rules or events take place in the world. As I felt the need to provide some structure, I decided that, in addition to using this textbook, this class would follow a more theoretical approach built on readings that explain culture within the business world. At the same time, the course discusses in depth some important topics of every Spanish-speaking country, including the Hispanic world within the United States.

4.2 Spanish for Business II (MLSP312)

On the other hand, MLSP312 is a more hands-on course. The first time I taught this course and because I wanted to provide continuance in the curriculum, I decided to use the *Éxito Comercial* workbook. The workbook mirrors the textbook in many ways but offers several more exercises, ranging from audio practice to translation. However, students voiced the repetitiveness and predictability of activities on every chapter. These included translations from Spanish to English and vice versa, brief readings, and a short list of vocabulary words. After receiving this feedback, I realized that this workbook complimented the textbook well if both are used at the same time. It is for this reason that I decided to use other sources, many of which I explain further in this article.

4.3 Advanced Writing and Composition (MLSP203)

A popular choice among the students minoring in Spanish for Business is Advanced Grammar and Composition, which is essentially a writing class. Because this course is exclusively designed for L2 learners of Spanish, it is closed to those students who finished their primary and secondary (K-12) schools in a Spanish-speaking country. Currently, I use the textbook *Talleres de Escritores* (by Guillermo Bleichmar and Paula Cañón), which is a neatly divided textbook that uses a scaffolding approach. In effect, the book begins with some grammar points, such as adjectives and the use of metaphors and similes, among others. The closing activity of this first chapter is a basic description using the aforementioned writing tools. The book continues with a similar layout in the subsequent chapters. The sixth and final chapter ends with an academic research paper writing assignment. The ML Department offers this class every fall, and since 2015 I have incorporated certain topics related to business.

For example, in Chapter 5, which focuses on argumentation, I plan activities, such as interviews and poll questions, that prompt my students to choose between two sides of an argument and write a persuasive essay. These activities are designed with the aim to help students prepare argumentative essays based on current topics. They tend to bring friendly discussions about relevant topics, such as the effects of the legalization of marijuana. For this particular theme, my students go around the classroom and discuss with their peers the pros and cons of this recent trend in the world. After gathering information, they submit an argumentative essay in favor or against the legalization of marijuana from a business standpoint. Given the fact that as of 2016 the use of marijuana for recreational purposes is legal in Massachusetts, the conversations have evolved to more interesting ideas. For example, students have written about the opening of marijuana dispensaries and their marketing plans.

4.4 Translation (MLSP305)

Bentley University has a significant number of international students (comprising over 10% of the student population), and many of them come from various Spanish-speaking countries. Since many businesses use their workers as translators (Piekkari, Welch, and Welch 2014, 29), I selected Spanish Translation as a course option for this minor. Although I do not teach this course, I believe the course can be extremely beneficial to precisely those international students as well as Spanish heritage speakers. This class has recently undergone restructuring, but the main objective of the course is to teach students about the various techniques of translation as well as the importance of communicative translation. Throughout the semester, students work on translation from English to Spanish and vice versa. This important class feature allows students to expand their appreciation of both languages as they consider how to best translate structures, words, texts, and discourse styles unique to each respective language, while simultaneously acquiring a valuable and highly marketable skill. Starting in 2019, this class now offers an embedded service-learning project. In this project, students interact with Hispanic families who are learning English and together they discuss various topics, ranging from comparison and contrast of the education in various Hispanic countries and the United States, gender equality, and family life, to name a few. In addition, students can also advance their skills in a real-life setting, such as through visits to the Waltham Housing Authority, an organization that "provides low-income families, seniors, and people with disabilities the opportunity to live in safe, decent, affordable and accessible housing" (n.d.). During these visits, students help the local government office with the translation of various documents.

5 Examples of classroom activities

I would like to dedicate this section to the various activities that I have incorporated into my courses for this minor. Some of the activities have been assimilated from past language courses I have taught throughout the years, while others have stemmed from conversations with colleagues or from feedback that students have shared with me.

5.1 Vocabulary and review games

As I have previously stated, MLSP302 is a highly theoretical class. The textbook introduces up to 100 words per chapter. In an effort to make the class more conducive to dialogue, the class plays vocabulary games, and this usually occurs at the beginning of each chapter. For students want continuity, I separate the class into five to six groups (on average, each team has four to five members), and they must remain with that group for at least four chapters. The game consists of having one student from each group stand and face their team so that they cannot see the board where I display a selected word from that chapter. The remaining teammates must try to describe the word to their partner by providing hints and clues in the target language within a business context. For example, the word *tenedor* has two different meanings in Spanish; it can mean "fork," but it can also translate as "bearer" or "holder." It is relevant to highlight a recent push in the United States to take into consideration the process of language production as the starting point of learning another language, rather than the grammatical rules that can restrict students at times (VanPatten 2015, 3). Following this mindset, I emphasize to the students that they do not need to focus so much on grammar, but rather emphasize the content. Therefore, I guide my students to remain within the business context in all the words that they are given. Each team receives one point if the person standing can only get the English word, and two if they get it in Spanish as well. At the end, I calculate the points, and the winning team gets an extra point on the upcoming exam. I usually pick about seven words per group, for a total of 35. This ensures that everyone has a chance to be the guesser at least once, providing them opportunities to continue developing their listening skills.

Another popular game is the famous American TV show Jeopardy. Fortunately, several websites share their templates online, although most use the game for vocabulary purposes. However, I have found that this game is extremely useful in my writing course whenever I introduce difficult topics, such as the use of tildes, diphthongs, and hiatus. It is a fun and interactive game that I usually implement as a review before an exam.

5.2 Students as teachers

At Bentley, the language proficiency levels of the students taking content courses[5] range from intermediate mid to L1 users of Spanish, which allows me to pair students in mixed-proficiency dyads and lead classroom discussions in the MLSP302 course. In effect, before every class session, students provide discussion questions stemming from the assigned readings. As part of this assignment, students must ask thought-provoking questions. An important and highly specific rule I give to my students is that questions should be about "why" and "how," rather than "yes" or "no" questions. I also require them to introduce a YouTube video that further explains the main topics of the reading. Typically, the students lead, and they can often spark lively discussions. It is important to note that, although the students act as teachers, I act as the facilitator because some hot-button topics (e.g., gender equality) can trigger some controversy.

5.3 Launching marketing campaigns

One of the most acclaimed activities that I introduce in my MLSP312 course is the launch of products and the creation of a business plan. This assignment takes place over the span of two to three weeks. In pairs, students choose an

---

[5] At Bentley, these are what the Modern Languages Association refers to as advanced undergraduate courses—those in the fifth through eighth semesters.

American product they wish to launch in a Spanish-speaking country of their choice. (Countries cannot be repeated, and I always tell each group to have a plan A, B, and sometimes even C). They also import a product of that country into the United States. The project consists of four main parts, and the students must present them all to the class:

1. portfolio for each product that addresses several aspects, such as the reason to choose each product, customs tariffs that they must inquire about online on government sites, rental agreement drafts for product storage, market analyses, earnings and expenses, and projected sales for each product,
3. television commercial for the product to be launched in the Spanish-speaking country,
4. a billboard for the product to be launched in the United States,
5. a social media campaign for both products.

On presentation day, students must treat the class as if they were a group of investors. Therefore, I give extra credit points to those students who ask questions to the class. As previously stated, this is one of the most highly regarded activities from this class. It provides the students with the optimal opportunity to practice their business skills as well as showcase their creativity using platforms of their choice.

5.4 The human resources chapter

In the MLSP312 course, students learn some important cultural aspects about human resources in Hispanic culture. For example, they learn that providing photos, revealing marital status, or even date of birth in a curriculum vitae (CV) is not rare. At the same time, they are able to compare and contrast the format of CV and letters of application in Spanish compared to those in the United States. This interactive chapter provides a great opportunity for my students to be interviewers as well as interviewees. In effect, in groups of three or four, students create a business and design ads for a job position. This activity focuses heavily on forms because oftentimes a grammar rule can make a difference in job ads. Because of this, and using authentic materials, I highlight mistakes in both job ads and application materials. After presenting the business names and job ads, students proceed to work on their CVs as well as draft application letters. After students complete writing their application materials, they send them to the respective companies using the contact information provided in the groups' ads, and I hold mock interviews. Since this lesson encourages students to go beyond their comfort zone, students need a certain structure; therefore, I provide a rubric for an interviewer and interviewee for these mock interviews, which can be found in Figures 5.1 and 5.2 below.

Figure 5.1: MLSP312 rubric for mock interview (interviewee)

CATEGORY	4	3	2	1
Speaking	Student speaks clearly and enunciates words to the best of his or her abilities. There are no errors in pronunciation	Student speaks clearly most of the time. The student takes the necessary time to enunciate words that although there may have errors, he or she can be understood by someone whose first language is Spanish.	Student speaks clearly some of the time. There are some glaring errors in pronunciation, but he or she can be understood by someone whose first language is Spanish but is familiar with L2 Spanish learners.	There are too many errors throughout the interview, which makes it extremely difficult to understand.
Vocabulary and delivery	Student can answer all questions accurately. Student expands beyond the scope of what is required.	Students can answer most of the questions accurately, but there are some gaps. Student does not expand beyond the scope what is required.	Student can answer some of the questions accurately, but there are several gaps that leave the interviewers wondering. Student does not attempt to go beyond the scope of what is required.	Student cannot answer questions accurately and often asks for explanation of the questions.
Eye contact and delivery	Student maintains eye contact all the time, delivers content in a clear and concise manner. The volume and gestures enhance the interaction.	Student maintains eye contact most of the time. Student shows little hesitation. The volume and gesture support the interaction.	Student maintains eye contact some of the time. Student shows hesitation but does not hinder the flow of the conversation. The volume and gesture display some support the interaction.	Student maintains very little eye contact. Student shows hesitation that hinders the flow of the conversation. Student speaks at very low volume and there is no gesture throughout the interaction.
Grammar	Student interacts using best sentence structure and grammar, which enhance the interaction. There is use of slang and	Student interacts using some proper sentence structure and grammar, which support the interaction. There is some	Student interacts using proper sentence structure and grammar, but only to stay within the topic. There is	Student interacts using incorrect sentence structure and grammar, which hinders the interaction. There is no

	business jargon in some parts of the conversation.	attempt to use slang and business jargon.	some attempt to use business jargon.	attempt to use slang or business jargon.

Figure 5.2: MLSP312 rubric for mock interview (interviewer)

CATEGORY	4	3	2	1
Content	Student displays complete control of conversation and uses business jargon and slang. Student follows up answers with questions.	Student displays control of conversation most of the time and makes attempt to use business jargon and slang. Student makes an attempt to expand on answers from interviewee.	Student displays some control of conversation and makes attempt to use business jargon. Student makes some attempt to expand on answers from interviewee.	Student displays no control of conversation and makes no attempt to use business jargon and slang. Student does not attempt to expand on answers from interviewee.
Speaking	Student speaks clearly and has no errors in pronunciation.	Student speaks clearly and has a few errors in pronunciation, but it does not hinder flow of the interaction.	Student speaks clearly and has errors in pronunciation, but they understandable for a Spanish speaker who is familiar with the accent.	There are many errors throughout the conversation, and they hinder the flow of the interaction.

The Future

In 2007, the Modern Language Association Ad Hoc Committee on Foreign Languages published a report about the future of teaching foreign languages in HE. It stated that "[t]he standard configuration of university foreign language curricula, in which a two- or three-year language sequence feeds into a set of core courses primarily focused on canonical literature [...], represents a narrow model" (MLA n.d.). This has fostered a culture of two sides. On the one hand, there are the language instructors who teach basic and intermediate courses and, on the other, academic researchers—mostly tenured faculty—who teach the content-based classes, mostly beyond the intermediate level. Because of this environment, language instructors and academic researchers have worked in silos, which has increased the gap between these two groups. Due to this lack of collaboration, instructors may not have significant input in missions of foreign language programs. Worsening the issue is the fact that most doctoral programs do not emphasize language teaching, but once their students graduate, they attain positions in HE institutions and are the ones who affect the curriculum (VanPatten 2015, 8).

This reality coupled with the fact that LSP has been "an applied field with little funding, support, or recognition for in-depth research" (Sánchez-López, Long, and Lafford 2017, 13) has compelled American universities to be creative. As a result, several universities have started launching majors that meet the needs of employers, such as the Foreign Language and International Economics major offered by the University of Kentucky and Foreign Language and International Trade Concentration offered by the University of Alabama in Huntsville, to name two. In a globalized world, where students grow up in the digital age, universities must explore modes of creativity, meet the demands of the market, and spark interest in the students. It is for this reason that during the fall 2019, soon after I took the role of Chair of the ML Department, I spearheaded the redesign of the Hispanic Studies; and using various models, including Clemson University Language and International Business and American University Business, Language and Culture Studies, the Department launched a new major—Language, Culture, and Business with a specialization in the four languages taught at Bentley University. The newly founded program is truly interdisciplinary. It uses the Bentley Business Core to its advantage and includes courses from several business departments. At the same time, it encompasses courses within the chosen language in writing, language for the profession, and culture. It also contains a guaranteed Global Experience through the office of Study Abroad and the Pulfiser Career Development Center, Bentley University's career office.

In conclusion, as it was shown in this chapter, the time to begin thinking outside the box and start a true collaboration between researchers and instructors is now. In a world in which the landscape of HE is often questioned, and when languages are scrutinized and challenged, I argue that we can be creative in the topics we teach and the programs we design. As someone who has published on the end of the 19th century in Spain—specifically about Krausism—I can attest that, through some creativity and partnership with other disciplines and researchers, foreign languages can have a place at the forefront of new programs.

References

Bentley University. 2021. "Undergraduate Catalogue 2021–2022." Accessed May 17, 2022. https://catalog.bentley.edu/undergraduate/.

Bentley University. 2017. "Graduate Catalogue." Accessed May 17, 2022. https://d2 f5upgbvkx8pz.cloudfront.net/sites/default/files/inline-files/GR-Catalog%202017-18_0.pdf.

Bentley University. 2022. "Mission and Vision." Accessed May 17, 2022. https://www.bentley.edu/about/mission-and-values.

Bleichmar Guillermo, and Paula Cañón. 2016. *Talleres de Escritores*. Second edition. Boston: Vista Higher Learning.

Cammarata, Laurent, Diane J. Tedick, and Terry A. Osborn. 2014. "Content-Based Instruction and Curricular Reforms." *Content-Based Foreign Language Teaching: Curriculum and Pedagogy for Developing Advanced Thinking and Literacy Skills*, edited by Laurent Cammarata, 1–21. New York: Routledge.

Cummings Joy, and Roy Lister. 2014. "Integrating CBI into High School Foreign Language." In *Content-Based Foreign Language Teaching: Curriculum and Pedagogy for Developing Advanced Thinking and Literacy Skills*, edited by Laurent Cammarata, 77–98. New York: Routledge.

Doyle, Michael Scott, and T. Bruce Fryer. 2017. *Éxito Comercial*. Seventh Edition. Boston: Cengage.

EFMD Global. 2022. "About EFMD Global." Accessed May 17, 2022. https://www.efmdglobal.org/about-efmd-global/.

MLA Ad Hoc Committee on Foreign Languages. N.d. "Foreign Languages and Higher Education: New Structures for a Changed World." Accessed 1 September 1, 2020. https://www.mla.org/Resources/Research/Surveys-Reports-and-Other-Documents/Teaching-Enrollments-and-Programs/Foreign-Languages-and-Higher-Education-New-Structures-for-a-Changed-World.

Henrichs, Helen. 2022. "Bentley Named a Top University for Long-Term Return on Investment." Bentley University Newsroom. Accessed May 17, 2022. https://www.bentley.edu/news/bentley-named-top-university-long-term-return-investment.

Henrichs, Helen. 2019. "New Bentley Graduates Report Successful Outcomes: 99 Percent are Employed or in Graduate School." Bentley University Newsroom. Accessed August 15, 2020. https://www.bentley.edu/prepared/new-bentley-graduates-report-successful-outcomes-99-percent-are-employed-or-graduate-school.

Piekkari, Rebecca, Danice E. Welch, and Lawrence S. Welch. 2014. *Language in International Business: The Multilingual Reality of Global Business Expansion*. Northampton: Edward Elgar.

Sánchez-López, Mary K. Long, and Barbara Lafford. 2017. "New Directions in LSP Research in US Higher Education." In *Language for Specific Purposes: Trend in Curriculum Development*, edited by Mary K. Long. Washington, DC: Georgetown University Press.

The Best 385 Colleges 2020 Edition. 2020. Accessed September 10, 2020. https://www.princetonreview.com/college-rankings?rankings=best-career-services.

VanPatten, Bill. 2015. "Hispania White Paper: Where Are the Experts?" *Hispania* 98 (1): 2–13.

Waltham Housing Authority. N.d. "Homepage." Accessed December 1, 2020. http://walhouse.org.

CHAPTER 6

Tailoring an LSP course: Threading the needle with sociolinguistic tenets

Yliana V. Rodríguez

Universidad de la República, Uruguay

Lucía López Risso

Universidad de la República, Uruguay

Abstract

One of the many consequences of the expansion of British colonial power and the emergence of the USA as a leading economic state is the growing demand for using English (Crystal 1997, Penycook 2007). Good reading skills in English have become part of the indispensable toolkit of students, instructors and researchers. In response to this reality, the Center for Foreign Languages of Universidad de la República (Uruguay) offers English reading comprehension courses which aim to provide university students with the necessary strategies to access specialized literature. However, when it comes to the design of LSP courses, there are very few methodological guidelines. Hence, practitioners face the challenge of developing both the curriculum and the teaching strategies almost from scratch. In this chapter we argue that language education lags behind with respect to making the most of other disciplines and that sociolinguistics in particular has a lot to offer when it comes to the tailoring and execution of LSP courses. The aim of this work is to present the sociolinguistic tenets that were taken as guiding principles for the design and execution of the English reading comprehension course of the Faculty of Psychology. Within such context, we elaborate on how raising awareness on some sociolinguistic principles can aid the LSP instructor run a successful practice.

Keywords: sociolinguistics, LSP, curriculum design, language awareness, English reading comprehension

***

Introduction

Having proficient reading skills is fundamental when it comes to studying, teaching, and carrying out research, not to mention lifelong education. As a result of the expansion of Britain's colonial power and the economic leadership of the USA in the world's economy, using English has become essential (Crystal 1997, Penycook 2007). Without such a skill, keeping up to date with the latest scientific findings becomes a difficult enterprise. Due to this scenario, the Center for Foreign Languages has been offering ongoing courses of *English Reading Comprehension* in many faculties of Universidad de la República (Uruguay). The courses aim to provide university students with the necessary strategies to tackle frequent genres in their disciplinary areas in order to access specialized literature. Unfortunately, there are very few guidelines when it comes to the design of Language for Specific Purposes (LSP) courses, and instructors end up developing the curriculum and the teaching strategies all by themselves.

Even though current approaches to foreign language education call for an understanding of sociocultural theory and sociolinguistics (Bayrutt 2013), language education is in arrears with profiting from other disciplines. In this chapter, we argue that sociolinguistics in particular has a lot to offer when it comes to the tailoring and execution of an LSP course, given that resorting to sociolinguistic insights can be used for teaching towards a better world (Penycook 2010, 82). In the present work, we present some sociolinguistic tenets that were used as guiding principles for the design and execution of the aforementioned reading comprehension course and explain how raising awareness of these principles can help LSP instructors in their challenging endeavor. Three tenets were considered, namely: monolingualism is not the normal state of humankind, languages change over time, and languages are in contact with each other.

In Section 1 we describe the main characteristics of the course, in Section 2 we elaborate on each one of the principles, explain their relevance for teaching and learning a foreign language, and present some practical examples of how the tenets were orchestrated, and in Section 3 we present some students' reflections during the course, on the grounds that students' opinions have a potential to improve teaching effectiveness. All observations made in this work are circumscribed to this particular LSP course and its students: young adult graduates and undergraduates of the Faculty of Psychology.

1 The context: A reading comprehension course

The *English Reading Comprehension* course is a semester long, and it is offered to both graduate and undergraduate students of the Faculty of Psychology.[1] It is a requisite for students to take a foreign language reading course (either English or Portuguese) unless they certify that they already know one of these languages either by sitting for an exam or by presenting corresponding credentials. The course is blended in nature, so students attend half the classes on the faculty premises and the rest in the university's virtual learning environment EVA (Spanish acronym for *Entorno Virtual de Aprendizaje*). The learning environment is supported by Moodle,[2] a free web-based open-source learning management system.

The course is divided into five units, each with two authentic texts. Like the majority of LSP courses, it is centered on students' present needs and future professional challenges, so units tackle topics that are relevant for psychology students: *Today's world (Busy and stressed), Technology (From electricity to robots), Addictions (No escape?), Social inequality (Privilege and racism),* and *Gender (From the body to the mind).* The issue of which topics to tackle was discussed in focus groups of undergraduate students. After deciding upon these, the same students suggested a myriad of texts connected to the degree program as well as the issues that professional psychologists are dealing with at present. The ten texts used in the course were finally selected by instructors. The genres include: narrative, procedural, expository, hortatory, and descriptive. Each text has pre-reading and post-reading questions (Solé 1992) with automatic guiding feedback programmed by the instructors. However, because students sometimes feel unsure about their answers (given that most questions are open-ended), a forum was created for them to ask questions. The online forum is meant for communication between students and instructors as well as students themselves.

Since readers' motivations, attitudes, goals, and interests need to be accounted for in a full model of reading (see Bernhardt 2005, Finkbeiner 2005), during the course students are asked to evaluate both the text and all the stages that precede and follow it. These assessments are used to evaluate the course's success and to design improved versions of the course since the course is being continuously refreshed. New texts are provided by both students and instructors, and questions and activities are re-evaluated regularly.

---

[1] It is worth noting that Universidad de la República is a public university, which leads to the student body being very diverse.

[2] Written in PHP and distributed under the GNU General Public License.

2 Sociolinguistics and language awareness

Within linguistics, sociology, and other social sciences, sociolinguistics has become an increasingly important and popular field of study (Wolfram 2019). Sociolinguistics shows the relationship between language use and the social basis for such use (Hudson 1996). Even though there are several definitions, for the purpose of this work we focus on sociolinguistics as the discipline that examines how language and culture are related (Bell 1976) and whose main task is to uncover, describe, and interpret the socially motivated choices speakers make (Coulmas 2013).

Language awareness generally denotes "explicit knowledge about language, and conscious perception and sensitivity in language learning, language teaching and language use" (*ALA Definition* 2016).[3] Sadly, language teachers seldom reflect on how the other languages of their learners' can be activated to the benefit of acquiring the target language faster and more effectively (Haukås 2015). Furthermore, they rarely contemplate how knowledge of language phenomena can aid in the process.

In this section, we elaborate on three precepts from sociolinguistics, a field that offers a plethora of knowledge that is yet to be fully exploited by language instructors, and point out why and how they can become part of an LSP instructor's toolkit. The tenets—embroidered with language awareness—constitute the ground rules of the aforementioned course. Such tenets helped run a successful teaching practice, and although they were used in the context of a reading comprehension program, we believe they could prove useful in other LSP settings as well.

2.1 Monolingualism is not the normal state of humankind

> Societies are multicultural in nature. It is estimated that there are far more bilingual and multilingual speakers than there are monolinguals (Baker and Prys Jones 1998; Hamers and Blanc 2000; Crystal 1987; Dewaele, Housen, and Wei 2003).

We do not know the exact number of languages spoken in the world (in part because of the difficult distinction between language and dialect). According to *Ethnologue* (Eberhard, Simons, and Fennig 2020)—the most comprehensive catalogue of the world's languages—there are 7105 living languages. However, we do know that many people speak more than one of these languages. Even

---

[3] Hernandez and Li (2007) propose that learning early in life is based more on sensory and motor brain systems whereas learning later in life is based on higher-level cognitive brain systems that develop later in life. Language awareness is part of the latter.

though many societies see monolingualism as the norm, this is not the case when considering the whole population of our planet. Multilingualism is a well-established phenomenon across the globe (Eisenchlas, Schalley, and Guillemin 2015). Despite this reality, the so-called monolingual bias is present in many western societies. Unfortunately, this bias is also present in the majority of foreign language classrooms. In most contexts worldwide, language teaching is predominantly based on monolingual instructional principles, with minimal or no reference to students' other languages (Cummins 2017). This is a consequence of the traditional teacher-training model which considers language autonomous, placing the focus only on the target language (Otwinowska-Kasztelanic 2017).

There is no reason why the target language should be the only language used in the classroom or be taught separately from other languages that students know. In fact, in the case of English, imposing the English-only policy lends continuity to the imperialistic practices of English-speaking countries by presenting the economically and politically dominant groups as the only right and standard ones (Otwinowska-Kasztelanic 2017; Byram and Feng 2004; Young, Sachdev, and Seedhouse 2009). We agree with Otwinowska-Kasztelanic in that there is "no reason why English should be the only language used in the classroom and should be taught separately from other languages known to learners" (2017, 305). What is more, the monolingual bias should be debunked in both societal and classroom levels.

In the reading comprehension course, students' native language as well as other languages known to them are welcome, and multilingualism is treated as a common phenomenon within human communication. (It is worth noting that all instructors are knowledgeable in at least two foreign languages.) Accordingly, when tailoring the course, students' languages were taken into account by designing instances of reflection in which the target language was compared with students' L1 (Spanish) and other foreign languages. (A questionnaire is carried out at the beginning of the course to find out about learners' foreign languages. See Appendix 6.1.) Even though mastering English is the target, students' L1 is used as a scaffold to reach that aim. For instance, we ponder how Spanish is a synthetic language while English is analytic and weigh up the pros of this difference for learners of the latter. Furthermore, we study the Latin and Greek etymology of the English lexicon in order to speed up the learning process (see Table 6.1). In this experience, contrasting linguistic systems helped students gain confidence in resorting to their own language knowledge to better learn a foreign tongue.

Table 6.1: Words with Latin or Greek roots that denote states of feeling
(adapted from Green 2020, 128).

Love and desire		
Greek or Latin word	**English meaning**	**English derivative**
amor, amoris	love	amorous
amicus, amici	friend	amicable
cupido, cupidinis	longing, desire	cupidity
philia (φιλια)	affection, friendship	
phile-, -phile (used as noun-forming prefix or suffix in English)	loving	bibliophile, philharmonic
eros (ερως)	desire	erotic
Hatred and disapproval		
Greek or Latin word	**English meaning**	**English derivative**
odium, odii	hatred	odious
hostile, hostilis	enemy (adjective)	hostile
hostis, hostis	enemy (noun)	host
fallo-fallere-falsum	deceive	fallacy
pseudon (ψευδον)	lie	
pseudo- (prefix used as a learned borrowing)	false	pseudonym

2.2 Languages change over time

> "Unless they are dead, languages are always adapting to the needs of their users. This isn't a bad thing, if English hadn't changed since, say, 1950, we wouldn't have words to refer to modems, mobile phones, or technology in general" (Birner 2019).

Linguistic change is the diachronic process that begins as an individual innovation and then propagates to the rest of the community of speakers. Eugenio Coseriu has done one of the most remarkable studies on that process. In his words, "what becomes different through change is the specific language itself as a historical product, as a set of traditions; and in this sense, we can speak of 'linguistic change', i.e., of change in a language or in languages. But properly speaking this does not mean that a language as an objective product (ergon) changes: it means that a language is produced. In the right perspective, languages are not continually changing, they are continually being produced, being done" (Coseriu 1983, 55).

For Coseriu, linguistic change does not consist of alterations in the products of language; instead, it is a creation of linguistic traditions, and the material for this change may come from another language. By not seeing the change as a product, he considers that it does not exist as a special category, different from the other general manifestations of language. For him, the change is no more than the normal functioning of language. In the same vein, Adolfo Elizaincín

(2011) explains that linguistic change is as inevitable as it is unpredictable and that it is not unidirectional, given that it does not start unequivocally at a certain time and place, and from there it begins its uninterrupted trajectory over a period of time until it finishes. On the contrary, according to Elizaincín, usually its beginnings are barely perceptible, and its concretion often does not materialize; and to reinforce this idea he quotes Givón: "we must remind ourselves periodically that language never rests, it is always in the middle of change, in pronunciation, in lexicon and in syntax" (1984, 44).

Although they know that languages change, students might not always bear in mind this variation phenomena. For example, sometimes they are perplexed when they do not find a word in a dictionary, failing to see that neologisms occur in any natural language. They are puzzled to find out that there are many "correct" ways of saying the same thing in the same language, overlooking the fact that English in particular has many varieties around the globe and that the form depends also on the context and the register, among many other factors. Additionally, they tend to see irregular verb lists as tedious and nonsensical, and they wonder why "dream" has two possible past-tense and past-participle forms. Nonetheless, if instructors make them aware of the behind-the-scenes of such phenomena, their learning becomes more significant.

During the course, whenever an irregularity comes up, students are invited to discuss their hypothesis for such a "distortion." By means of practice, they begin to see how variation and change are natural in any human language and how irregular forms respond to the history of languages. For instance, students are presented with verb lists and asked to analyze them in terms of their form and frequency (see Tables 6.2 and 6.3). They soon realize how new verbs adjust to the rules of our synchrony and how the most frequent ones still respect the commands of past times. This helps students see irregularities as meaningful phenomena, which leads to more purposeful learning.

Table 6.2: Non-past to past tense conjugation of
Modern English Internal Vowel Alternation

IVA pattern	Non-past tense form	Past tense form
[ɪ] → [ʌ]	dig	dug, *digged*
[ɪ] → [ʌ]	string	strung
[ɪ] → [ʌ]	stick	stuck
[ɪ] → [ʌ]	ding	dung

(IVA) verbal forms (adapted from Even-Simkin and Tobin 2013, 236).

Table 6.3: Fronting process in nouns from singular to plural formation in Modern English (adapted from Even-Simkin and Tobin 2013, 51)

Singular form of Modern English nouns with the following phonological representation of the vowels: [u, au, æ]	Plural form of Modern English nouns with the following phonological representation of the vowels: [, i, a]	Fronting process (+) of IVA
man (mann)	men (menn)	[æ] [ ] = (+)
woman (wīfmann)	women (wīfmenn)	[æ] [ ] = (+)
foot (fōt)	feet (fēt)	[u] [i] = (+)
tooth (tōð)	teeth (tēð)	[u] [i] = (+)
goose (gōs)	geese (gēs)	[u] [i] = (+)
mouse (mūs)	mice (mys)	[au] [a] = (+)
louse (lūs)	lice (lys)	[au] [a] = (+)

2.3 Languages are in contact with each other

Linguists have yet to find a language that has remained completely isolated or developed in isolation. Even though we tend to think of languages as watertight compartments, language contact is the norm, and its results should not be overlooked.

David Crystal (2006) defines *language contact* as a term used in sociolinguistics to refer to a situation of geographical continuity or social proximity—and therefore mutual influence—of languages or dialects. Its consequences can be observed in the *emergence of loanwords, patterns of phonological or grammatical change, mixed forms,* such as pidgins and creoles, and a general increase in *bilingualism.* In a narrow sense, languages are considered to be in contact if they are used interchangeably by the same people. As regards loanwords, Peter Durkin (chief etymologist of the *Oxford English Dictionary*) points out that

> loanwords have a key role in the development of the lexicon, whether they offer ways of expressing new concepts, or new ways of expressing existing concepts. [...] Indeed, fine-grained analysis offers the potential to gain insight into a plurality of cultures and societies that share a common core of vocabulary but within which there are significant differences in the lexicons of particular groups or individuals. Ultimately, language is a vehicle of thought and expression, and the reception of loanwords into the system of a language is one of the ways in which a language changes and develops, and with it the resources of that language for formulating thoughts and communicating them to others (2015, 428).

With respect to the case of English in contact with other languages, John Algeo states that Britain underwent waves of invasion by Celts, Romans, Anglo-Saxons, Danes, and Norman French, each of them contributing to the life and language of the islands (2010, 247). In a very similar way, the American population, despite being British at its origin, is the product of a combination of genes, cultures, and speechways, as Algeo explains. And being the case that English is spread throughout the world, it has influenced and been influenced by many languages. The result is a mongrelized vocabulary and culture (Algeo 2010, 247). But despite this intense contact, English core vocabulary continues to be patrimonial. Words used daily to refer to kinship relationships, actions, addresses, numbers, and grammatical lemmas[4] are native. Even though words used daily to refer to kinship relationships, actions, addresses, numbers, and grammatical lemmas are native, most of the words present in any extensive dictionary of English have their origin in other languages or were coined from foreign words. In sum, English has an important number of foreign components.

Relevant for the instruction of foreign languages—and in particular for those Romance language speakers studying English—is the fact that many of the words English has borrowed from other languages work as cognates. Moreover, its more learned and formal vocabulary shows a huge influence of French and Latin in its basic constituents as well as in its derivational processes (Durkin 2015). Making learners aware of lexical borrowing as one of the linguistic consequences of cultural contact between societies and knowing that English in particular has borrowed a sensational number of words from other languages can help students identify such words more easily.

The aforementioned reading comprehension course starts with the narrative of William the Conqueror: the onset of the colossal number of words with Latin origin present in English. The Norman invasion set up a language contact state of affairs that ultimately benefited Romance language speakers that learn English almost one thousand years later. Students realize that Spanish and English have much more in common than one may think. It is noteworthy that these loanwords work as cognates, which helps readers recognize words more easily (Heuven, Dijkstra, and Grainger 1998; Dijkstra and Heuven 2002; Kroll and Dijkstra 2002; Kroll et al. 2002; Lemhöfer and Dijkstra 2004; Otwinowska-Kasztelanic 2009; among others). See Figure 6.1 for an example of cognates identified in an abstract.

---

[4] E.g., earth, tree, stone, sea, hill, dog, bird, house, land, roof, sun, moon, time, friend, foe, mother, father, son, daughter, wife, husband, hate, love, fear, greedy, help, harm, rest, walk, ride, speak, one, two, three, ten, top, bottom, north, south, up, down, I, you, he, to, for, from, be, have, after, but, and, etc. (Algeo 2010, 247).

Figure 6.1: Cognates identified in an abstract (Dhont et al. 2019, 29)

Abstract
Despite being **animals, humans distance** themselves **physically** and **mentally** from
(most) other **animals** and **prioritize human interests.** We **exploit** other **animals** to feed,
clothe, and **entertain** ourselves, to name just a **few animal exploitation practices.** Such
discrimination against other **species,** or *speciesism,* is the **central focus** of the **present**
chapter. Drawing on **recent specific** findings, we **reveal** the **psychological connections**
between **speciesism** and **prejudices** such as **racism** and **sexism.** Those who **support**
animal exploitation also tend to endorse **sexist** and **racist** views and rely on belief in
group dominance and **human supremacy** to **justify systems** of **inequality** and
oppression. The **common denominator** is that the **interests** of **disadvantaged groups**
like **animals,** women, and **ethnic minorities,** are **considered subordinate** to the
interests and **privileges** of **advantaged groups** like **humans** in **general,** and white men
in **particular.** Although **recognizing** this **intersectionality** is **critical** to the understanding of
human-animal relations, explicitly referring to such **parallels** in **animal** advocacy
campaigns can be easily misunderstood, and may be **ineffective** or even **counterproductive.**
We see **value** in **experience-** and behavior-**based interventions** where people learn to
connect psychologically with **animals** to change their **animal-relevant** beliefs, and
more **generally,** to broaden the mind and challenge **exploitative societal traditions.**

3 Students' reflections

Language courses should allow students "to be aware of the pedagogical goals
and content of the course, to help them go beyond the classroom, and to make
links between the content of the classroom and the world beyond" (Nunan and
Lamb 1996, 12). Our understanding of the world beyond includes language
phenomena and in order to rest assured that the aforementioned "links" are
established, questionnaires were carried out throughout the course. Furthermore,
it is widely agreed that "it is important to reflect on students' attitudes to
improve teaching quality" (El-Halees 2011), especially when it comes to online
teaching as students' perspectives and experiences have the potential of
providing an in-depth understanding of the effectiveness of web-based learning
(Vonderwell 2003). The questionnaires have proven effective in improving student
learning as well as student satisfaction with the course.

In the questionnaires students are asked to evaluate different aspects of each
of the five units as well as to provide a final assessment of the reading
comprehension course. Concomitantly, students are encouraged to share how
they navigate the course. This exchange is intended to improve the course and
to keep it relevant to students through their academic journey. Every question
is presented in Spanish, and students are expected to answer in the like
manner. Therefore, all questions and answers were translated from Spanish to
English for the purpose of this article.

From the beginning of the course, students are introduced to loanwords,
particularly to those that work as cognates with Spanish. Most students (76%)
state that they were not aware of the existence of cognates before taking the

course when asked in the first questionnaire (Were you aware of the phenomenon of cognates? / *¿Ya conocía el fenómeno de los cognados?*).

The vast majority of students tend to be surprised when the similarities between English and Spanish are highlighted. As an example, some students compare the course with their previous experiences:

i. "Making comparisons with cognates, for example. Even though I speak English, I have never seen it explained with comparisons like these." / *La comparación con los cognados, por ejemplo. Si bien sé inglés nunca vi que lo explicaran con comparaciones así.*

ii. "Spanish cognates and their history. In my years of study, it had never been explained that way. It was very interesting." / *Los cognados del español y su historia. En los años de estudio nunca lo habían explicado de esa forma. Fue muy interesante.*

This way, from the first class, students are introduced to one of the tenets that guide the course: languages are in contact with each other. Over the course of the semester, they incorporate new vocabulary and acquire vital skills to navigate an academic text by themselves. By unit two, *Technology (From electricity to robots)*, students encounter unknown words that cannot be found in their dictionaries. This situation usually gives rise to a debate among students through which they realize languages change over time, allowing for the creation of new words. Exploring this idea, students are further aware of the resemblance between languages. For instance, as they notice the presence of neologisms and acronyms in the texts, they make comparisons with their L1 and start to see change as natural in every language, which they mostly did not consider before. As an example, when asked about what they found new about the unit (Which aspects of this unit did you find newfangled? / *¿Qué cuestión de esta unidad le resultó novedosa?*), a student writes:

iii. "There are many new and current words, such as bullied, diagnosed, mental health." / *Palabras nuevas y muy actuales como bullied, diagnosed, mental health.* (Most answers to the question referred to the use of neologisms, acronyms, and initialisms.)

By the end of unit five, *Gender (From the body to the mind)*, students evaluate and reflect on the past course. When asked, What conclusions have you made about English vocabulary? / *¿Qué conclusiones ha sacado sobre el vocabulario de la lengua inglesa?*, most students agree on the fact that English and Spanish have more in common than they previously realized. Here, some of them highlight the importance of identifying cognates when reading:

iv. "Like in Spanish, a word has diverse meanings. And there are a lot of them that share an origin with words in Spanish. Identifying cognates is the new thing about vocabulary that I take from this course. I found it very useful. In the six years of English I had in high school, no teacher ever mentioned them. And recognizing them helps a lot with reading." / *Que al igual que en el español, una palabra tiene diversas acepciones. Y que hay muchas que comparten un origen común con palabras en español. La identificación de los cognados es lo más novedoso con respecto al vocabulario que me llevo de este curso. Me resultó muy útil. En seis años de inglés que tuve en el liceo, ningún profesor los nombró. Y el reconocerlos ayuda mucho con la lectura.*

v.   "We find English tricky and difficult due to the number of unknown words, but its syntactic organization is not difficult to learn, and when acknowledging the number of cognates (words of Latin origin that then have similarities to Spanish) the approach to reading seems much easier." / *La lengua inglesa nos resulta engorrosa y hasta nos causa sensación de dificultad por la cantidad de palabras desconocidas, pero su organización sintáctica no es difícil de aprender, y al notar la gran cantidad de cognados (palabras con origen en latín, que por ende, tienen similitud con el español) resulta mucho más fácil el acercamiento a la lectura.*

It is clear from most of the comments that being aware of language contact and one of its consequences—loanwords—is what students find most riveting when it comes to the learning process. This goes in line with the fact that noticing cognates has been proven to be beneficial as research confirms that when students are aware of the existence of cognates, the probability that they recognize and learn them increases (Craik 2002, Horst 2005, Hulstijn 2003, Laufer and Hulstijn 2001, Webb 2007).

Final remarks

In this work, we have presented well-established precepts from sociolinguistics that can serve in the LSP learning and teaching scenario. We started by examining the fact that monolingualism is not the norm, hence it should not be privileged over plurilingualism. Secondly, we looked into how languages are always changing and how students can profit from being aware of this reality. Last but not least, the birth of loanwords that end up working as cognates was also posited as an asset. Each tenet was introduced in terms of its potential for a language class, and although they were used in the context of a reading comprehension course, they should also prove useful in other LSP schemes. Needless to say, all the tenets are intertwined, and there are many more ways in which we can take them into account in the diverse stages of our professional practices.

Furthermore, keeping track of students' perceptions and assessment during the course was key to better accompany their process. This chapter has the merit to cruise into the under-researched area of the overlapping of language teaching and sociolinguistics. Our main goal has been to show how sociolinguistic findings can aid the language instructor. We are convinced that awareness of language phenomena can improve teaching practices as well as learning experiences, given that students responded positively to the approach, reporting that being aware of them helped tackling their reading in English. Our intention was to share a successful experience with colleagues and to invite them to reflect on how sociolinguistics can aid the sometimes-lonely LSP instructor. We are convinced that in the current state of play in language education—where we are still in arrears with benefiting from other fields—sociolinguistics is a potential contributor to language pedagogy.

References

ALA Definition. 2016. S.v. "Language Awareness Defined." Association for Language Awareness. Accessed September 20, 2020. www.lexically.net/ala/la_defined.htm.

Algeo, John. 2010. *The Origins and Development of the English Language*. Boston: Wadsworth.

Baker, Collin, and Sylvia Prys Jones. 1998. *Encyclopaedia of Bilingualism and Bilingual Education*. Clevedon: Multilingual Matters.

Bayrutt, Yasemin. 2013. "Current Perspectives on Sociolinguistics and English Language Education." *Journal of Language Teaching and Learning* 1: 69–78.

Bell, Roger T. 1976. *Sociolinguistics: Goals, Approaches, and Problems*. London: Batsford.

Bernhardt, Elizabeth. 2005. "Progress and Procrastination in Second Language Learning." *Annual Review of Applied Linguistics* 25: 133–50. https://doi.org/10.1017/S0267190505000073.

Birner, Betty. 2019. "Is English Changing?" Linguistic Society of America. Accessed March 11, 2019. https://www.linguisticsociety.org/content/english-changing.

Byram, Michael, and Anwei Feng. 2004. "Culture and Language Learning: Teaching, Research and Scholarship." *Language Teaching* 37: 149–68. https://doi.org/10.1017/S0261444804002289.

Coseriu, Eugenio. 1983. "Linguistic Change Does Not Exist." *Linguistica Nuova ed Antica, Rivista di Linguistica Classica Medioevale e Moderna* 1: 51–63.

Coulmas, Florian. 2013. *Sociolinguistics: The Study of Speakers' Choices*. Cambridge: Cambridge University Press.

Craik, Fergus. 2002. "Levels of Processing: Past, Present ... and Future?" *Memory* 10: 305–18.

Crystal, David. 1987. *The Cambridge Encyclopaedia of Language*. Cambridge: Cambridge University Press.

Crystal, David. 1997. *English as a Global Language*. Cambridge: Cambridge University Press.

Crystal, David. 2006. *A Dictionary of Linguistics and Phonetics*. London: Blackwell.

Cummins, Jim. 2017. "Teaching for Transfer in Multilingual School Contexts." In *Bilingual and Multilingual Education*, edited by Ofelia García, Angel Lin, and Stephen May, 103–15. Cham: Springer International.

Dewaele, Jean-Marc, Alex Housen, and Li Wei. 2003. *Bilingualism: Beyond Basic Principles*. Clevedon: Multilingual Matters.

Dhont, Kristof, Gordon Hodson, Ana C. Leite, and Alina Salmen. 2019. "The Psychology of Speciesism". In *Why We Love and Exploit Animals: Bridging Insights from Academia and Advocacy*, edited by Kristof Dhont and Gordon Hodson, 29–49. Routledge. https://doi.org/10.4324/9781351181440.

Dijkstra, Ton, and Walter J. B. van Heuven. 2002. "The Architecture of the Bilingual Word Recognition System: From Identification to Decision." *Bilingualism: Language and Cognition* 5: 175–97. https://doi.org/10.1017/s1366728902003012.

Durkin, Philip. 2015. *Borrowed Words: A History of Loanwords in English*. New York: Oxford University Press.

Eberhard, David M., Gary F. Simons, and Charles D. Fennig (eds.). 2020. *Ethnologue: Languages of the World*. Twenty-third edition. Dallas, Texas: SIL International. http://www.ethnologue.com.

Eisenchlas, Susana A., Andrea C. Schalley, and Diana Guillemin. 2015. "Multilingualism and Literacy: Attitudes and Policies." *International Journal of Multilingualism* 12 (2): 151–61. https://doi.org/10.1080/14790718.2015.1009371.

El-Halees, Alaa. 2011. "Mining Opinions in User-Generated Contents to Improve Course Evaluation." In *Software Engineering and Computer Systems*, edited by Jasni Mohamad Zain, Wan Maseri bt Wan Mohd, and Eyas El-Qawasmeh. Berlin: Springer. https://doi.org/10.1007/978-3-642-22191-0_9.

Elizaincín, Adolfo. 2011 "Motivación y origen de los cambios lingüísticos" [Motivation and Origin of Language Changes]. In *Español al Sur*, edited by María José González and Cristina Pippolo, 257–89. Montevideo, Uruguay: Luscinia.

Even-Simkin, Elena, and Tobin Yishai. 2013. *The Regularity of the "Irregular" Verbs and Nouns in English*. Amsterdam: John Benjamins Publishing Company.

Finkbeiner, Claudia. 2005. *Interessen und Strategien beim fremdsprachlichen Lesen: Wie Schülerinnen und Schüler englische Texte lesen und verstehen* [Interests and Strategies in Reading in a Foreign Language: How Students Read and Understand English Texts]. Tübingen: Narr.

Givón, Thomas. 1984. *Syntax*. Amsterdam: John Benjamins.

Green, Tamara M. 2020. *The Greek & Latin Roots of English*. Vancouver: Rowman & Littlefield Publishers.

Hamers, Josiane F., and Michel H. A. Blanc. 2000. *Bilinguality and Bilingualism*. Second edition. Cambridge: Cambridge University Press.

Haukås, Åsta. 2015. "Teachers' Beliefs about Multilingualism and a Multilingual Pedagogical Approach." *International Journal of Multilingualism* 13: 1–8.

Hernandez, Arturo, and Ping Li. 2007. "Age of Acquisition: Its Neural and Computational Mechanisms." Psycholical Bulletin 133(4): 638–50.

Heuven, Walter J. B. van, Ton Dijkstra, and Jonathan Grainger. 1998. "Orthographic Neighborhood Effects in Bilingual Word Recognition." *Journal of Memory and Language* 39: 458–83. https://doi.org/10.1006/jmla.1998.2584.

Horst, Marlise. 2005. "Learning L2 Vocabulary through Extensive Reading: A Measurement Study." *Canadian Modern Language Review* 61 (3): 355–82.

Hudson, Richard A. 1996. *Sociolinguistics.* Cambridge: Cambridge University Press.

Hulstijn, Jan H. 2003. "Incidental and Intentional Learning". In *The Handbook of Second Language Acquisition,* edited by Catherine J. Doughty and Michael H. Long, 349–81. Oxford: Blackwell.

Kroll, Judith F., and Ton Dijkstra. 2002. "The Bilingual Lexicon." In *Handbook of Applied Linguistics,* edited by Robert B. Kaplan, 301–21. Oxford: Oxford University Press.

Kroll, Judith F., Erica Michael, Natasha Tokowicz, and Robert Dufour. 2002. "The Development of Lexical Fluency in a Second Language." *Second Language Research* 18: 137–71. https://doi.org/10.1191/0267658302sr201oa.

Laufer, Batia, and Jan Hulstijn. 2001. "Incidental Vocabulary Acquisition in a Second Language: The Construct of Task-Induced Involvement." *Applied Linguistics* 22: 1–26.

Lemhöfer, Kristin, and Ton Dijkstra. 2004. "Recognizing Cognates and Interlingual Homographs: Effects of Code Similarity in Language-Specific and Generalized Lexical Decision." *Memory & Cognition* 32: 533–50. https://doi.org/10.3758/BF03195845.

Nunan, David, and Clarice Lamb. 1996. *The Self-Directed Teacher: Managing the Learning Process.* Cambridge: Cambridge University Press

Otwinowska-Kasztelanic, Agnieszka. 2009. "Raising Awareness of Cognate Vocabulary as a Strategy in Teaching English to Polish Adults." *Innovation in Language Learning and Teaching* 3: 131–47.

Otwinowska-Kasztelanic, Agnieszka. 2017. "English Teachers' Language Awareness: Away with the Monolingual Bias?" *Language Awareness* 26 (4): 304–24.

Penycook, Alastair. 2007. "ELT and Colonialism." In *International Handbook of English Language Teaching,* edited by Jim Cummins and Chris Davison, 13–24. New York: Springer.

Penycook, Alastair. 2010. "Nationalism, Identity and Popular Culture." In *Sociolinguistics and Language Education,* edited by Nancy H. Hornberger and Sandra Lee McKay, 62–86. Clevedon: Multilingual Matters

Solé, Isabel.1992. *Estrategias de lectura* [Reading Strategies]. Barcelona: Graó.

Vonderwell, Selma. 2003. "An Examination of Asynchronous Communication Experiences and Perspectives of Students in an Online Course: A Case Study." *Internet and Higher Education* 6 (1): 77–90. https://doi.org/10.1016/s1096-7516(02)00164-1.

Webb, Stuart. 2007. "The Effects of Synonymy on Second-Language Vocabulary Learning." *Applied Linguistics* 19 (2): 120–36.

Wolfram, Walt. 2019. "Sociolinguistics." Linguistic Society of America. Accessed March 11, 2019. https://www.linguisticsociety.org/resource/sociolinguistics.

Young, Tony, Itesh Sachdev, and Paul Seedhouse. 2009. "Teaching and Learning Culture on English Language Programmes: A Critical Review of the Recent Empirical Literature." *International Journal of Innovation in Language Learning and Teaching* 3 (2): 149–69. https://doi.org/10.1080/17501220802283178.

Appendix 6.1

SAMPLE QUESTIONNAIRE ITEMS

1. Sample questions of the questionnaire carried out at the beginning of the course.
   - Which is your first language?
   - Do you speak any other language(s)? Which?
   - How proficient are you in it/them? Indicate it in the following scale, 1 being not much and 5 very. [A five-point Likert scale followed this question]
   - How similar do you believe English and Spanish to be?

2. Sample questions of the questionnaire carried out throughout the course.
   - How useful were the pre-reading activities for a good understanding of the text?
   - Which aspects of this unit did you find newfangled?
   - From a scale of 1 to 5, 1 being not at all and 5 very, how engaging did you find the text? [A five-point Likert scale followed this question]
   - Did you feel the questions and tasks help you tackle your reading? Why? Why not?

3. Sample questions of the questionnaire carried out at the end of the course.
   - Were you aware of the phenomenon of cognates?
   - What conclusions have you drawn about English vocabulary?
   - How similar do you believe English and Spanish to be?

CHAPTER 7

Harnessing learners' domain expertise for ESP curriculum development: Experience-based best practices and strategies

Katherine Guertler

Ostbayerische Technische Hochschule Regensburg, Germany

Eric Koenig

Technische Hochschule Nuremberg, Germany

Jolana Tluková

Brno University of Technology, Czech Republic

Abstract

The instruction of English for Specific Purposes (ESP) including Technical English (TE) at university level represents a daunting challenge for the language instructor. Not only is ESP training an underserved qualification, but the sheer range of specialist technical domains virtually guarantees that the TE instructor will at some point enter an environment far removed from their primary training in English linguistics. This paper reviews available strategies for the ESP practitioner to acquire and integrate specialized terminology and concepts in a new technical domain via student input, drawing on the authors' decades of experience with numerous technical target domains. Best practice techniques with a high degree of in-class application focus on the development and active use of domain-specific vocabulary via the productive skills of speaking and writing, with additional discussion of cultivating willingness to communicate among oftentimes reticent technical students. Technical ESP practitioners can benefit greatly from curiosity and an eagerness to learn, not only about their chosen profession of language education but also their learners' respective domains of specialization.

Keywords: English for Specific Purposes, higher education, curriculum development, terminology, willingness to communicate

***

Introduction

Teaching English for Specific Purposes (ESP) poses an array of challenges for instructors who do not yet have an adequate background in the target domain. Upon first encountering a new specialized—often technical—ESP course, the instructors may feel intimidated or overwhelmed and will almost certainly invest many hours in reading, researching, and discussing with specialists to provide themselves with some fundamental knowledge in the new field. Even so, there is still much to learn, and developing a solid curriculum will typically require several course repetitions.

Based on the authors' combined experience of over 70 semesters teaching various ESP formats at six technical universities in the Czech Republic and Germany, this paper presents best practices in ESP instruction and advises on language instructors' own development of technical terminology and concepts as what Hutchinson and Waters deemed "reluctant dwellers in a strange and uncharted land" (1987, 158). The techniques and best practice recommendations are additionally informed by presentations and collegial discussions at renowned international conferences (e.g., Koenig and Guertler (2018b) at CercleS or Koenig and Guertler (2018c) at the GELS Network). Building on this broad experiential foundation, specific strategies are identified for bridging the gap between language-oriented instructors and their technology-oriented students through interaction and student-guided input.

Instruction of ESP and specifically Technical English at university entails several factors which can contribute to the challenges of successfully attaining the course objectives. National education systems vary widely, but at the authors' technical universities in the Czech Republic and Germany, language courses often play only a marginal role in technical students' higher education (e.g., as little as 1% of total ECTS required for graduation). Students have limited time for language classes, standardly 90 minutes per week over a 12- to 15-week semester. Additionally, the duration of the language program at technical universities tends to be limited as well, frequently as short as a single semester and therefore inadequate for making significant learner progress. Even multiple-semester language programs may not be coordinated, with a student able to select any Technical English course in any year of study, resulting (especially for learners) in heterogeneous levels of knowledge in their field of specialization and the accordant specialized English discourse, and (for the instructor) in an inability to conceive consecutive, accumulative courses progressing toward a more advanced outcome.

Moreover, depending on the degree program, ESP courses may be completely optional. Elective-only program designs further reinforce the (mis-)conceptions that communicative competence is subsidiary to specialized content knowledge or that English language proficiency is not essential for professional success in a globalized economy. For instructors, elective courses represent a double-edged sword: as students have chosen to attend the course, their motivation is generally higher, but they also frequently expect higher entertainment value as a reward.

In addition to structural constraints circumscribing university ESP courses, it is important for the instructor to recognize that students of Technical English are a distinct sub-community of learners as opposed to generalist language learners. Based on the authors' decades of experience, students of engineering tend to be highly pragmatic or instrumental regarding their language competence and ergo courses (cf. Gardner and Lambert 1972, Keller 1983); as such, applied methods such as task-based learning (Skehan 2003) are strongly preferred by most technical language learners. Technical English students are by and large output-oriented, and clear communication regarding when a particular language skill can be applied in the workplace is a great motivator (cf. Kennedy and Bolitho, 1991). Relatedly, they consistently prioritize the attainment of communicative goals over formalist concerns, such as grammar (e.g., Weyreter and Viebrock 2014, Koenig and Guertler 2018a). Observationally, technical students often have an affinity for haptic or spatial relationships so activities involving tangible objects are well-received.

Beyond Technical English learner preferences, instructors should also be aware that this sub-community of students may come with some language-learning baggage. Technical students often have had prior negative experiences with language classes at school (possibly contributing to their decision to study a technical field in the first place). Some students may even be convinced they do not have a talent for languages, which can lead to anxiety and thereby lower motivation, lower willingness to communicate, or inhibitions regarding further language development or performance (Horwitz, Horwitz and Cope 1986; Gardner and Macintyre 1993). Naturally, school curricula show a high degree of variation, but in the authors' states of Germany and the Czech Republic, secondary school language programs are not geared towards technical or applied language usage—not even at *technical* secondary schools (cf. e.g., BStMUK 1998 and 2004, MŠMT 2007). Thus, technical students may have little relevant experience or positive expectations regarding a Technical English course at the university level.

Even among teachers of English as a Foreign/Second Language (EFL/ESL), instructors of ESP and Technical English are to some extent exotic and underserved, and formal training in ESP is relatively rare (Master 1997, Basturkmen 2010, Kirkgöz 2019). Pre-service training programs often neglect to incorporate explicit preparation for (Technical) ESP, be they university degrees or certificate programs, instead typically placing focus on core language instruction elements, such as grammar and pragmatics, with little domain-specific support (see e.g., Luo and Garner 2017, 84–85). Most English teacher-education programs abroad are designed to train teachers for primary or secondary school English, which, as mentioned above, also overwhelmingly focus on generalist language. Certificate programs can be described as "bootcamps" for non-linguists, so again the emphasis is on fundamental linguistics/EFL without much or any discussion of ESP including Technical English (cf. e.g., CELTA syllabus 2018).

In summary, the Technical English classroom may represent a potentially alienating environment where students with an applied engineering background convene with language instructors who frequently have humanistic training in linguistics or philology. Instructors are unlikely to have been formally trained for ESP or more specifically for the target (sub-)domain of their students—the "subject knowledge dilemma" described by Wu and Badger (2009, 20)—and will need to invest significant effort in "self-training" (Chen 2000, 389) to become effective. To support teachers of ESP and in particular Technical English, this paper presents experience-based best practices and shares techniques intended to give novice instructors a head start when encountering a new field of ESP. Although the paper is not directly supported with data from quantitative surveys, the methods and activities have been developed and classroom-tested over the last 15 years in our lessons of Technical English and thus may be of great use to all Technical English instructors wishing to meet their Technical English students' language expectations. Further development and intensification of an ESP curriculum is a unique challenge requiring more extensive instructor experience and is not directly addressed in this chapter.

1 Developing a new technical ESP (sub-)domain through student interaction

Assuming an ESP course for a new technical domain is a daunting prospect for any instructor, novice EFL/ESL instructors often have little formal preparation for technical ESP, and even experienced instructors may be stymied by the sheer breadth of technical fields and the associated disciplinary cultures. To wit, experience in teaching Technical English for computer science has limited translational advantage when preparing a course in Technical English for architecture, biochemistry, mechanical engineering, etc.

The importance of integrated and interdisciplinary approaches to ESP, bridging language and content, has been thoroughly discussed (see especially Swales 1988, Dudley-Evans and St John 1998). Ideally, subject specialists from the target domain will collaborate with the LSP instructor in the form of team-teaching or at least in a consultative role (Hutchinson and Waters 1987, Dudley-Evans and St John 1998). However, experience has shown that this starry-eyed constellation is rarely borne out in teaching practice, often attributable to "unreasonable prejudice" of content teachers (Ghafournia and Sabet 2014, 6).

As a content outsider, selecting appropriate topics and the accordant terminology is one of the first challenges awaiting the new instructor. The initial course topics may be based on recommendations from a domain specialist providing a list of core topics in their field (cf. Butt 2015), but these suggestions may be very broad and therefore too large or unrefined to produce an acceptable outcome for the students. Compounding this situation, low student participation or motivation—for example, when class attendance is optional or the course is de-prioritized by learners due to a low number of credits—make it difficult to conduct a comprehensive needs analysis.

Even the most thorough planning for a new technical ESP course is unlikely to fully prepare the novice instructor for the lived reality of a discipline. By introducing a process and classroom culture in which students and instructors can symbiotically learn from one another, the development of a new technical ESP curriculum can be accelerated and concomitantly tailored to best serve the learners' goals.

When first encountering a new technical discipline, the instructor has a readily available resource: the course participants. The students in a Technical English course have already exhibited a profound interest in that specific discipline and frequently have already garnered some experience in the field, be it through coursework, occupational training, or professional experience. The students' underlying competence in the technical domain (Hutchinson and Waters 1988), though imperfect, can help guide the novice instructor in setting course topics and curricular priorities.

The role of student input in developing teaching skills and curricula for Language for Specific Purposes has long been recognized. Early (1981, 42) provided an initial argument that ESP instructors frequently possess less knowledge about the specialist domain than their students. And such "dealing with unknown discipline-related elements" might be perceived as "sources of anxiety for many language teachers at the start of their career" (Suchomelová-Polomska 2021, 93). In this vein, Hutchinson and Waters (1987, 27) emphasized mutual respect and interest between instructor and learners as an important criterion for effective classroom communication and ultimately LSP skill development. Dudley-Evans and St John (1998, 4) described the ESP instructor as a "language consultant," who may often defer to the subject-matter expertise of the students, with the learning process ultimately based on collaboration between teacher and student. Other researchers have discussed the role of ESP learners as active, responsible "student participants" in the learning process (Ghafournia and Sabet 2014, 3).

Specifically, when the ESP course is a component of a university-degree program, the participating students often already have some specialist knowledge or underlying competence in their field; the ESP course is often held in a more advanced semester so the students will already have completed several semesters of coursework before attending class and thus have some insight into the most important concepts and terms in their chosen field. As the communication between language instructors and those of the core subject courses is frequently inadequate (at least from the point of view of the language teacher), the students may be the best or at least most willing and accessible resource for learning more about the subject area. Moreover, using the student-generated content "allows teachers to bring student experiences and voices into the community of practice and acknowledges the importance of their prior experiences in knowledge production" (Snowball and McKenna 2017, 604).

Additionally, depending on the national education system, higher education students may already have completed a training program or apprenticeship or even gained professional experience in their chosen field before attending university. For example, an ongoing investigation of students in tertiary-level Technical English courses in Germany has found that around 90% of students already have work experience, with 82% having held positions generally relevant to the technical field of study, such as internships, apprenticeships, or as full-time employees (Koenig and Guertler 2018a). Students' pre-matriculation exposure to the target domain is especially valuable in programs where the technical ESP course is placed early in the curriculum when students have not yet completed much relevant coursework.

Finally, when the technical ESP course is contracted by a company, for example in the form of English classes for their employees, the wealth of relevant experience that the course participants can provide for the language instructor is indisputable. The willingness to format on-site ESP courses as a dialogue between a language specialist and a group of technical professionals is generally quite high for all involved parties.

2 Applications to incorporate student domain expertise in the ESP classroom

Scenarios where the ESP teacher can incorporate technical students' knowledge in the language classroom enable both parties to rapidly expand their respective proficiency in the other's field of expertise. Open and honest dialogue is certainly a valuable approach, but the implementation of interactive exercises can further support the mutual development of knowledge while targeting specific language acts.

This section outlines in-class communicative activities that the ESP instructor can implement in order to promote interaction and content generation from the student participants as a form of self-training through action research following Chen (2000).

2.1 Speaking activities

Oral communication along with presentation skills (which are likely to be needed in a professional setting) can be trained through a variety of activities. The productive nature of speaking activities makes them an ideal in-class format for teacher self-training. Not only are students providing high-priority, subject-specific content (while training their own communicative skills), but the instructor has the opportunity to promote and confirm their own understanding by asking questions about the material.

Classical presentations

Prepared with or without presentation software, student-led presentations can develop the instructor's knowledge regarding a given topic by giving students specific themes, or they can allow for exploration and novel topics when open to student-selected themes. This activity is especially beneficial for ESP content rookies because the instructor's attention can be focused on a single source of student input.

Expert interviews

Each student prepares at home to become a subject-matter expert on a particular topic, with in-class interviews designed to explore their knowledge. This activity encourages self-learning and preparation while students can train flexibility and responsiveness by asking and answering novel questions.

Info marketplace

This small-group activity offers the opportunity for students to work together to create a visual display and then practice delivering an ad hoc presentation. Groups of around four students work together to create a poster explaining a field-relevant concept, entailing group discussions about which information to present and how to communicate effectively. Once the posters are complete, the students are reshuffled to form new groups with one member from each poster. The groups then rotate from poster to poster, with each member explaining the content of their respective poster to the other members. In addition to the oral elements, the posters provide the instructor with a written record of the generated content.

Speed-dating

The course participants sit at a long table in pairs across from each other and exchange their knowledge or ideas on a given piece of authentic information, such as a chart or diagram. After about three to five minutes, they rotate around the table so that each is matched with a different partner and has a new topic for discussion. By observing these conversations and especially listening in on topics for which there is a relative knowledge deficit, the instructor can quickly learn more about a range of relevant content areas. Alternatively, instead of discussion topics, the students can play the roles of a hiring manager (who devises requirements for a position) and a job applicant (who can present his or her own qualifications). This task is especially useful information for the teacher on which skills are highly valued in the field.

Student-led speaking activities provide the novice ESP instructor with an opportunity to learn from and interact with relative-expert students on a range of topics. Additionally, they provide an ideal inflection point as instructors develop their content-area knowledge by providing opportunities for the instructor to ask questions or eventually make their own contributions. As the instructor's familiarity with the field grows, the topics and activity details can be continuously refined for higher specificity, updated to reflect a new concept or technology, or simply changed to allow the instructor to learn more about other relevant areas.

2.2 Writing activities

Writing tasks for ESP should reflect the communication style of the target field to provide students with authentic or at least realistic practice. While practicing engineers are rarely or never called on to write essay-style texts, the written word plays an essential role in the clear, precise transmission of knowledge required for technical communication. Writing in engineering fulfills distinct functions, such as instructing (e.g., handbooks), specifying (e.g., technical specifications), initiating (e.g., a project proposal), reporting (e.g., technical reports), advising (e.g., feasibility studies), or publishing (e.g., research publications; cf. Irish and Weiss 2009, 31). The skill of writing can be practiced as an ad hoc exercise in class or with a stronger preparatory or research-based lien at home.

Brainwriting

Each student selects a field-relevant topic and writes an introductory sentence at the top of the page. The papers are then continuously rotated to the next student who reads the previous text and contributes a sentence of their own before rotating once more. In this way, teachers are exposed to a range of student-selected topics, while students practice reading and writing with an especially taxing element of coherence as the student has no influence over the topic or previous entries.

Technology timeline

Students work in small groups to identify a current concept or technology, then use recall or reference resources to outline the important steps in historical development, the status quo, and possible directions for future development. The information can be presented as a simple timeline or as full text. In this manner, the instructor can learn important contextualized information about the state of the field, and students are challenged to integrate past, present, and future developments communicatively and grammatically correctly.

Long-form writing

Longer written tasks, such as reports or process descriptions, can be completed at home, especially to encourage students to conduct their own research on relevant topics and the associated terminology. The fundamental structures of a traditional essay (introduction, body, and conclusion) are universally applicable to the majority of communicative acts which engineers will require on the job. This research-oriented task additionally trains students how to use (online) resources to learn more about their area of interest using English language sources. Examples of various writing products can be elicited to improve students' expressive range and to practice different communication styles. For their part, instructors can acquire in-depth knowledge about a range of relevant topics with the ability to read and reread at their own pace.

While the limited amount and duration of university-level language courses lead many instructors to deprioritize writing tasks, especially during class time, they provide a valuable window into novel technical content. Given the slower pace and ability to integrate outside research, written tasks often reflect a higher level of detail and precision than spoken interaction.

2.3 Kinesthetic activities to promote willingness to communicate

Recommendations for interacting with specialist students to promote teacher-knowledge development on a new subject for ESP instruction are fundamentally predicated upon the students' ability and willingness to communicate. The interplay of personality and foreign language competence point to a multi-layered model of willingness to communicate (WTC) in L2, integrating enduring trait-like factors like self-confidence with situational influences, such as the desire to communicate with a specific person (MacIntyre et al. 1998). The ESP practitioner should strive to engender WTC as a key to fostering learner success and proficiency in productive language modalities, especially oral skills and interpersonal communication (Kang 2005).

While individual factors, like personality and motivation as well as situational influences, such as instructional style and group dynamics, have received extensive attention in the WTC literature, the consideration of WTC in the ESP classroom additionally necessitates discussion of the elements of content and task. Regarding content, student selection of lesson topics and in particular the learner's familiarity with the subject matter influence WTC (MacIntyre et al. 1998), and students have reported that the ability to select topics where they feel secure and have an inherent interest positively contributes to their WTC (Kang 2005, Zarrinabadi 2014). Notably for ESP practitioners, a drop in dynamic WTC has been associated with the inability to effectively recall vocabulary items (MacIntyre and Legatto 2011).

Significantly less attention has been paid to the mundane issue of which specific tasks can be employed in the language classroom to raise learner WTC. On a conceptual level, students have been found to be more willing to communicate when participating in familiar tasks (MacIntyre and Legatto 2011) or preferred tasks (Mystkowska-Wiertelak and Pawlak 2014), but investigations into the relationship between task type and WTC are currently lacking.

Given the underrepresentation of broad-range empirical or action research on which classroom tasks can best promote WTC, the authors draw upon their combined experience to report that spatial and kinesthetic (especially tactile) learning activities generally encourage student's WTC. Observationally, the presence of a physical object as a reference point results in higher levels of oral production among technical ESP students, both in interactive dyads or small group activities as well as in frontal presentations or monologues.

Show-and-tell

Students select and bring a relevant technical device to class, which allows participants to practice explaining a functionality or an operation. This activity can be tweaked to reflect numerous technical applications, for example practicing a sales pitch or explaining a defect.

Seek-and-find

Authentic visual information, such as graphs or images, are posted around the classroom. Based on a list of descriptions of the posted items, students move around the room trying to find a match. Subsequently, students can explain to one another or to the instructor the role of this information in their fields, such as methods for data generation, experimental processes, or the significance of the results.

Student-led tours

Technical students often spend a significant amount of time working in a laboratory or production facility. A field trip into these environments allows students to explain machinery or processes, and the high level of familiarity with the environment feeds into WTC. For the teacher, a tour gives deep insight into students' actual workplace, instead of being restricted to the language classroom.

Other task-based learning

A range of technical, inductive task-based learning activities depending on the target field may involve materials, such as construction kits, building blocks, circuit boards, magnets, etc. While the tasks should be tailored to the respective area of specialization, requiring somewhat greater familiarity with the field, the benefit is that students are able to better apply their existing specialist knowledge, and the instructor can gain important insights into how students have been trained to approach and execute the task.

In summary, kinesthetic activities have observationally been found to promote WTC in the technical LSP classroom, and a range of activities can be used by the teacher to channel this willingness into a valuable opportunity to learn more about the target field from the students.

2.4 Receptive skills

The present exploration of classroom activities to create a forum for the ESP instructor to learn more about the target field via input for the specialist students naturally focuses on productive modalities. However, the receptive skills of listening and reading can be leveraged to a certain extent to support teacher learning. For receptive modalities, content is king. By encouraging students to share writing products specific to their field (e.g., technical reports, documentation, publications) or listening samples (e.g., podcasts, video channels), the instructor can absorb topics and sources pertinent to the target domain, arguably with a higher level of quality or accuracy than the students could provide.

Alternatively, a receptive skill like reading can be expressly linked to oral production, which has the benefit of ensuring that the source input is high quality while learners actively recode the information into a productive modality.

Three-way information gap

The class of students is divided into three groups, with each group assigned a different topic. Within these groups, students prepare their topic by reading an authentic text and then discussing, including mutual recall to supplement the content comprehension, taking notes on the key points as needed. Then groups of three are formed with one member from each discussion group, and each student reports on their group's findings to the other two. (For larger classes, the number of original groups may require adaptation.)

Terminology happy hour

Working in pairs, students read a relevant technical text and extract five key terms from their reading. Together, they develop definitions for these terms, checking their work against an outside source, like the instructor or a technical dictionary as required, as a quality assurance measure. Then the learners swap the definitions with another group who try to identify the term based on definition alone. If a hint is needed, they can also refer to the reading to search for the relevant term in the original authentic source.

Finally, examinations can also be viewed as a learning opportunity. Especially for students with low motivation or WTC, an examination environment may be one of the only situations in which oral or written production is guaranteed. By posing open essay themes or allowing for student-selected topics for oral examination presentations, students are encouraged to integrate their own knowledge into the language development process.

Discussion and outlook

The instruction of ESP and Technical English presents unique challenges even for experienced instructors. The broad range of (sub-)domains presents a virtually endless panoply of specialized content, frequently far afield from the instructor's primary training in linguistics and education. Regardless of preparation or experience, a language instructor in a classroom full of technical specialist students will at some point encounter foreign terrain.

To facilitate the ESP practitioner's adaptation to a new specialist domain, (relative) specialist students can help guide the instructor's knowledge development by means of targeted activities, such as presentations, expert interviews, or laboratory tours. By incorporating interactive exercises where students have an opportunity to share their technical knowledge with the (novice) ESP practitioner, both parties can learn from and inspire each other to create a culture in which each party benefits from the other's expertise.

Crucially, the content-focused activities described here can also be tied to specific grammar points as needed, for example using the passive voice to describe a technical process, conditionals to hypothesize or speculate about future developments in the field, or pragmatic strategies for hedging or dealing with uncertainty. Depending on the level of English proficiency of the class as well as the relative strengths and weaknesses, the instructor may choose to emphasize different aspects and exercises for the development of these core language skills.

While pre-class preparation and post-class analyses are beneficial for every type of teaching, the alienation and steep learning curve of teaching ESP heighten the importance of reflection before and after each lesson. By taking extensive notes on their successes and indeed failures, instructors can accelerate the development of their personal domain specialization and be better prepared for future iterations of the ESP course.

Novel inroads were described towards creating specific recommendations for classroom tasks to foster WTC, in contrast with the wealth of research focusing on factors of personality, motivation, and classroom climate. Specifically, the authors' extensive experience teaching ESP for various technical domains overwhelmingly points to kinesthetic or haptic activities as successful promoters of student WTC. The underpinnings of this observation have yet to be explored. With regards to trait-like or enduring factors, one possible explanation is that by directing attention towards an object or physical activity, the learner's self-awareness is lowered and thus known inhibitors of WTC, such as apprehension, anxiety, or low self-confidence, are cognitively de-prioritized. Equally, the situational factors related to the task may motivate students to focus on producing a specific, tangible output, in contrast to the conceptualized structures required for effective oral or written communication. Of course, the issue is further confounded by the acknowledgment that technical students are as a group highly receptive to haptic and kinesthetic applications, as these personal preferences are quite possibly what initially led them to pursue a technical degree. Still, the simple element of enjoying a task has been shown to increase motivation and WTC (Mystkowska-Wiertelak and Pawlak 2014).

Despite these tools, the admission and acceptance that students may be more knowledgeable about their discipline can be an uncomfortable experience for some instructors, especially those who associate their role with authority and relative proficiency in the course subject matter. Additionally, this vulnerability may beget doubts about the instructor's professional competence in cultural contexts in which teachers are viewed as knowledge providers rather than guides for student self-development (see Wu and Badger 2009, Luo and Garner 2017). However, by lowering potential barriers and expressing a willingness to learn from students, a symbiotic relationship can be developed, in which the instructor can learn about the technical target domain from the relative content experts participating in the course, while the students can develop communicative proficiency in the target language under the guidance of the technical ESP practitioner.

As the instructor's experience, confidence, and domain-specific knowledge base grow, they can develop their own materials to more accurately target particular content areas. With increased fluency in the target technical domain, the instructor's focus can switch from basic content comprehension to optimizing delivery methods for learner training. No matter the level of experience, the instruction of English for Specific Purposes will require a high degree of teacher dedication, the acquisition of new terms and concepts, and a willingness to collaboratively learn from and with their specialist students.

References

Basturkmen, Helen. 2010. *Developing Courses in English for Specific Purposes.* Basingstoke: Macmillan.

Bayerisches Staatsministerium für Unterricht und Kultus/ISB (BStMUK). 1998. "Lehrplan für die Berufsoberschule, Jahrgangsstufe 12 und 13 für Englisch" [Vocational Secondary School English Curriculum for 12th and 13th Grades]. Accessed April 5, 2019. https://www.isb.bayern.de/download/13469/lp_bos _englisch_12_13.pdf.

Bayerisches Staatsministerium für Unterricht und Kultus/ISB (BStMUK). 2004. "Gymnasiumlehrplan für Jahrgangsstufe 11/12 für Englisch" [Grammar School English Curriculum for 11th and 12th Grades]. Accessed April 5, 2019. http://www.isb-gym8-lehrplan.de/contentserv/3.1.neu/g8.de/index.php? StoryID=26513.

Butt, Sophia. 2015. "Authenticity in ESAP Course Design: Managing Departmental and Student Expectations." *CASALC Review* 5 (1): 171–80.

Cambridge English. 2018. *CELTA Certificate in Teaching English to Speakers of Other Languages: Syllabus and Assessment Guidelines.* Fifth edition. Cambridge: Cambridge English Language Assessment.

Chen, Tsai-Yu. 2000. "Self-training for ESP through Action Research." *English for Specific Purposes* 19: 389–402.

Dudley-Evans, Tony, and Maggie Jo St John. 1998. *Developments in English for Specific Purposes: A Multi-disciplinary Approach.* Cambridge: Cambridge University Press.

Early, Patrick. 1981. "The ESP Teacher's Role: Implications for the 'Knower-Client' Relationship." *The ESP Teacher: Role, Development and Prospects.* ELT Documents 112. 42–52. London: The British Council.

Gardner, Robert C., and Wallace E. Lambert. 1972. *Attitudes and Motivation in Second Language Learning.* Rowley, MA: Newbury House Publishers.

Gardner, Robert C., and Peter D. MacIntyre. 1993. "On the Measurement of Affective Variables in Second Language Learning." *Language Learning* 43 (2): 157–94.

Gharfournia, Narjes, and Shokoofeh Ahmadian Sabet. 2014. "The Most Prominent Roles of an ESP Teacher." *International Education Studies* 7 (11): 1–9. http://dx.doi.org/10.5539/ies.v7n11p1.

Horwitz, Elaine K., Michael B. Horwitz, and Joann Cope. 1986. "Foreign Language Classroom Anxiety." *Modern Language Journal* 70: 125–32.

Hutchinson, Tom, and Alan Waters. 1987. *English for Specific Purposes. A Learning-Centred Approach.* Cambridge: Cambridge University Press.

Hutchinson, Tom, and Alan Waters. 1988. "ESP at the Crossroads." In *Episodes in ESP*, edited by John Swales, 174–87. Hemel Hempstead: Prentice Hall International.

Irish, Robert, and Peter Weiss. 2009. *Engineering Communication: From Principles to Practice.* Oxford: Oxford University Press.

Kang, Su-Ja. 2005. "Dynamic Emergence of Situational Willingness to Communicate in a Second Language." *System* 33: 277–92.

Kennedy, Chris, and Rod Bolitho. 1991. *English for Specific Purposes.* London: MacMillan.

Keller, John M. 1983. "Motivational Design of Instruction." In *Instructional-Design Theories and Models: An Overview of Their Current Status*, edited by Charles M. Reigeluth, 383–436. Hillsdale, NJ: Lawrence Erlbaum.

Kırkgöz, Yasemin. 2019. "ESP in Teacher Education: A Case Study." In *ESP Teaching and Teacher Education: Current Theories and Practices*, edited by Salomi Papadima-Sophocleous, Elis Kakoulli Constantinou, and Christina Nicole Giannikas, 13–26. S.l.: Research-publishing.net. https://doi.org/10.14705/rpnet.2019.33.923.

Koenig, Eric, and Katherine Guertler. 2018a. "Parlaying Students' Work Experience into Practice-Oriented ESP." *Journal of Teaching English for Specific and Academic Purposes* 6 (2): 277–84.

Koenig, Eric, and Katherine Guertler. 2018b. "Technical and Interpersonal Communication Prioritization in Engineering ESP." Presented at XV CercleS International Conference *Broad Perspectives on Language Education in the Globalized World*, Poznan University of Technology, Poznan, Poland, 6–8 September.

Koenig, Eric, and Katherine Guertler. 2018c. "Report: Longitudinal Study of Undergraduate Engineers." Presented at GELS Training Week, KTH Royal Institute of Technology, Stockholm, Sweden, April.

Luo, Jing, and Mark W. J. Garner. 2017. "The Challenges and Opportunities for English Teachers in Teaching ESP in China." *Journal of Language Teaching and Research* 8 (1): 81–86. http://dx.doi.org/10.17507/jltr.0801.10.

MacIntyre, Peter D., Zoltán Dörnyei, Richard Clément, and Kimberly A. Noels. 1998. "Conceptualizing Willingness to Communicate in an L2: A Situational Model of L2 Confidence and Affiliation." *Modern Language Journal* 82 (4): 545–62.

MacIntyre, Peter D., and James Jason Legatto. 2011. "A Dynamic System Approach to Willingness to Communicate: Developing an Idiodynamic Method to Capture Rapidly Changing Affect." *Applied Linguistics* 32 (2): 149–71.

Master, Peter. 1997. "ESP Teacher Education in the USA." In *Teacher Education for LSP*, edited by Ron Howard and Gillian Brown, 22–40. Clevedon: Multilingual Matters.

Ministerstvo školství, mládeže a tělovýchovy (MŠMT). 2007. "Rámcové vzdělávací program" [Framework Educational Programmes]. Accessed March 20, 2019. http://www.msmt.cz/vzdelavani/stredni-vzdelavani/ramcove-vzdelavaci-programy.

Mystkowska-Wiertelak, Anna, and Mirosław Pawlak. 2014. "Fluctuations in Learners' Willingness to Communicate During Communicative Task Performance: Conditions and Tendencies." *Research in Language* 12: 245–60. http://dx.doi.org/10.2478/rela-2014-0019.

Skehan, Peter. 2003. "Task-Based Instruction." *Language Teaching* 36: 1–14.

Snowball Jen D., and Sioux McKenna. 2017. "Student-Generated Content: An Approach to Harnessing the Power of Diversity in Higher Education." *Teaching in Higher Education* 22 (5): 604–18. https://doi.org/10.1080/135625 17.2016.1273205.

Suchomelová-Polomska, Agnieszka. 2021. "What Is Expertise in Language Teaching? Balancing between LAP and LSP." *CASALC Review* 11 (1): 93–103. https://doi.org/10.5817/CASALC2021-1-8.

Swales, John. 1988. *Episodes in ESP*. Hemel Hempstead: Prentice Hall International.

Weyreter, Martina, and Britta Viebrock. 2014. "Identity Construction in Adult Learners of English for Specific Purposes (ESP): Exploring a Complex Phenomenon." In *Plurilingualism and multiliteracies*, edited by Dagmar Abendroth-Timmer and Eva-Maria Hennig, 145–58. Frankfurt: Peter Lang.

Wu, HuiDan, and Richard G. Badger. 2009. "In a Strange and Uncharted Land: ESP Teachers' Strategies for Dealing with Unpredicted Problems in Subject Knowledge during Class." *English for Specific Purposes* 28: 19–32.

Zarrinabadi, Nourollah. 2014. "Communicating in a Second Language: Investigating the Effect of Teacher on Learners' Willingness to Communicate." *System* 42: 288–95. https://doi.org/10.1016/j.system.2013.12.014.

CHAPTER 8

Lexical approach and social reading in CLIL settings: Two strategies to support LSP students with functional vocabulary and discipline-specific communication skills

Emma Abbate

Cambridge International IGCSE® High School Armando Diaz, Italy

Abstract

In the early nineties, Lewis overcame the dichotomy between vocabulary and grammar which may arise during a second language (L2) learning process by proposing the lexical approach in order to recuperate the dimension of the language as a whole in which lexicon plays a pivotal role. In the same period, CLIL (Content and Language Integrating Learning) was capturing growing attention from researchers all over Europe. The recent European language policies, aimed at promoting multilingualism, have presented a fertile soil for the dissemination and application of this innovative methodology. The social dimension of CLIL approach, which is strongly student-centered, has not been investigated as it deserves. The use of social reading techniques in L2 courses in the pupils' content area represents a tool to improve language awareness and academic language proficiency in LSP students. This paper intends to suggest a few practical examples of adopting digital lexical approach and social reading strategies in CLIL settings in order to prepare students to pass IMAT (International Medical Admission Test), a very selective and difficult entry test for admission to Degree Programme in Medicine and Surgery taken in Italy, and other subject-specific admissions tests in L2 at tertiary level instruction.

Keywords: Lexical Approach (LA), CLIL (Content and Language Integrated Learning), Social Reading, Language for Specific Purposes (LSP)

***

Introduction

In Italy, some universities[1] have adopted an aptitude test as part of the admissions process at the degree program in Medicine and Surgery: IMAT (International Medical Admissions Test), a 100-minute subject-specific test in English for applicants for medicine, surgery, and dentistry courses taught in English and open to both home and overseas applicants.[2] The format of the test is 60 multiple-choice questions with five options each; it is divided into four sections: 1 Logical Reasoning and General Knowledge[3], 2–4 Scientific Knowledge (covering Biology, Chemistry, Physics and Mathematics)[4]. The first part of the IMAT is worth half of the total points: in this exam section, students need to show their skills at analyzing short texts (critical thinking) and choose which sentences complete or contradict the argument in the text. Problem-solving involves solving logical problems of different types. IMAT is set by the Italian Ministry of Education, Universities and Research (MIUR)[5] in conjunction with Cambridge Assessments Admissions Testing.[6] For non-native English students, it is required to have obtained an English language certification at least equal to B2 of the CEFR (Common European Framework of Reference for Language) even though the scientific and technical terms used in IMAT are considered higher than the B2 level of competence. Thus, to pass IMAT, it is essential to have an in-depth knowledge of the subjects' terminology and target-language use (TLU) domain in order to predict language performance in specific contexts, such as the workplace (Douglas 2001).

IMAT implies the use of English to learn academic subjects (in this case Medicine and Surgery) in countries in which English is not the first language of the majority of the population: the application of English as a Medium of Instruction (EMI) is part of this increasing process of internationalization that universities face all over the world (Dearden 2014, 29).

---

[1] To check which courses require IMAT in Italy, see https://www.admissionstesting.org/Images/473210-universities-requiring-imat.pdf.

[2] https://www.admissionstesting.org/for-test-takers/imat/about-imat/

[3] This section tests generic skills in problem solving, understanding argument, data analysis and inference, and general knowledge. It is made up of 22 multiple-choice questions.

[4] These sections test a candidate's ability to apply scientific knowledge from school science. They are made up of 38 multiple-choice questions: Biology (18 questions), Chemistry (12 questions), Physics and Mathematics (8 questions).

[5] https://www.miur.gov.it/web/guest/-/accesso-programmato-on-line-decreto-con-modalita-e-contenuti-delle-prove-di-medicina-e-chirurgia-in-lingua-inglese-imat-

[6] https://www.admissionstesting.org

At the primary and secondary level, this kind of bilingual education is often referred to as CLIL (Content and Language Integrated Learning). In both CLIL and EMI, subjects are taught in English. The difference results from the way the teacher or lecturer sets the lesson/lecture goals. In CLIL settings, there is a clear dual aim: teaching's focus is on language and the subject content. Delivering a university course with the EMI approach implies that the content teacher should have a linguistic background to deal with language issues even though the lecturers typically do not think of themselves as language teachers (and the same often happens to CLIL teachers). However, it seems necessary for both CLIL and EMI teachers to dedicate time to language explanations in order to reduce the language barriers that may affect and jeopardize the content knowledge. This indicates that at the tertiary level, research on the effectiveness of the CLIL approach (with an ideal balance and positive integration of language and content) is still a challenging area.

Another important distinction to consider is that between CLIL and LSP (Language for Specific Purposes) teaching: LSP is single-focused on foreign language competence activated by students' linguistic and communicative needs while CLIL should simultaneously teach language as well as subject content through partial or total immersion in L2. Thus, the two approaches have different learning aims and outcomes (Fernández 2009, 13; Górska-Porȩçka 2011; Yang 2016, 46–47).

However, recent studies show the benefits of integrating CLIL and LSP in the context of tertiary education (Dorović and Zavišin 2018, 29; Vilkancienė 2011, 113). The importance of the continued study of "language" in the context of upper-level courses for learners critically engaging with "content" leads us to consider the combination of CLIL and LSP as beneficial (e.g., Byrnes, Maxim, and Norris 2010; Thoms 2011; Thoms and Poole 2017).

CLIL classes may then be considered the LSP learning environment par excellence. In both methodologies, Data-Driven Learning (DDL), a corpus-based language teaching, represents an excellent scaffolding method to support both teachers and students to foster skills in moving away from simple surface features of text to detecting and understanding meanings and structures (Corino and Onesti 2019, 2–3). Furthermore, the interactive, participatory nature of CLIL based on Cooperative Learning suggests a collection of tools to exploit. For example, the social reading strategy represents a good exercise for improving LSP students' reading and comprehension skills. This chapter suggests some practical and easy-to-use social reading tools based on lexical approach strategies to apply in CLIL settings in order to prepare students to attend academic courses taught in English.

1 CLIL's core elements

The definition of CLIL as dual-focused education based on using languages to learn and learning to use language clarifies the educational goals of this methodology which aims at enhancing both language and content knowledge (Marsh and Langé 2000, 6). CLIL activities are built on the vehicular use of a target language in order to complete assigned tasks in a collaborative approach (Guazzieri 2007, 173). This theoretical-methodological framework is addressed to increase cognitive and study skills: in CLIL environments students are engaged in context-embedded activities aimed at "producing" rather than merely "re-producing" language.

In CLIL approach, to consolidate the content and language acquisition in addition to the understandable input proposed by Krashen (1985), it is also necessary to develop an understandable output. The cognitive process of negotiating and producing meaningful, comprehensible output as part of language learning is called *Languaging*, a term coined by Swain (1985). Languaging occurs when students produce speech in the target language in order to negotiate and accomplish a CLIL task. It supports the development of Cognitive and Academic Language Proficiency (CALP) which consists, according to Cummins (2008), of knowing how to use the L2 to understand complex linguistic constructs and to analyze, explore, and decode concepts explained in the textbooks.

In short, CLIL promotes the acquisition of the "academic" language, which does not imply only the ability to comprehend and use the specific vocabulary related to a certain disciplinary area but rather the ability to develop the cognitive process indicated in Bloom's taxonomy, the hierarchy of thinking skills or educational objectives, which serves as a useful framework for designing and planning various classroom activities (Chadwick 2012, 5–7).

2 Lexical approach's fundamentals

The opportunity to integrate the lexical approach into CLIL framework is an emerging research area (Cardona 2008; Eldridge, Neufeld, and Hancioglu 2010). According to the lexical approach developed by Lewis (1993), language is composed of four types of lexical units:

1.   words and polywords,
2.   collocations,
3.   institutionalized utterances,
4.   sentence frames or heads.

Words and polywords refer to lexical items assumed as independent units. Part of this category are the terms of professional scientific micro-languages. The second type indicated by Lewis consists of a group of two or more words that usually go together. Collocations in L2 may represent a problem for students because they are hard to recognize; they noticeably vary in different languages. In the lexical approach, collocations play an important role, and the teacher should make learners aware of their structure within the language, planning activities that support their acquisition through semantic connections and long-term memorization. The third category is units of speech, i.e., formulaic and idiomatic expressions that are often used in the oral code. Finally, the last category includes sentence frames used to structure the text. Basically, these are part of the written language code (expressions such as *firstly, secondly, finally*), and they are extremely useful for decoding academic texts.

The study of these structures depends on the course's objective. In the case of foreign students who need to access academic courses or pass a subject-specific entry test, the knowledge of these types of lexical chunks is pivotal. By reflecting on language *chunks*, i.e., words that are often used together, students become able to recognize them (comprehensible input) and use them correctly in the production phase (output). The analysis of chunks through inductive approach allows one to understand L2's structure and functioning; the focus is not on language acquisition, but on the chunks' reuse in the production phase.

3 Why integrate CLIL with lexical approach?

The focus on highly-specialized language is certainly one of the central aspects in CLIL. The student is basically required to develop understanding and production skills through tasks (Task-Based Learning) that improve the use of a target language (L2) within a "learning-by-doing" approach. The CLIL teacher, who is the subject expert, can provide valuable input on linguistic functioning through relevant learning materials, such as academic/scientific literature, technical reports, and more practical documents (e.g., subject-specific language texts).

The complexity of the subject's micro-linguistic wordlist and the use of a precise vocabulary repertoire are related to the development of the learner's lexical competence; each discipline is characterized by fixed terminology (language requirement of the domain) that may represent an obstacle for students in achieving the planned learning objectives. The lexical approach, however, represents a tool for investigating the standard textbook that can be positively used by CLIL students to approach the target discipline in their second language. A corpus linguistics mindset offers a range of tools and methodologies to CLIL teachers depending on their specific needs, aims, and contexts. It can also help CLIL students with different levels of L2 proficiency to approach the subject-specific language (Abbate 2019, 290–91).

In the following pages, the possible convergences between Lewis's lexical approach, CLIL methodology, and social reading techniques will be explored in order to establish whether the combination and integration of them can represent a valid support for the development of lexical competence in tertiary students taking subject-specific admissions tests in a second language.

As part of the scaffolding technique, in CLIL settings timely activities for the expansion and reinforcement of subject-specific lexicon should be proposed before approaching the study text, together with basic micro-linguistic vocabulary and a corpus of topic key terms. It is also possible to train students to identify lexical chunks that structure a certain type of text, reflecting on the specific collocations and their frequency. It is not enough, though, to focus on activities that develop the vocabulary from a quantitative point of view. It is also necessary to make a reflection on the language so as to ignite in students a metalinguistic awareness that can help them handle the study material in a foreign language; a rule which learners come up with on their own by reflecting on key words in context is more likely to be meaningful and relevant to them. Through CLIL methodology, it is possible to foster associative lexical links working on semantic fields determined by the subject content. This knowledge is not acquired passively but is used in tasks and group activities.

Moving the focus from "how to say" to "what to say" produces lexical enrichment of both productive and receptive skills. CLIL activities are cognitively challenging, therefore an adequate lexical competence is an essential prerequisite for task comprehension and completion: it can be boosted by providing a rich linguistic input that stimulates the students' HOTS (high-order thinking skills) (Meyer 2013, 305–06). In CLIL settings, the linguistic input is contextualized, meaningful, and semantically rich: this guarantees its decoding and assures a learning process deeply integrated in the semantic memory. Words are learnt by students according to their value, i.e., the meaning they have in a specific context, and not simply according to their dictionary definition. In the following section, I will examine how to combine lexical approach activities with CLIL methodology.

4 Chunks of text

In this chapter, I endorse a language-pattern-focused approach to study a text. Students must get used to noticing structures and lexical sets which prevail in the chosen passage. A good exercise could be writing down, for example, adjective-noun combinations or verb-adverb combinations or differentiating factual sentences from judgmental ones. Salient pattern detection is a natural inductive process that reduces the cognitive load of managing text and allows students to become aware of the formulaic/phraseological nature of language (Meunier 2012, 115–16). A good strategy to "attack" a text is to "chunk" it: in order to read, speak, and write fluently, students need to know general and topic-specific chunks. Moving the emphasis from a single word to multiword units will increase conceptual comprehension and production in CALP.

Technology may support students in developing their understanding of how words work together and which words are commonly used together, providing easy access to chunks in order to identify language formulation. IdiomSearch tool,[7] born from a project of Dr Jean-Pierre Colson at Leuven Catholic University, makes it possible to extract most set phrases from any text. Therefore, it is a useful tool to support students' hypothesis formation process.

Teachers or students type or paste a text and select the language then click on "Start search" to start the extraction of phrases; the results page will display the set phrases identified in the input text. In Figure 8.1 below, you can see the extraction of lexical items operated by IdiomSearch on a passage taken from IMAT past paper in the academic year of 2015–16.[8]

Figure 8.1: Extraction of phrases on IdiomSearch

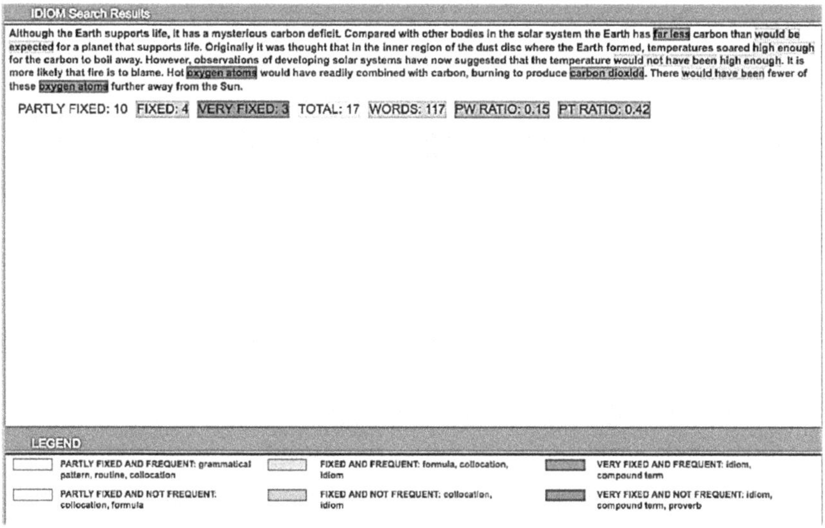

The colors used in the legend below the passage correspond to the degree of language chunks' fixedness ranging from pale yellow to red. Under the colored

---

[7] http://idiomsearch.lsti.ucl.ac.be/

[8] https://www.admissionstesting.org/Images/311133-imat-specimen-paper-.pdf

text appear the number of partly fixed, fixed and, very fixed combinations, as well as the number of words. Using this tool makes students explore and be aware of the regularities of patterning in the target language. The frequencies and chunks highlighted from the program can be used for targeted exercises of content-specific vocabulary building.

Students may be asked to detect general and topic-specific chunks in order to activate semantic associations on the basis of phrases extracted using IdiomSearch. The teacher may structure cloze exercises which are good tools for assessing vocabulary comprehension and for helping students to interpret context clues. They are also good scaffolds for enforcing vocabulary building and reading comprehension.

It is possible to find many online cloze-test creators to design tailor-made learning activities. Thanks to an online gap-fill generator,[9] the same IMAT test passage mentioned above can be used to plan a subject-specific cloze activity to let students train linguistic chunks and keywords erased on the grounds of their frequency scores calculated using IdiomSearch. Having pasted the text in the first page box, the teacher clicks on the target words to make gaps as follows:

Figure 8.2: Online cloze passage exercise generated by
http://www.johnsesl.com/generators/gapfill/gapfill.shtml

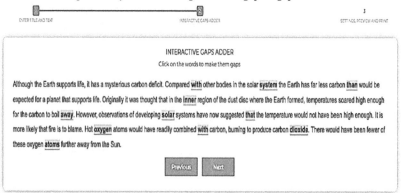

The teacher then selects gap-word options listed in a drop-down menu in order to customize the exercise to suit a larger range of students' learning styles as well as different levels of content and language proficiency:

---

[9] http://www.johnsesl.com/generators/gapfill/gapfill.shtml

Figure 8.3: Dropdowns to select gap word option on
http://www.johnsesl.com/generators/gapfill/gapfill.shtml

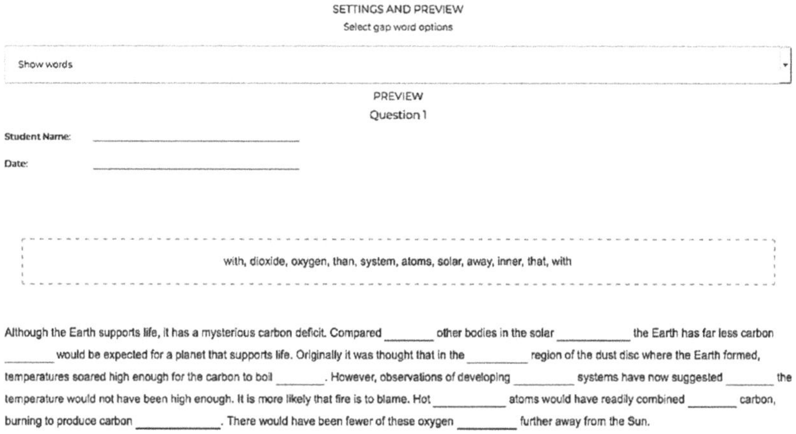

SETTINGS AND PREVIEW
Select gap word options

Show words

PREVIEW
Question 1

Student Name:

Date:

with, dioxide, oxygen, than, system, atoms, solar, away, inner, that, with

Although the Earth supports life, it has a mysterious carbon deficit. Compared _____ other bodies in the solar _____ the Earth has far less carbon _____ would be expected for a planet that supports life. Originally it was thought that in the _____ region of the dust disc where the Earth formed, temperatures soared high enough for the carbon to boil _____. However, observations of developing _____ systems have now suggested _____ the temperature would not have been high enough. It is more likely that fire is to blame. Hot _____ atoms would have readily combined _____ carbon, burning to produce carbon _____. There would have been fewer of these oxygen _____ further away from the Sun.

This exercise, provided in a PDF format, can be used as a reading task to focus learners' attention on content-specific vocabulary items and collocations.

5 CLIL and social reading: A blend that works

Over the past few years, language teaching has increasingly developed from the traditional teacher-centered classroom setting to more multifaceted, learner-centered and/or digital scenarios, allowing learners to examine authentic content through collaborative work to create sophisticated and socially relevant products. The recognition of the basic social nature of learning has led to the development of a sociocultural pedagogical framework for CLIL based on the idea of the active participation of the learner as a member of a learning community (Moate 2010, 39). Therefore the CLIL instructor is requested to design socially-based classroom activities that support second language acquisition within a dynamic process in which a subject's contents and concepts are developed, internalized, and used for further development of HOTS.

From this perspective, one activity that mostly fits the CLIL methodological framework is *social reading*. Social reading, meant as a shared reading practice within the Web environment with the help of tools such as social media networks and collaborative annotation tools (Blyth 2014, 212–13), can be seen as an effective learning tool that plays a pivotal role in the construction of personally meaningful understanding within CLIL settings.

Digital literacies (e.g., computer literacy, information literacy, media literacy) are becoming significant components of L2 learning and teaching (Thorne and Reinhardt 2008, 560–61). Promoting reading in the digital environment in order to encourage access and audience development is the aim of the European Union's "Work Plan for Culture" (2016). Social reading is a great tool to reach the EU goal. As a particular form of collaborative learning that facilitates the process of meaningful negotiation, it also offers many possibilities to CLIL students in order to increase information acquisition and technological skills together. It also provides the opportunity to improve the interaction between students and teacher and students in pairs when they cooperate during the reading comprehension activities, developing critical and information literacy abilities and higher-order cognitive skills (Tian et al. 2016). Exploratory studies that analyze learner-learner interactions within a virtual environment when collaboratively reading L2 texts in courses at college level show the benefits of this approach in terms of the impact on students' reading progress (Thoms and Poole 2017, Zapata and Morales 2018).

Another important consideration about the opportunity to apply the social reading strategy stems from the gap between the growing emphasis on the use of e-texts, massively increased after the shift to online learning due to COVID-19, and the unexpected lack of software to support close reading;[10] this gap may be revealed by any CLIL teacher, especially nowadays.

Applying social reading in a CLIL lesson means giving students agency (student-centered approach), allowing them to share their notes on a given text by collaborating in interpreting the content (peer-to-peer learning). Social reading and discussion activities on study texts in formal education can be supported by web annotations / commenting tools, such as the ones that will be presented in the next section. These tools facilitate the development of new digitally-based reading strategies (Chang and Hsu 2011; Nor, Azman, and Hamat 2013; Tseng, Yeh, and Yang 2015) and scaffold learning allowing students to co-construct meaning while engaged in close reading (Tian 2020).

In the midst of COVID-19, the rapid and mandatory adoption of distance teaching during lockdown forced instructors to find efficacious strategies to engage with students both socially and virtually in online classes with Web resources. The use of annotation tools within social-reading-based lessons allows teachers to design, with no effort, argumentation and group activities on the textbook in order to process domain-specific language knowledge and improve literacy skills (Zhu et al. 2020, 267–68). Commenting and annotating online texts also reduces the difficulty of reading a digital text versus a traditional, print-based one. Researchers suggest that the incorporation of digital annotations in reading instruction in online courses can effectively enhance low-achieving students' reading comprehension in L2 (Sheng-Shiang

---

[10] The detailed examination and interpretation of short extracts down to word level.

and Yeh 2018; Yeh, Hung, and Chiang 2017), especially in LSP settings (Tian et al. 2016, 432).

This method, strongly dialogic and collaborative, offers interesting opportunities for application in CLIL at tertiary level—it is salient under the disciplinary (any discipline can be involved) and relational profiles (it assures the social benefit of building a sense of community), and at the same time it provides a model for training digital citizenship and soft skills. Furthermore, it is predictable that the application of the lexical approach techniques mentioned in the previous paragraph can promptly and successfully integrate social reading in CLIL, giving inspiration for working on language acquisition during content-instruction lessons in L2.

6 Web tools for CLIL social reading

In the lexical approach framework, learners are encouraged to notice language within texts; social reading is the right strategy to develop this skill. In this section I describe the use of three social reading platforms that work as digital learning spaces used to collectively discuss L2 study texts as opportunity for CLIL. Before using these tools in class, the teacher should model effective annotation skills and productive discussion practices in order to let students fully benefit from this approach.

VocabKitchen

The first one, VocabKitchen,[11] is a tool that enables teachers to share digital texts with a class and monitor how students deal with them and which words they choose to learn because best definitions from the dictionary entries can be chosen and shared with learners in real time. This site speeds up the process of learning unknown words from any text; it focuses on teaching words which come from the General Service List (GSL) by Michael West (1953) and the Academic Word List (AWL)[12] by Averil Coxhead (2000).

The aim of the VocabKitchen social reading tool is to quickly detect which words students do not know in a text and return a specific word meaning based on context. The app helps teachers gather data so that they can make an informed decision about which terms to teach. It also helps students by reducing the time and energy it takes to sort through multiple word meanings in a dictionary entry.

----

[11] http://vocabkitchen.com

[12] https://www.wgtn.ac.nz/lals/resources/academicwordlist

The VocabKitchen learning app has two sections: a teacher page and a student page. In the teacher area by clicking on "Add a new text," the CLIL teacher can copy and paste a passage to examine with the class. If students are registered, they can work on it because every uploaded text has a ticket number that, having been entered in the learning area,[13] links directly to it.

Having inserted the text, teachers can click on a word and add their own definition or view the complete dictionary entry for that word and select a specific sub-entry that matches the sentence context. In this way, teachers can create individualized vocabulary lists simply by clicking on new words in a reading activity.

Teachers may also use the *vocabulary profiler* option. A vocabulary profiler is a tool that checks if a piece of text contains words from a vocabulary list. It can be useful for identifying the level of a reading text or as a way of finding which words in a text should receive more focus and scaffold. Students can use it to see which words might be most useful for them to learn. After copying the text in the section, which is the same passage I mentioned in the previous paragraphs, words change color according to their CEFR level,[14] like in Figure 8.4 below.

Figure 8.4: CEFR Vocabulary Profiler on VocabKitchen.com

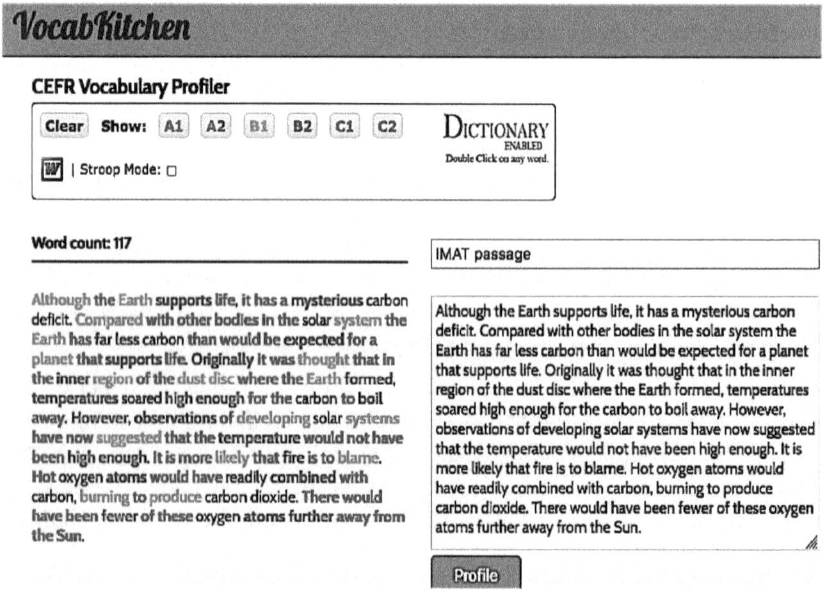

---

[13] vocabkitchen.com/learn/student

[14] https://www.coe.int/en/web/common-european-framework-reference-languages/level-descriptions

The grey words are defined off-list because they are less common and cannot be saved. These words do not appear on GSL or AWL and are normally proper nouns, topic-specific words, or acronyms; the teacher can use them to make a glossary or a word bar for a gap exercise (see Section 4).

From the teacher's perspective, the main pedagogical benefit of incorporating collaborative reading in a higher education level L2 course via VocabKitchen is that it helps the instructor understand his or her students' weaknesses and strengths better. For students, it is possible to register predictable performance benefits; reading activities in a digital environment allow for more time to scan texts and this scaffolding strategy brings a more informed reaction to the different Web sources given as study material. Moreover, the use of the different colors, as shown in Figure 8.4, represents a further visual scaffolding that supports the student in memorizing and understanding the vocabulary that characterizes the proposed text.

eMargin

Another good "text attack" visual strategy to use in CLIL is a color-coding task that I usually assign to my students in eMargin[15] when they initially approach a new text. It is an online collaborative annotation tool developed by the Research and Development Unit for English Studies at Birmingham City University.

Digital annotation tools simplify the progress of new digitally-based reading strategies by allowing learners to highlight digital texts with multiple colors, insert text-, video-, and picture-based annotations, as well as offering functions, such as tag/comment clouds, heat maps of annotations, and combined dictionary search fields. The eMargin user can underline, color-code, write notes, and assign tags to single words or passages of a text. The annotations can be visible and shared amongst class groups, generating discussions and allowing analyses and interpretations to be integrated. eMargin replicates manual annotation in a digital form and is beneficial for close reading of text-based disciplines. It can specifically be used for cooperative activities and in CLIL settings as a versatile and efficacious learning tool to facilitate the L2 vocabulary acquisition process.

The same IMAT sample cited above can be uploaded by teachers on eMargin and shared with the class for an activity based on the color-coding technique. Students are asked to decide which words to color-code based on how familiar they are with them according to the color labels as in Figure 8.5 below.

---

[15] https://emargin.bcu.ac.uk

Figure 8.5: Exercise social reading with eMargin

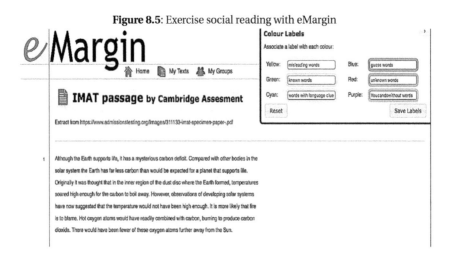

Learners can break unfamiliar vocabulary into six categories by highlighting words in the text with a different color according to the following associations:

- yellow: misleading words,
- green: known words,
- cyan: words containing a language hint,
- blue: words that students can easily guess from the context,
- red: unknown words which students cannot interpret from the context,
- purple: "youcandowithout" words, words that students can manage without while still understanding the main point of the sentence.

Students read the extract, as in the example above (Figure 8.5), using marginalia to highlight words or phrases which seem important and to elicit themes and topics gradually on each rereading. The teacher facilitates this exercise by monitoring the procedure of academic study of texts. Clicking on the highlighted words enables one to look them up in the Oxford English Dictionary, Etymology Dictionary, Dictionary.com, Wikipedia, Google, and WebCorp Live to have a prompt explanation of their meaning.

Personalization is the core of the system, allowing teachers to tailor colors, layout, and annotation styles to the class's individual needs. The synchronous reading of the same digital text enables students to develop their skills in both hyper reading and machine reading, simplifying close reading.

With eMargin, users cooperate to build a shared online interpretation of a text in a more approachable form offering a new kind of study experience— collective and instantaneous. Students can review their earlier predictions, analyses, and observations of text and also dynamically give feedback to their peers in a mutual manner.

eMargin is a versatile tool transferable to any text-based discipline taught in CLIL. It is usable for online synchronous and asynchronous lessons to take notes of emergent language and give well-directed feedback to students on language use; they can go back and review what they have annotated, see what classmates have created, and leave one another comments related to the text's interpretation.

In a user-friendly interface, with eMargin the CLIL the teacher has the opportunity to:

- create threaded discussions linked to precise spans of text (from word to paragraph),

- provide explicit linguistic information to the learner, such as information regarding grammatical structures or lexical meaning,

- tag content/subject-specific keywords crucial to students for understanding the text's meaning,

- add and share annotations on the texts as a scaffolding strategy,

- plan insights related to textual analysis, such as tasks on learner's interpretation of a text's meaning,

- encourage learners to express their opinions about pairs' comments on the text under analysis (e.g., indicating agreement or disagreement),

- focus class discussion on particular themes and passages from the study text,

- ask students to evaluate the meaning of key terms collectively,

- stimulate learners to reflect on cultural differences described in the texts compared with their own cultural background (intercultural competence).

A "wiki" feature allows an "official" interpretation to be formed at class level once consensus has been reached. Using the "tag cloud" command, all the words in a given text are automatically displayed in a word cloud, an iconic representation of frequency—the more frequent the word in the text, the bigger the word in the cloud. Learners can collect important information at a glance by scanning a text's word cloud and detecting keywords.

NowComment

NowComment[16] is a collaborative environment aimed at creating and managing online discussions on any type of document. It is a free application for student-led reading practices. The basic idea is very simple: this tool exploits the possibilities offered by the Web to create an environment in which one can conduct a discussion focused on a document, an image, a quote, a paragraph of a text, or a video.

In NowComment, the CLIL teacher uploads a document to create and manage discussion groups on a specific subject-related topic. Through a code sent by e-mail, learners are invited to comment on the document. Each member of the group can develop a "conversation" linked to any part of the document just by selecting it with a double-click of the mouse. In this way, a conversation is activated and displayed to be shared with other users. Students can rotate the responsibility for taking over and asking questions, annotating, and starting discussions.

Like the other aforementioned tools, NowComment has a very intuitive interface. The screen is divided into two windows: the one on the left shows the document uploaded by the teacher and the title of the discussion; on the right the users find the conversations stemmed from different parts of the document and initiated by the various members of the group. The comments of the group members are ordered in threads. Using search tools and scrolling the threads, it is possible to find the most interesting comments. A system of e-mail notification updates about each new discussion. It is possible to create groups and subgroups of any size. All group participants can upload and share their documents and insert links in the discussion. The teacher helps students chunk readings, guides the conversation, and adds key questions to the text to foster their authentic participation.

NowComment is a very interesting application because it offers an environment for online communication and discussion, which presents the characteristics of a digital forum focused on the disciplinary content we decide to upload. It can be very useful in CLIL blended-learning approach to analyze a study text and sources and keeping track of them.

In distance or flipped learning, often the "management" of videos and documents for individual viewing and/or reading places students in a poor communicative situation and prevents them from interacting and dialoguing about what they have seen/read to deepen knowledge, ask for clarifications, raise objections, make hypothesis, debate, etc. NowComment fills this gap

---

[16] https://nowcomment.com/

because it provides tools for long-term online discussions on specific topics in a rich communicative environment. Figure 8.6 below is an example of social reading on NowComment of an IMAT 2019 passage in biology.

Figure 8.6: Exercise social reading with NowComment

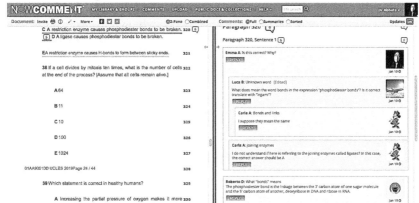

Conclusion

CLIL represents an ideal learning environment in which the concept of language is that of an individual resource for communication, not abstract knowledge to gain. Every subject is characterized by its micro-language, a definite corpus of specific terms, and by its own speech composed of lexical units, collocations, chunks, phrases, and expressions that contribute to the internal coherence, cohesion, and connotative dimension of a given text. When students learn a subject in L2, they need to develop a linguistic meta-competence that allows them to successfully acquire the content and deeply understand technical texts. Therefore, the use of corpus-based tools for vocabulary acquisition appears an important support for students' acquisition process of L2 grammar and vocabulary skills.

If this process happens within the framework of social reading, it is facilitated and improved by the transformation of the learning space into a dynamic, interactive environment where the teacher guides students in text interpretation as they apply their own reading strategies. The combination of the lexical approach with social reading in online CLIL courses has the advantage of integrating language and content learning goals that can be easily applied in lower-level courses as well as upper-level ones.

The annotations on text with tools and methods, shown in the previous pages, can be tagged online in such a way that they can be aggregated, viewed, and discussed by the other students, offering a precious meta-reading opportunity to learners and encouraging them to carry out a close reading of study texts, especially in preparation for tests. Also, reluctant hand-raisers interact with the text and participate in discussions responding in the margins, looking for definitions in real time and reflecting on classmates' comments.

The Web provides users with several student-centered social reading platforms as I have illustrated. They can be easily adapted to CLIL settings with activities aimed at the development of text-reading and comprehension skills in L2, the collaborative construction of contents, the customization of learning thanks to the enhancement of the individual contribution, and the increase of study motivation.

The possibility to enrich the text's passages with hypertext links (to videos, images, or sources) provides scaffolding for students in reading and understanding: adding media supports/complements the most difficult parts of the reading allowing a personalized and multimodal approach to the text. Once the students start to engage with the uploaded materials, the teacher will be able to track their activities very easily. These platforms are also useful tools to get an overall view of the class when the test is approaching. Within them, the learners are immersed in a virtual environment full of possible meanings that become progressively decodable as they act and interact with this environment. The implementation of CLIL with lexical approach and the social reading strategy transfers lessons into a scenario of authenticity and naturalness that represents the essential condition for developing the socio-pragmatic aspects of linguistic interaction.

Finally, in times of imposed social distancing and online learning due to the dramatic spread of COVID-19, it should be highlighted that the methodological and practical approach outlined in this chapter represents a way to mitigate the sense of alienation perceived by learners and their instructors forced to operate from home and leads to the creation of a true and more open learning community beyond the barriers of isolation and loneliness.

References

Abbate, Emma. 2019. "DDL and CLIL Integration: Learning Activities and Resources Based on the Use of Corpora for CLIL Geography in a Cambridge International IGCSE® High School in Italy." *EL.LE Educazione Linguistica / Language Education* 8 (2): 287–304. https://doi.org/10.30687/ELLE/2280-6792/2019/02/002.

Blyth, Carl. 2014. "Exploring the Affordances of Digital Social Reading for L2 Literacy: The Case of eComma." In *Digital Literacies in Foreign and Second Language Education*, CALICO Monograph Series, Volume 12, edited by Jamel Pez Guikema and Laurence Williams, 201–26. San Marcos, TX: CALICO.

Byrnes, Heidi, Hiram H. Maxim, and John M. Norris. 2010. "Realizing Advanced Foreign Language Writing Development in Collegiate Education: Curricular Design, Pedagogy, Assessment." *Modern Language Journal* 94: i–vi.

Cardona, Mario. 2008. "L'insegnamento e apprendimento del lessico in ambiente CLIL. Il CLIL e l'approccio lessicale: Alcune riflessioni" [Teaching and Learning Vocabulary in CLIL settings. CLIL and the Lexical Approach: Some Reflections]. *Studi di Glottodidattica* 4: 1–21. https://ojs.cimedoc.uniba.it/index.php/glottodidattica/article/viewFile/188/59

Chadwick, Timothy. 2012. *Language Awareness in Teaching: A Toolkit for Content and Language Teachers.* Cambridge: Cambridge University Press.

Chang, Chih-Kai, and Ching-Kun Hsu. 2011. "A Mobile-Assisted Synchronously Collaborative Translation-Annotation System for English as a Foreign Language (EFL) Reading Comprehension." *Computer Assisted Language Learning* 24 (2): 155–80. https://doi.org/10.1080/09588221.2010.536952.

Corino, Elisa, and Cristina Onesti. 2019. "Data-Driven Learning: A Scaffolding Methodology for CLIL and LSP Teaching and Learning." *Frontiers in Education* 4. https://doi.org/10.3389/feduc.2019.00007.

Coxhead, Averil. 2000. "A New Academic Word List." *TESOL Quarterly* 34 (2): 213–38.

Cummins, Jim. 2008. "BICS and CALP: Empirical and Theoretical Status of the Distinction." In *Encyclopedia of Language and Education*, Second Edition, Volume 2, edited by Nancy H. Hornberger, 71–83. New York: Springer. https://pdfs.semanticscholar.org/d032/e468026f45f0d0537521e4d0caf7762200a9.pdf.

Dearden, Julie. 2014. *English as a Medium of Instruction: A Growing Global Phenomenon.* Oxford: British Council. https://www.britishcouncil.es/sites/default/files/british_council_english_as_a_medium_of_instruction.pdf.

Dorović, Daniela, and Katarina Zavišin. 2018. "Integrating Elements of LSP Language Teaching and CLIL Methods in the Context of Tertiary Education." *Scripta Manent* 13 (1): 26–44. http://scriptamanent.sdutsj.edus.si/ScriptaManent/article/view/262.

Douglas, Dan. 2001. "Language for Specific Purposes Assessment Criteria: Where Do They Come From?" Language Testing 18 (2): 171–85. https://doi.org/10.1177/026553220101800204.

Eldridge, John, Steve Neufeld, and Nilgun Hancioglu. 2010. "Towards a Lexical Framework for CLIL." *International CLIL Research Journal*, 1 (3): 88–103. https://www.unifg.it/sites/default/files/allegatiparagrafo/20-01-2014/eldridge_et_al_towards_a_lexical_approach_to_clil.pdf

European Commission. 2016. "European Agenda for Culture. Work Plan for Culture. Promoting Reading in the Digital Environment." Accessed January 15, 2021. https://op.europa.eu/en/publication-detail/-/publication/d1964bfe-2ecd-11e6-b497-01aa75ed71a1.

Fernández, Daniel J. 2009. "CLIL at the University Level: Relating Language Teaching with and through Content Teaching." *Latin American Journal of Content and Language Integrated Learning* 2 (2):10–26. https://doi.org/10.5294/laclil.2009.2.2.11.

Górska-Poręçka, Bozena. 2011. "The LSP-CLIL Interface in the University Context." Paper presented at the 4th edition of ICT for Language conference,

Florence, Italy, 20–21 October. https://conference.pixel-online.net/conferences/ICT4LL2011/common/download/ Paper_pdf/CLIL13-422-FP-Porecka-ICT4LL2011.pdf

Guazzieri, Anna Valeria. 2007. "Participation in CLIL: Cooperative Learning in CLIL." In *Diverse Contexts—Converging Goals, CLIL in Europe*, edited by David Marsh and Dieter Wolff, 171–84. Frankfurt am Main: Peter Lang.

Krashen, Sthephen. 1985. *The Input Hypothesis: Issues and Implications*. New York: Longman.

Lewis, Michael. 1993. *The Lexical Approach*. Hove: Language Teaching Publication.

Marsh, David, and Gisella Langé. 2000. *Using Languages to Learn and Learning to Use Languages: An Introduction to Content and Language Integrated Learning for Parents and Young People*. Jyväaskyla: University of Jyväaskyla. http://archive.ecml.at/mtp2/clilmatrix/pdf/1uk.pdf.

Meunier, Fanny. 2012. "Formulaic Language and Language Teaching." *Annual Review of Applied Linguistics* 32: 111–29. https://doi.org/10.1017/S0267190512000128.

Meyer, Oliver. 2013. "Introducing the CLIL-Pyramid: Key Strategies and Principles for CLIL Planning and Teaching." In *Basic Issues in EFL Teaching*, Second Edition, edited by Maria Eisenmann and Theresa Summer, 295–312. Heidelberg: Universitätsverlag Winter.

Moate, Josephine. 2010. "The Integrated Nature of CLIL: A Sociocultural Perspective." *International CLIL Research Journal* 1 (3): 38–45. http://www.icrj.eu/13/article4.html.

Nor, Fariza Mod, Hazita Azman, and Afendi Hamat. 2013. "Investigating Students' Use of Online Annotation Tool in an Online Reading Environment." *3L: The Southeast Asian Journal of English Language Studies* 19 (3): 87–101. http://journalarticle.ukm.my/6586/1/3655-9500-1-PB.pdf.

Sheng-Shiang, Tseng, and Hui-Chin Yeh. 2018. "Integrating Reciprocal Teaching in an Online Environment with an Annotation Feature to Enhance Low-Achieving Students' English Reading Comprehension." *Interactive Learning Environments* 26 (6): 789–802. https://doi.org/10.1080/10494820.2017.1412989.

Swain, Merrill. 1985. "Communicative Competence: Some Roles of Comprehensible Input and Comprehensible Output in its Development." In *Input in Second Language Acquisition*, edited by Susan M. Gass and Carolyn G. Madden, 235–56. New York: Newbury House.

Thoms, Brian. 2011. "A Dynamic Social Feedback System to Support Learning and Social Interaction in Higher Education." *IEEE Transactions on Learning Technologies* 4 (4): 340–52. https://doi.org/10.1109/TLT.2011.9.

Thoms, Joshua J., and Frederick Poole. 2017. "Investigating Linguistic, Literary, and Social Affordances of L2 Collaborative Reading." *Language Learning & Technology* 21 (1): 139–56. https://scholarspace.manoa.hawaii.edu/bitstream/10125/44615/1/21_02_thomspoole.pdf

Thorne, Steven L., and Jonathon J. Reinhardt. 2008. "Bridging Activities: New Media Literacies and Advanced Foreign Language Proficiency." *CALICO Journal* 25 (3): 558–72. https://pdfs.semanticscholar.org/bfa3/4dd59ed39a9ece65e1b131ec0cffc11d221e.pdf.

Tian, Jennifer Pei-Ling, Simon Yang, Elizabeth Koh, and Christin Jonathan. 2016. "Fostering 21st Century Literacies through a Collaborative Critical

Reading and Learning Analytics Environment: User-Perceived Benefits and Problematics." In *Proceedings of the Sixth International Conference on Learning Analytics & Knowledge* (*LAK '16*), 430–34. New York: Association for Computing Machinery. https://doi.org/https://doi.org/10.1145/2883851.288 3965.

Tian Jianqiu. 2020. "Investigating Students' Use of a Social Annotation Tool in an English for Science and Technology Course." In *Emerging Technologies for Education*, edited by Elvira Popescu, Tianyong Hao, Ting-Chia Hsu, Haoran Xie, Marco Temperini, Wei Chen, 299–309. Cham: Springer. https://doi.org/ 10.1007/978-3-030-38778-5_33.

Tseng, Sheng-Shiang, Hui-Chin Yeh, and Shih-hsien Yang. 2015. "Promoting Different Reading Comprehension Levels through Online Annotations." *Computer Assisted Language Learning* 28 (1): 41–57. https://doi.org/10.1080/ 09588221.2014.927366.

Vilkancienė, Lilija. 2011. "CLIL in Tertiary Education: Does it Have Anything to Offer?" *Kalbų Studijos: Studies About Languages* 18: 111–16. https://etalpykla. lituanistikadb.lt/object/LT-LDB-0001:J.04~2011~1367174913450/J.04~2011~ 1367174913450.pdf.

West, Michael. 1953. *A General Service List of English Words*. London: Longman, Green and Co.

Yang, Wenhsien. 2016. "ESP vs CLIL: A Coin of Two Sides or a Continuum of Two Extremes?" *ESP Today* 4 (1): 43–45. https://www.esptodayjournal.org/pdf/ current_issue/3.6.2016/ WENHSIEN-YANG-full%20text.pdf

Yeh, Hui-Chin, Hsiu-Ting Hung, and Yu-Hsin Chiang. 2017. "The Use of Online Annotations in Reading Instruction and Its Impact on Students' Reading Progress and Processes." *ReCALL* 29 (1): 22–38. https://doi.org/10.1017/S095 8344016000021.

Zapata, Gabriel, and Maybel Mesa Morales. 2018. "The Beneficial Effects of Technology-Based Social Reading in L2 Classes." *Lenguas en Contexto* 9: 40– 50. https://doi.org/10.13140/RG.2.2.33960.83202.

Zhu, Xinran, Bodong Chen, Rukmini Manasa Avadhanam, Hong Shui, and Raymond Zhuo Zhang. 2020. "Reading and Connecting: Using Social Annotation in Online Classes." *Information and Learning Science* 121 (5–6): 261–71. https://doi.org/10.35542/osf.io/2nmxp.

Websites

https://emargin.bcu.ac.uk
http://idiomsearch.lsti.ucl.ac.be/
http://nowcomment.com
http://vocabkitchen.com
http://www.johnsesl.com/generators/gapfill/gapfill.shtml

CHAPTER 9

The influence of the Romanian academic style on student writing in English

Loredana Bercuci

West University of Timişoara, Romania

Mădălina Chitez

West University of Timişoara, Romania

Abstract

Romanian English for Academic Purposes tutors often complain that students write in the "Romanian style" instead of adopting the Anglo-American style in their English papers. The "Romanian style" of academic writing has not yet been fully defined, but a cursory look at papers written in Romanian reveals traits such as an impersonal style, a plethora of unnecessary detail, and distinctive turns of phrase. This chapter aims to define this "Romanian style" of academic writing and to show how it influences student writing in English. First, we survey research that has so far sought to define the style. Then, we analyze student papers published at the Faculty of Letters, History and Theology of the West University of Timişoara in Romania, both in Romanian (five issues of the journal *Literacum*) and in English (seven issues of the *Journal of Student Research in Languages and Literatures*), using corpus linguistics methods. We look at frequencies and phraseology patterns as well as prominent rhetorical features. Several conclusions are drawn regarding the interlanguage profile of such linguistic features.

Keywords: academic writing, learner corpus, L1 interference, Romanian-English

***

Introduction

The typical traits of introductions in scholarly works have been studied extensively (e.g., Swales 1990). As the most formulaic parts of scholarly writing, introductory moves are also one of the first tricks students learn in academic writing courses in LSP, particularly in English for Academic Purposes. The process through which students learn these moves is a laborious one, a major step of which is publishing in student journals when students first encounter the professional community that they later might wish to join. Those who write in two different languages face a further challenge: writing for two academic writing audiences with different genre expectations. Even though published articles are selected and edited by professors and are thus considered successful student work, generic interference from one language into another is still seen as an issue by the faculty. In this study, we analyze the influence of Romanian language traits and academic genre norms with a view to offering a basis, as well as some suggestions, for making students aware of this interference. We seek to answer the following questions:

- What are the defining traits of the Romanian academic style?

- Which linguistic features are prominent in student writing in English?

- Which structures typical of the Romanian academic style occur frequently in student writing in English?

- Which didactic strategies can be used to make students aware of L1 interference in their own writing?

1 Literature review

1.1 Academic writing in Romania

In the first part of this study, we will offer an overview of the relatively few research works that have contextualized and defined academic writing in Eastern Europe, discussing the particularities of the Romanian context in more depth. We also point to current research conducted in the field in an attempt to address some of the gaps still present in the endeavor of defining the academic culture of Eastern Europe in general and of Romania in particular. We thus provide a working definition of the "Romanian style" that will be expanded in the second part of this paper as we perform our corpus analyses.

Academic writing produced by scholars at Romanian universities has seen numerous fluctuations in the past three decades. While before 1945 Romanian higher education showcased an affinity towards the Napoleonic model of organization (cf. Charle 2004), the post-war context saw the Soviet model imposed in the region (cf. Rüegg and Sadlak 2011). This state of facts is reflected in academic writing norms. Since 1989, and especially since the adoption of the Bologna Process in 2004 and Romania's accession to the European Union in 2007, academic writing norms have tended to follow the Anglo-American model due especially to "the widespread use of English in scientific and professional communities" (Borchin and Doroholschi 2016, 179). However, this complex history of intersecting writing-community norms has resulted in a rather unique blend of the abovementioned writing cultures.

Recent studies on research writing in Romania in L1 Romanian and L2 English have identified several tendencies that can be explained in light of the transition from the French to the Soviet and toward the Anglo-American writing culture. For example, Băniceru et al. note that "[t]he 'traditional' Romanian practice of writing can be characterized as implicit, 'author oriented,' 'concerned with style,' lacking theoretical reflection and an appropriate methodological approach" (2012, 321). However, as they show through the analysis of student writing in B.A. theses written in L1 Romanian and in L2 English (Literary Studies and Linguistics), the influence of the Anglo-American models is discernible. Their study identifies seven rhetorical "moves most typically used in the corpus of diploma paper introductions, and conclude[s] that the 'descriptive' moves and steps (introducing the topic, presenting the structure of the paper) prevailed over the more 'reflective' moves (summarising previous research, indicating a gap in previous research)" (Băniceru et al. 2012, 320).

Student perceptions, too, reflect these tendencies, writing being associated more with terminological accuracy, the use of figurative language, and avoiding first-person pronouns, and less with convincing arguments and critical thinking (Băniceru and Tucan 2018, 107). This is reflected at the level of form as well. Bercuci and Chitez (2019, 743) show that, compared to student writers whose L1 is English, Romanian students writing both in L1 Romanian and in L2 English have a tendency to depersonalize their texts, this being more apparent when they write in their L1 Romanian.

In "Corpus Linguistics Meets Academic Writing: Examples and Applications in the Romanian EFL Context" (2018), Mădălina Chitez discusses linguistic features of writing in English by students with L1 Romanian. The frequency of certain parts of speech was computed and the study indicates that the "most frequent nouns coincide with the most used nouns by native speakers" (Chitez 2018, 205). In the case of verbs, on the other hand, the highest occurring words are not the same as in Romanian. The nouns that are subject to overuse by Romanian L2 writers are *life, world, way, society, man, fact, person, death, problem,* and *child.* Several verbs are also used more frequently by Romanian speakers than by L1 English speakers (e.g., *think, want, know,* and *say*).

In the last decade, two research projects at the West University of Timișoara in Romania have attempted to research and tackle these issues. First, project

LIDHUM (Literacy Development in the Humanities)[1] was an institutional cooperation project in which each partner aimed at creating a favorable context for the development of academic writing initiatives (i.e., academic writing centers, academic writing courses). A work package in the project was dedicated to the comparison of academic writing cultures of the various national representatives in the project. At the same time, case studies were conducted on the difference between academic writing in L1 and L2. In this way, common and culture-specific characteristics and trends could be identified and interpreted (Chitez et al. 2018). Second, project ROGER (Academic genres at the crossroads of tradition and internationalization: Corpus-based interlanguage research on genre use in student writing at Romanian universities)[2] lies at the intersection between two disciplines within the humanities: Academic Writing and Corpus Linguistics. In the frame of the project, a corpus was compiled between 2017 and 2022 which includes academic genres from Romanian universities, written both in Romanian and English, in several disciplines. The relevance of contrasting academic genres in both languages is justified by the increasing offer of courses taught in English, attended by both Romanian and foreign students, in all disciplines. In the context of curricular transition to international norms, it is important to highlight the differences of use in L1 and L2 within the same discipline, i.e., the use of research report in Romanian and English courses in humanities departments or the mixture of genre norms between L1 and L2 due to linguistic interferences and norm borrowing from L1 into L2 and vice versa.

A comparison to ESP students' writing in L1 Romanian offers the missing perspective regarding the cause for overuse or underuse of certain linguistic elements which might be related to the interference with the mother tongue.

1.2 Corpus approaches to academic writing

Though there is little theoretical (or corpus-based) contrastive research on academic writing in Romanian versus English (see Chitez 2014, Chitoran 2013), the proposed study can build on the body of contrastive research on academic discourse in other languages (D'Angelo 2012; Fløttum, Dahl, and Kinn 2006; Mauranen 1993; Mauranen 1994; Siepmann 2005). The beginning of this research line was Kaplan's study of essays (1966) from students originating from different cultures in which he analyzed paragraph structures and identified five

---

[1] More information available at https://www.zhaw.ch/no_cache/en/research/research-database/project-detailview/projektid/751/.

[2] The ROGER corpus is available at https://roger-corpus.org/.

types of thematic progress which he believed to be typical thought patterns of the English, Russian, Semitic, and Romance languages. The global attribution of textual features to culture-based thought patterns was characteristic for the first phase of intercultural research. Connor showed that Kaplan's thinking was strongly influenced by the Sapir-Whorf hypothesis, if not in its strong version ("language controls thought") then in its weak one ("language influences thinking") (2002, 495). What is relevant to the proposed project is the main hypothesis that "writing is culturally influenced in interesting and complex ways" (Connor 2002, 495). However, we will not disregard voices which have been warning that cultures are not "monolithic entities" (Atkinson 1999, 627), but rather that they are inhomogeneous and in continuous change. Most influential, besides Kaplan, was the research by Clyne (1981, 1987) comparing sociological texts from German and English speakers with regard to the hierarchy of text, dynamics of text, symmetry, and uniformity. His results, for example, indicate that German texts show more digressiveness, are worse organized, and use fewer topic sentences at the paragraph level. Both Kaplan's and Clyne's approaches were situated in the field of English as a Second Language (ESL) or English for Specific Purposes (ESP). The studies following this line since then have been summarized as "contrastive rhetoric" (or intercultural rhetoric) by Connor (2002) or Connor, Nagelhout, and Rozycki (2008). Connor's perception of genres as not-static products and "as functional parts of dynamic cultural contexts" helped shaping this field (2002, 493).

A few studies have investigated salient features in academic writing of different L1 users. For example, a corpus investigation of syntactic transfer (from L1 into learner language) was conducted by Borin (2004), bringing into discussion the topic of "translationese" seen as "the set of 'fingerprints' that one language leaves on another when a text is translated between the two" (Gellerstam 1985). Partially replicating Aarts and Granger's N-gram interlanguage comparisons (1998), Borin (2004) performed a POS-tag n-gram analysis (Mann-Whitney test) in order to identify phenomena of underuse or overuse in L2[3] (learner corpus English) compared to L1 (native corpus English) and M (mother tongue Swedish) for uni-, bi-, tri- and 4-grams. Similar to Aarts and Granger (1998), Borin (2004) anticipated that, with the help of χ^2 statistical tests, L1-specific patterns can be identified.

---

[3] The L1 (native English) / L2 (EFL) / M (mother tongue) system has the following configuration in Gilquin (2008): L2/IL/L1.

2 Method and data

2.1 Method

Based on the results of our literature review in the previous section, we analyzed frequency and phraseology patterns in the JAWS corpus which consists of two learner sub-corpora. JAWS contains introductions to research articles written by undergraduate and master's students in English and in Romanian. The corpus contains 36 introductions in English and 41 in Romanian, being made up of a total of 21,083 words. The corpus was tagged for rhetorical moves and a native-speaker corpus, LOCNESS, was used for reference. For the analysis, we used Words, Whelk, and N-grams tools of programs LancsBox (Brezina and McEnery 2020) and WordSmith (Scott 2016).

LancsBox and WordSmith have similar functions which can be used to analyze both expert and learner corpora. They are concordancing programs that permit the analysis of large corpora based on the frequency of occurrence. For example, both programs have a function that results in a list of the most frequent words in the corpus (Words in LancsBox; WordList in WordSmith). Another function in both programs permits the visualization of a word or phrase in a variety of contexts (KWIC in LancsBox; Concord in WordSmith). As such, these programs offer a variety of opportunities for teaching as well as self-directed learning: to learn new words and collocations, to compare texts from the same genre in different languages, to find examples of use, or to compare one's own writing with an expert text.

2.2 Data

The first learner corpus, JAWSEN, written in English, is made up of research articles published in the *Journal of Student Research in Languages and Literatures*, which is an open-access edited journal dedicated to original research by undergraduate and master's students of language, literature, and related areas. Its aim is to provide young researchers with an opportunity to work in more depth on the issues they are interested in and with a platform for sharing their ideas.

The journal is edited by the Department of Modern Languages and Literatures, in collaboration with the Center for Academic and Professional Writing at the Faculty of Letters, West University of Timișoara, Romania. The majority of the papers have been presented at the annual Symposium of Students in English organized by the Department of Modern Languages and Literatures. The Symposium of Students in English aims to offer young researchers the opportunity to share their research, network with faculty and peers from other departments, providing them with first-hand experience of an academic conference. It is an attempt to acquaint students with the practical side of a research career, which is an insufficiently addressed part of the curriculum.

The second learner corpus, JAWSRO, written in Romanian, is made up of introductions to research papers published in the student journal *Literacum*. *Literacum* is an open-access edited journal dedicated to original research by undergraduate and master's students of Romanian literature. It is an online platform where the authors of the articles share their interests and research. The journal is edited and published by the Literacum Student Research Center of the West University of Timișoara, Romania, whose members are primarily students. Several faculty members act as research and editing advisers to the student editors. The language of publication is Romanian.

Many of the studies published in *Literacum* have been presented at student conferences at various Romanian universities. Further, they have received commendations from conference juries, such as prizes or honorable mentions. Thus, the papers follow the guidelines requested by the conference where they were presented. Organized by Romanian departments, these conferences typically suggest very different quality parameters from the Symposium of Students in English, which seeks to prepare students for their integration in Western European and American academia. More about the traits of Romanian academia and academic writing will be outlined in what follows.

The student texts were pre-processed for the corpus analysis. The following steps were taken to ensure the corpus would be ready for analysis:

1. Selecting the text that deals directly with our research objective: In our case, we selected the introduction to the students' essays in both English and Romanian. The student texts had been edited before publication.

2. Getting the text in the right format: i.e., transform .pdf into .txt. Each introduction was saved as an individual document in the .txt format. The documents were given codes which included abbreviations for the name of the corpus, the number of the text, and the batch (the issue where the text appeared).

3. Cleaning text: i.e., by removing title page, content page, introductory statements, executive summary, annexes/appendices, reference list, headers and footers, links.

4. Encoding (UTF8): There are special characters that are not recognized. Special characters, typical of Romanian, were removed.

5. Removing stop words: most common words in a language that provide no content (i.e., and, for, in, to).

LancsBox and WordSmith permit stop words to be removed to allow for an analysis of content words. In our case, stop words were removed only for the second round of analyses as we were interested in comparing the use of prepositions, conjunctions, and articles in both languages.

When using corpora for teaching, or within teaching processes, it is advisable that these steps be followed. They ensure the proper functioning of the programs. What is more, the results of the analyses will be accurate.

3 Results

3.1 Basic frequencies and N-grams

The frequency analysis of the Romanian text corpus, JAWSRO, indicates that the most used linguistic tokens are prepositions (*de* – EN: *of*, *in* – EN: *in*, *la* – EN: *to*, *at*, *ca* – EN: *like*, *such as*), indefinite articles (*o*, *un* – EN: *a*), conjunctions (*si* – EN: *and*), and pronouns (*care* – EN: *which*, *who*, *that*). Table 9.1 shows the ten most used lexical tokens in JAWSRO. The frequency and dispersion of these common words are typical of Romanian in general, so they may be used as grounds for comparison to the English corpus.

Table 9.1: Most frequent words in JAWSRO

	Word RO	Freq.	%
1.	DE	459	4.24
2.	IN	308	2.85
3.	SI	285	2.63
4.	A	283	2.61
5.	O	181	1.67
6.	CARE	171	1.58
7.	SA	143	1.32
8.	LA	134	1.24
9.	CA	121	1.11
10.	UN	118	1.09

In the JAWSRO corpus (see Table 9.2), the collocations used by students are either general formulaic expressions (e.g., *de a-si exprima sentimentele—to express feelings*), typical LSP units (e.g., *si a incadrarii acestuia in literatură—and situating it in the current research*), or standard academic writing clusters (*in cadrul lucrarii de fata—in the present study*). The inclusion of phrases typically taught in academic writing classes suggests that the students have some command of the academic register. However, the high frequency with which they appear points to a lack of variety in the use of these terms.

Table 9.2: Frequent collocations in JAWSRO

DE	DE + a (Romanian: [de + a + Infinitive Verb]	de a comunica (EN: to communicate) de a-si exprima sentimentele (EN: to express feelings) de a transmite (EN: to transmit)
	DE + la (Romanian : [de + at + noun]	de la principiile indicate (EN: from the principles indicated) de la o perioada la alta (EN: from one period to another)
	DE + o (Romanian: [de + o + noun]	pe de o parte (EN: on the one hand)
IN	IN + care (Romanian: [in + care/relative pronoun]	Unul in care (EN: one in which) Modul in care (EN: the way in which) Perioada in care (EN: the period in which)
	IN + cadrul (Romanian: [in + cadrul/complex preposition]	In cadrul prelegerilor sale (EN: as part of their lectures)
SI	SI + a (Romanian: [si + a + noun]	Si a unor metode recente (EN: and of some recent methods) si a incadrarii acestuia in literatura (EN: and situating it in the current research)

To measure L1 interference, we compared the frequency with which equivalent terms appear in Romanian and in English. As shown by Figure 9.1, similar tokens occur very often in both Romanian and English introductions, even though the highest occurring 15 rank differently in Romanian versus English. The variation in rank and frequency is minimal, apart from some cases, namely *and, in, a, is, that/which.*

Figure 9.1: Comparison of the most frequent tokens in JAWSRO vs JAWSEN

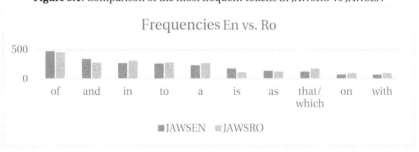

Considering the apparent specificity of the lexico-grammatical patterns in the Romanian academic written discourse, a double-shifted comparison with the English LSP corpus and the English L1 corpus is necessary. Table 9.3 shows differences in use between such two salient structures: *in care / in which* and *pe de o parte / on the one hand.*

Table 9.3: Lexico-grammatical patterns in JAWSRO vs JAWSEN

RO	EN	JAWSRO	%	JAWSEN	%	LOCNESS	%
[In care]	[In which]	5	0.007	6	0.009	20	0.001
[pe de o parte]	[on the one hand]	8	0.011	0	0.000	8	0.0003

A first overview of the correspondent terms in English of the most frequent tokens plus their collocations in Romanian demonstrates that the style of the student writing in English LSP is strongly influenced by Romanian in cases such as expressions involving pronouns (e.g., *which*) or structures connected to introductory moves more typical of the Romanian academic style (e.g., *one of the most, at the same time*). On the other hand, typical formulaic Romanian expressions (*pe de o parte* / EN: *on the one hand*), although also present in the English academic writing vocabulary, are avoided (see Figure 9.2).

Figure 9.2: Equivalent structures in JAWSEN vs JAWSRO

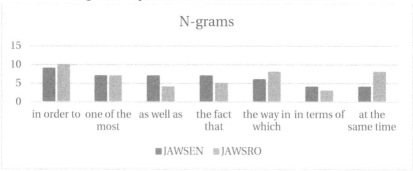

Less affected are the expressions that are grammatical equivalents. For example, the use of the preposition *de* in Romanian is not mirrored in the use of the infinitive-to construction in LSP texts. This means that students know how to make the necessary stylistic adaptation from one language to the other. Similarly, structures such as *as well as, in terms of,* whose equivalents in Romanian are used in a similar manner, are subject to slight overuse in the L2 English corpus. This may be interpreted as being related to how confident the students feel when using a certain structure: if they know the usage is similar in their L1, they lean on it more when writing in L2.

The comparison between the lexis of the L2 English texts and L1 English texts (KWIC analysis) reflects, even more, the correspondence between terms in the native language and those transferred in the foreign language. Words such as *language, body, story, paper, narratives, character,* and *adaptation* appearing as typical keywords for the L2 English corpus are also highly frequent in the L1

Romanian corpus. This can be attributed to the topics dealt with by the papers: linguistics, literary studies, cultural studies, and political science (Table 9.4).

Table 9.4: Frequent lexical items in JAWSEN

Word	Freq.	%
THE	832	7.83
OF	467	4.39
TO	254	2.39
BE	57	0.53
FOR	36	0.33
BODY	33	0.31
LANGUAGE	32	0.30
NOVEL	30	0.28
STORY	27	0.25
PAPER	21	0.19
CHARACTER	18	0.16
GOTHIC	17	0.16
CHARACTERS	15	0.14
WOULD	13	0.12
ELEMENTS	12	0.11
ANALYSIS	11	0.1
FOCUS	11	0.1
CHICANO	10	0.09
LANGUAGES	10	0.09
LITERARY	10	0.09

3.2 Use of *I*

As mentioned in the first part of this chapter, Romanian academic writing implicitly stresses the importance of using an impersonal style. Students are advised to avoid the first person when writing for academic purposes in order to achieve the appropriate register. Students of English at the West University of Timisoara, however, study Academic Writing in English as part of their core courses as well. In this context, they are encouraged to use the first-person singular perspective so as to take responsibility for their claims.

Table 9.5: Use of I in JAWSEN

Corpus: JAWSEN| Search Term: I| Occurrences: 17 (16.24)| Texts: 7/36|			
Index	**File**	**Left**	**Node**	**Right**
1	JAWSEN1005	of time and space. In this sense,	I	will pinpoint the contrasting views in shaping
2	JAWSEN1005	of the humanized monster. In other words,	I	will concentrate on the so-called taming of
3	JAWSEN1011	used in the analysis is my own.	I	have used the original Spanish version as
4	JAWSEN1011	as the source text (Borges 1974) and	I	have also consulted the Romanian translation of
5	JAWSEN1017	Rushdie and his novel Midnight's Children, which	I	will be analyzing in the following pages.
6	JAWSEN1017	in the following pages. In this paper	I	will make a presentation of the main
7	JAWSEN1020	up with earlier speculation. For this purpose,	I	shall take a more focused approach by
8	JAWSEN1022	hold of the subject. Throughout my essay	I	will be discussing the Hollywood stereotypes of
9	JAWSEN1022	and popular culture. Before starting my analysis,	I	would like to clarify the term 'stereotype.'
10	JAWSEN1026	social and economic vitality. In this essay,	I	apply Jane Jacobs' concept of sidewalk ballet
11	JAWSEN1026	a diverse urban neighbourhood. Considering her ideas,	I	examine the streetscape of contemporary Battery Park
12	JAWSEN1026	Lev Manovich's (2015: 1) proposition. Thus,	I	used data acquired from popular social media
13	JAWSEN1030	in gender, sexuality, ethnicity, religion and race.	I	will be focusing on the representation of
14	JAWSEN1030	they are not accepted. The characters that	I	will be analyzing are Santana Lopez (Glee)
15	JAWSEN1030	serve as examples for my theoretical basis.	I	believe that visual media, as opposed to
16	JAWSEN1030	have to face directly through real people.	I	do not deny that literature conveys a
17	JAWSEN1030	powerful image of the Chicano community, but	I	believe that in today's time the portrayal

The analysis of the two corpora shows that seven of the thirty-six texts written in English use the first-person perspective, i.e., about 20% (Table 9.5). This shows that a relatively low percentage of students have internalized academic norms related to author roles in English academic writing. When compared to the LOCNESS native-speaker corpus, Romanian students use *I* up to 3.5 times less. This points to the fact that, in the humanities if not in other disciplines, the use of first-person pronouns is much more common in English than it is in Romanian. As seen in examples 15, 16, and 17, slippage into an informal register is not uncommon. Furthermore, interference from Romanian is also evident (examples 2, 4). On the other hand, a majority of students use structures typical of academic writing in English (examples 1, 8, 10, 11).

When it comes to the Romanian texts, even fewer use the first-person perspective, namely six out of forty-one, i.e., about 14% (Table 9.6). Considering the tendencies in Romanian academic writing, it is striking that even these instances occur and that only 6% more students writing in English abide by their tutors' suggestions. The similarity in percentages can be accounted for by taking into consideration that undergraduate students at the West University of Timişoara have a double major, often English and Romanian, so many of the students writing for these journals have to negotiate the use of two sets of academic norms. The similar percentage of students who use *I* in English and in Romanian suggests that not only has Romanian academic writing influenced students' writing in English, but English norms have influenced Romanian writing as well. However, quite a few of the instances in which students have used the first person in Romanian stem from a failure to adhere to the formal register altogether ("I am saying this because"), suggesting a lack of experience with writing norms altogether. Even when disregarding these, English appears to influence Romanian writing.

Table 9.6: Use of I in JAWSRO

Use of I in JAWSRO	English translation
"Voi trata mai departe conceptul de"	I will proceed to discuss
"Am ales doua personaje masculine"	I have chosen two male characters
"Bukowski zicea asta, sa va citez si eu voua"	Bukovski said this, and I am quoting it for you
"Ma refer aici la faptul ca putem identifica doua posibilitati"	I am referring to the fact that we can identify two possibilities
"Spun acest lucru deoarece"	I am saying this because
"In urmatoarele randuri mi-am propus sa prezint"	In what follows, I wish to present

4 Teaching recommendations for the EAP and ESP classroom

4.1 For the EAP and ESP classroom where the student's first language is Romanian

Considering these results, we make the following recommendations to EAP and ESP instructors teaching writing to L2 English speakers whose L1 is Romanian:

- Assign exercises focused on decreasing the frequency with which the students use *that/which*, *of*, or *with*.

- Raise the students' awareness concerning the issue of false friends.

- Assign exercises focused on decreasing the frequency with which the students use *one of the most, at the same time.*

- Encourage students to use the first-person perspective when writing research in the field of humanities.

4.2 Corpus exercises for ESP and EAP

Effective ways to achieve the abovementioned goals include, first of all, expert and learner corpora as support for academic writing in L2 English. Students can be asked to compile learner and expert corpora, which can be used contrastively, especially for self-directed learning. They can also be used in class.

Activity example 1

The ESP instructor can ask students to create an expert corpus by finding research articles in their discipline. Each student may find 1–2 articles and pre-process them for analysis. The resulting corpus can be used by the whole group to discover specialized language by creating lists of the most frequent words. Similarly, word clusters and collocations can be discovered in the same way.

Activity example 2

Using the same corpus, the students may be asked to focus on functional language specific for their discipline. In this way, they may find language like text organizers, language used to show stance, and language used to describe data and commentary to data.

Activity example 3

The students may be asked to pre-process their own writing. The students' works can then be compiled into a corpus. This corpus may be compared to the expert corpus. Contrasting the frequency of use of certain words or phrases may help students correct their underuse or overuse tendencies when it comes to general or discipline-specific lexis.

Activity example 4

An L1 corpus may also be created for the purpose of contrasting it with the specialized corpus in English. Equivalent structures can be discovered in both languages, or differences in the use of some structures may be discussed.

Another way to achieve the goals is using corpora as control for reference instruments. Students can be given access to online corpora, which they can reference to improve their own writing.

Activity example 1

ESP and EAP instructors may use online corpora, such as the British National Corpus (BNC) or the Corpus of Contemporary American English (COCA), in their teaching. Students can be asked to use these corpora, which are freely available online, to search for words or phrases in their own writing. By finding examples of these words in context, students can be encouraged to correct their writing in this way.

Activity example 2

Students can be asked to explore online corpora to find examples of words and collocations in context. They may keep a glossary in which they keep track of new vocabulary along with examples lifted from corpora. The same can be done for collocates.

Conclusions

Linguistic features more frequent in Romanian, such as *that/which*, *of*, or *with*, occur with increased frequency in student writing in English. The students' vocabulary is also influenced by the Romanian vocabulary, irrespective of the register in which they have to write their texts. For example, correspondent vocabulary and expressions of both standard and academic Romanian terms can be identified in their LSP pieces of writing.

Similarly, some introductory structures typical of the Romanian academic style occur with increased frequency in student writing in English (e.g., *one of the most*, *at the same time*). Such phrases are typically used in a similar way in Romanian and their overuse is likely tied to how confident students are when using them. What is more, they are structures used to describe hierarchy and simultaneity, rather than other logical connections typical of argumentative texts. The Romanian academic style encourages students to be descriptive and historicizing rather than argumentative, and this is transferred into their writing in English through the overuse of these phrases.

Less than 20% of the texts written in English use the first-person singular, showcasing the influence of the Romanian academic style, in which students are taught to use the first-person plural, the third person, or passive voice. A similar number of papers in the Romanian corpus use the first person, which suggests that English influences Romanian as well. Moreover, it points to the difficulties young students face in shifting between sets of academic norms.

In the EAP and ESP class, corpus-related exercises can be used to improve students' writing. The use of corpora allows for the creation of creative exercises that permit focusing on the issues mentioned above as well as others discovered by the students or by the instructors. Apart from being versatile language-support tools, corpora may also increase student motivation and self-directed learning skills.

References

Aarts, Jan, and Sylviane Granger. 1998. "Tag Sequences in Learner Corpora: A Key to Interlanguage Grammar and Discourse." In *Learner English on Computer*, edited by Sylviane Granger, 132–141. London: Longman.

Atkinson, Dwight. 1999. "TESOL and Culture." *TESOL Quarterly* 33 (4): 625–54.

Băniceru, Cristina, Mirela Borchin, Claudia Ioana Doroholschi, and Dumitru Tucan. 2012. "Academic Writing in Romania: A Contrastive Analysis of BA Thesis Introductions in Romanian and English." *Quaestiones Romanicae* 1: 331–45.

Băniceru, Cristina, and Dumitru Tucan. 2018. "Perceptions About 'Good Writing' and 'Writing Competences' in Romanian Academic Writing Practices: A Questionnaire Study." In *University Writing in Central and Eastern Europe: Tradition, Transition, and Innovation,* edited by Mădălina Chitez, Claudia Ioana Doroholschi, Otto Kruse, Łukasz Salski, and Dumitru Tucan, 103–12. New York: Springer.

Bercuci, Loredana, and Mădălina Chitez. 2019. "A Corpus Analysis of Argumentative Structures in ESP Writing." *International Online Journal of Education and Teaching* 6 (4): 733–47.

Borchin, Mirela, and Claudia Ioana Doroholschi. 2016. "Romania." In *Exploring European Writing Cultures: Country Reports on Genres, Writing Practices and Languages Used in European Higher Education,* edited by Otto Kruse, Mădălina Chitez, Brittany Rodriguez, and Montserrat Castelló, 179–01. Winterthur: ZHAW Zürcher Hochschule für Angewandte Wissenschaften. https://doi.org/10.21256/zhaw-1056.

Borin, Lars. 2004. "New Wine in Old Skins? A Corpus Investigation of L1 Syntactic Transfer in Learner Language." In *Corpora and Language Learners,* edited by Guy Aston, Silvia Bernardini, and Dominic Stewart, 67–87. Amsterdam: John Benjamins.

Brezina, Vaclav, and Tony McEnery. *LancsBox: Lancaster University Corpus Tool.* Lancaster University, 2020.

Charle, Christophe. 2004. "Patterns." In *A History of the University in Europe, Vol. III: Universities in the Nineteenth and Early Twentieth Centuries,* edited by Walter Rüegg, 35–80. Cambridge: Cambridge University Press.

Chitez, Mădălina. 2014. *Learner Corpus Profiles: The Case of Romanian Learner English.* Bern: Peter Lang.

Chitez, Mădălina. 2018. "Corpus Linguistics Meets Academic Writing: Examples of Applications in the Romanian EFL Context." In *University Writing in Central and Eastern Europe: Tradition, Transition, and Innovation,* edited by

Mădălina Chitez, Claudia Ioana Doroholschi, Otto Kruse, Łukasz Salski, and Dumitru Tucan, 133–49. New York: Springer.

Chitez, Mădălina, Claudia Ioana Doroholschi, Otto Kruse, Łukasz Salski, and Dumitru Tucan, eds. 2018. *University Writing in Central and Eastern Europe: Tradition, Transition, and Innovation.* New York: Springer.

Chitoran, Dumitru. 2013. *Contrastive Studies in English and Romanian.* Bucharest: Bucharest University Press.

Clyne, Michael. 1981. "Culture and Discourse Structure." *Journal of Pragmatics* 5: 61–66.

Clyne, Michael. 1987. "Cultural Differences in the Organization of Academic Texts." *Journal of Pragmatics* 11: 211–47.

Connor, Ulla. 2002. "New Directions in Contrastive Rhetoric." *TESOL Quarterly* 36: 493–510.

Connor, Ulla, Ed Nagelhout, and William Rozycki. 2008. *Contrastive Rhetoric: Reaching to Intercultural Rhetoric.* Amsterdam: John Benjamins.

D'Angelo, Larissa. 2012. "Identity Conflicts in Book Reviews: A Cross-disciplinary Comparison." In *Academic Identity Traits. A Corpus-Based Investigation,* edited by Maurizio Gotti, 79–94. Bern: Peter Lang.

Fløttum, Kjersti, Trine Dahl, and Torodd Kinn 2006. *Academic voices.* Amsterdam: John Benjamins.

Gellerstam, Martin. 1985. "Translationese in Swedish Novels Translated from English." In *Translation Studies in Scandinavia: Proceedings from the Scandinavian Symposium on Translation Theory (SSOTT) II,* edited by Lars Wollin and Hans Lindquist, 88–95. Lund: Lund University Press.

Gilquin, Gaëtanelle. 2008. "Combining Contrastive and Interlanguage Analysis to Apprehend Transfer: Detection, Explanation, Evaluation." In *Linking up Contrastive and Learner Corpus Research,* edited by Gaëtanelle Gilquin, Szilvia Papp, and María Belén Díez-Bedmar, 3–33. Amsterdam: Rodopi.

Kaplan, Robert. 1966. "Cultural Thought Patterns in Inter-cultural Education." *Language Learning* 16 (1–2): 1–20.

Mauranen, Anna. 1993. *Cultural Differences in Academic Rhetoric: A Text-linguistic Study.* Frankfurt am Main: Peter Lang.

Mauranen, Ana. 1994. "Two Discourse Worlds: Study Genres in Britain and Finland." *Finlance* 13: 1–40.

Rüegg, Walter and Jan Sadlak. 2011. "Relations with Authority." In *A History of the University in Europe, Vol. IV: Universities Since 1945,* edited by Walter Rüegg, 73–123. Cambridge: Cambridge University Press.

Scott, Mike. 2016. *WordSmith Tools.* Stroud: Lexical Analysis Software and Oxford University Press. https://www.lexically.net/wordsmith/.

Siepmann, Dirk. 2005. *Discourse Markers Across Languages: A Contrastive Study of Second Level Discourse Markers in Native and Non-native Text with Implications for General and Pedagogic Lexicography. Routledge Advances in Corpus Linguistics.* London: Routledge.

Swales, John. 1990. *Genre Analysis: English in Academic and Research Settings.* Cambridge: Cambridge University Press.

CHAPTER 10

Developing writing competence for the future multilingual work environment of Belgian economists and sociologists

An Slootmaekers

Katholieke Universiteit Leuven, Belgium

Abstract

This chapter focuses on the development of a writing program for Dutch-speaking students in economic and social sciences at Leuven University (KU Leuven). Training for writing is part of a broader course of French for Specific Purposes, including also a training for reading and listening comprehension as well as for speaking. A framework of three different writing tasks has been developed in line with the key elements of effective adolescent writing instruction recommended by Graham and Perin (2007) in their large-scale examination of experimental studies on writing instruction. Besides the development of language materials and coaching tools specifically needed for the assignments, the design of the writing tasks themselves and the pre- and post-writing activities received special attention. The result is an individualized and process-oriented approach to teaching writing. The teaching program is constantly revised based on learners' writing outcomes.

Keywords: writing competence, multilingual working environment, process-oriented approach, flexible writing strategies, coaching tools, lexico-grammatical reference material

***

Introduction

This chapter focuses on the development of a writing program for Dutch-speaking students of economic and social sciences at Leuven University (KU Leuven) as part of a compulsory course of French for Specific Purposes (FSP), starting at the B1-level of the Common European Framework of Reference for Languages (CEFR). Students of economics take a compulsory course of one hour a week for four semesters. Students of sociology take a compulsory course of two hours a week for two semesters. Training students' reading, writing, listening, and speaking skills, so crucial in their future professional activities, lies at the core of the courses. The objectives for each of these skills are: (1) for reading—understanding newspaper articles and (later also) more specialized texts on economic or sociological topics; (2) for listening—understanding a presentation and a debate on a topic related to the field of study (video or audio fragments cover presentations and debates meant for a general audience, e.g., TV/radio programs, as well as more academically oriented spoken documents); (3) for speaking—presenting a study on an economic or sociological topic and participating in a debate on the same topic; (4) for writing—reporting on a current situation, summarizing texts, and presenting graphs. As for the other skills, the content of the three text types is also related to the field of study.

The development of the writing program that will be described here reflects the developer-teacher's cyclical learning process. I documented the development of the tasks, their presentation and application, and my reflection on the process and the outcome. It is this cyclical aspect of research, practice, and editing which the learner-writer also experiences. The first step in the development of this writing course was the selection of writing tasks. Simultaneously, a literature study on good practices of teaching writing skills was carried out. Then language materials and writing tools particular to the tasks were developed and put to the test in practice, always in agreement with the curriculum and the department's approach to foreign language learning and teaching. In the course of teaching and learning, the design of the pre- and post-writing activities received special attention: from on-campus to online writing activities, from individual work to peer and group work.

For various reasons, Graham and Perin's work (2007) was found to be the most relevant publication. The target audience of their report *Writing Next: Effective Strategies to Improve Writing of Adolescents in Middle and High Schools* matches the audience of the courses at hand. The authors analyze experimental studies on writing instruction for adolescents carried out between 1964 and 2005 and measure the effectiveness of these methods by using a statistical methodology called meta-analysis. The result is the identification of 11 instructional techniques or key elements for which the authors find experimental evidence that they enhance writing competence across a number of contexts. The framework based on the findings is solid and covers a wide range of practices from which instructional techniques most suitable for a particular teaching context can be selected and combined in various ways. A "blending" approach is strongly recommended, not only by Graham and Perin (2007, 11), but also by other researchers. Wingate, for example, states that writing pedagogy cannot be based on a single theoretical framework but rather enfolds a package of various approaches and methods that mostly suit the given context (2012, 2).

The complete set of "11 key elements of effective adolescent writing instruction" identified by Graham and Perin (2007, 11) comprises the following: *(1) Writing Strategies; (2) Summarization; (3) Collaborative Writing; (4) Specific Product Goals; (5) Word Processing; (6) Sentence Combining; (7) Prewriting; (8) Inquiry Activities; (9) Process Writing Approach; (10) Study of Models; (11) Writing for Content Learning.* In the course of the development of the writing program presented here, instructional techniques or key elements recommended by Graham and Perin (2007) were carefully selected, recombined, and put to the test in order to suit student needs in a changing teaching and learning environment. The description of this process, which inevitably led to a different ordering of the instructional techniques than the one presented by Graham and Perin, will show how the key elements "should not be seen as isolated but rather as interlinked" (2007, 11). Even more importantly, it will show the teacher's responsibility "to construct a unique blend of elements suited to specific student needs" (Graham and Perin 2007, 11). Table 10.1 summarizes what will be described in detail in the next sections.

Table 10.1: Instructional techniques or key elements of the writing program

Writing program FSP Economics and Sociology, KU Leuven			Key elements of effective adolescent writing instruction Graham and Perin (2007, 11–21)
Selection of three text types			
Reporting	Summarizing	Describing graphs	**Flexibility**: the final goal of a writing program **(2) Summarization**: explicit and systematic teaching how to summarize **(11) Writing for Content Learning**
Writing assignments			
Key words	Authentic texts	Authentic graphs	**(8) Inquiry Activities**: analysis of immediate, concrete data before writing
Guidelines of content and length			**(4) Specific Product Goals**: specific and reachable goals for the written product
Text models			**(10) Study of Models**: analysis of good texts
Pre-writing activities: organizing and verbalizing information			
Pre-writing activities: *Schema* technique and summarization			**(1) Writing Strategies**: explicitly teaching strategies for planning, revising, editing **(2) Summarization** **(7) Prewriting**: teaching to gather and organize information **(3) Collaborative Writing**: instructional arrangements whereby learners help each other with one or more aspects of their writing
Pre-writing activities: guided video watching			**(9) Process Writing Approach**: supportive writing environments with more extended and systematic instruction
Pre-writing activities: study of appropriate lexical and grammatical structures			**(6) Sentence Combining**: teaching learners to construct more complex, sophisticated sentences
Post-writing activities: revising and editing the text			
Post-writing activities: revising and editing the text by means of an on-line writing aid (*Inlato*) and peer correction (*Carrousel* technique)			**(1) Writing Strategies**: explicitly teaching strategies for planning, revising, editing **(3) Collaborative Writing**

1 Selection of three text types

Three different writing tasks have to be carried out, i.e., reporting, summarizing, and describing graphs. The writing program thus meets the goal of flexible writing competence defined by Graham and Perin as the competence of a writer who "can adapt to different contexts, formats and purposes for writing" (2007, 22).

The abovementioned types of texts were selected because they are relevant for the students' future work environment. Future managers or expert consultants are expected to be able to present short written reports of all kinds in the context of decision-making of government services and companies. In Belgium, this also entails being able to do so in at least two languages, i.e., Dutch and French. Moreover, mastery of English and German is definitely an asset. Although the French courses, of which the writing program is one component, are not proper Content and Language Integrated Learning (CLIL) courses, whereby economics and sociology are taught in French, their entire design takes as an anchoring point for future professional activities. All tasks to be carried out within these courses of FSP have been designed to fit real-life purposes. Still, the ultimate learning goals remain oriented toward language learning and communication rather than to content learning. This also applies to the writing program, where students learn to write for real-life purposes, not necessarily for content learning. Yet, the investment in a well-written report seems to enhance the students' understanding of topics of their field of study.[1] In conclusion, key element *(11) Writing for Content Learning* is not used as an instructional technique. Content learning rather is a positive side-effect of the writing program.

Another reason for selecting reporting, summarizing, and presenting graphs as the three writing tasks to be fulfilled is the observation that at the start of their French course many learners/L2 writers do not seem to master these text types. The following samples[2] of authentic texts written by learners of the target group demonstrate common problems. For each type of text, two samples are shown. Each sample consists of a series of three fragments, i.e., (1) the French text as it was originally written by the student, (2) a literal, not corrected translation of the French text (as the translation is close to the original student text in French, it may display odd or incorrect words), (3) the target text, i.e., the

---

[1] In informal comments in the classroom, various students commented on their better insight and interest in their field of study due to the writing assignments.

[2] All text samples of this article come from texts that were originally written by students of economics (n 781 first semester of 2018–2019) or sociology (n 32 first semester of 2017–2018; n 40 second semester of 2018–2019). For research purposes the texts were anonymized.

result of the learner's and teacher's joint effort in revising and correcting the text. The writing assignments that were given to the learners are described in more detail in the next section.

In order to identify problems in the students' texts, the following symbols are used: *, **?**, **#,** and Ø. Corrections are introduced by symbol > .

* Grammar error, e.g. **le* gestion* > *la gestion*.

? Incorrect choice of words, i.e., the word form is correct, but it is not combined in a correct way with other words so that argumentation becomes unclear, e.g., *le* ?*gestion de VW*: in French *gestion* is used to refer to the act of running a business, e.g., *un exemple de bonne gestion* / an example of good management, not to the actual managers > *les gestionnaires de VW*.

Argumentation problem often but not always linked to a language problem: lack of information or its opposite, i.e., unnecessary repetition of information, wrong ordering of information, contradictory information, and misinterpretation of the text or graph to be presented are the most common problems.

 # Ø In the case of text sample 1 (Figure 10.1), the company's identification by means of its nationality and line of business is lacking. Therefore, symbol # is complemented by symbol Ø: # Ø *Volkswagen* > *le constructeur automobile allemand Volkswagen*.

** Complex error, e.g., *des coûts **fortes*, is a combination of a grammatical and semantic problem; the noun *coûts* is not feminine and is not combined with the adjective *fort* > *des coûts élevés*.

Figure 10.1: Text samples at the start of the language course

---

Reporting

Original text 1: *Depuis 3 années, *le ?gestion de # Ø Volkswagen *a **souvenu des difficultés ?concernant des coûts **fortes. A cause ?des *nouveaux entreprises comme #Tesla, *leur part de marché diminue.*

Literal translation (not corrected) text 1: For 3 years, the management of Volkswagen has ?remembered difficulties concerning strong costs. Due to new companies like Tesla, their market share diminishes.

Target text 1: *Depuis 3 années, les gestionnaires du constructeur automobile allemand Volkswagen font face à des difficultés liées à des coûts élevés. A cause du succès de nouvelles entreprises comme le constructeur américain Tesla, sa part de marché diminue.*

Original text 2: *Ikea est une société anonyme, fondée plusieurs années ?passées. ?Le siège social se trouve *à la Soudaine et ?il y a beaucoup d'actionnaires qui investissent dans *cet entreprise afin qu'elle puisse continuer à développer de nouveaux ?immeubles.*

Literal translation (not corrected) text 2: Ikea is a limited company, established several years past. The head office is in Soudaine [sic] and there are a lot of shareholders who invest in this company so that it can go on developing new buildings.

Target text 2: *Ikea est une société anonyme, fondée il y a plusieurs années. Son siège social se trouve en Suède. Beaucoup de ses actionnaires investissent dans l'entreprise afin qu'elle puisse continuer à développer une nouvelle gamme de meubles.*

Summarizing

Original text 3: *L'article ? « Les *cites du futur » **écrivait par Monsieur Loumaye dans La Libre Belgique *à mars *en 2018. L'article *s'agit de #la plupart des *gents qui habitent en zone urbaine et une ?grande répercussion est la surconsommation des ressources ?de la Terre et la surpopulation *en monde *entière.*

Literal translation (not corrected) text 3: The article "The cities of the future" was writing by Mister Loumaye in La Libre Belgique at March in 2018. The article goes about most peeple (deals with people) who live in an urban zone and a great repercussion is the overconsumption of resources of the Earth and the overpopulation in entire world.

Target text 3: *L'article intitulé « Les cités du futur » publié par Monsieur Loumaye dans la Libre Belgique en mars 2018 porte sur la migration de la plupart des gens vers des zones urbaines et ses répercussions non négligeables en termes de surconsommation de ressources naturelles et de surpopulation dans le monde entier.*

Original text 4: *L'article, publié par La Libre Belgique en *Mars #2012, présente l'avenir *de villes ?en trois étapes. Tout d'abord, je *présentera le problème ?d'immigration vers les villes. Ensuite je **donnera les solutions *de ce problème et finalement, je **résumera ?l'article globalement.*

Literal translation (not corrected) text 4: The article, published by La Libre Belgique in March 2012, presents the future of cities in 3 stages. First of all, I will present the problem of immigration towards the cities. Then, I will give the solutions of this problem and, finally, I will summarize the article globally (briefly).

Target text 4: *L'article, publié par La Libre Belgique en mars 2018, présente l'avenir des villes du monde entier sous trois angles différents. Tout d'abord, je présenterai le problème de la migration vers les villes. Ensuite je décrirai les solutions à ce problème et finalement je terminerai par le message principal.*

Describing graphs

Original text 5: *?Ici, nous *voisons un *informathique. *L'informathique nous donne **information ?des ?immigrants qui *traversant la *méditerranée # Ø.* [The argumentation problem (#) comes from a lack of crucial information (Ø) with respect to the time frame.]

Translation original (not corrected) text 5: Here we sees (see) an informatics (infography). The informatics gives us information of the immigrants who crossing the Mediterranean.

Target text 5: *L'infographie ci-jointe donne des informations à propos des migrants qui ont traversé la Méditerranée entre 2015 et 2017.*

Original text 6: *L'infographie montre des variables *différents. *Il présente une ?situation *aux migrants traversant la Méditerranée. *Il *se présente #depuis 2015 *en 2017 et #entre des pays différents.*

Literal translation (not corrected) text 6: The infography shows different variables. It presents a situation to the migrants crossing the Mediterranean. It presents to itself from 2015 in 2017 and between different countries.

Target text 6: *L'infographie montre différentes variables, c'est-à-dire l'évolution entre 2015 et 2017 du nombre total de migrants traversant la Méditerranée et la comparaison des nombres en fonction du pays d'origine et du pays d'accueil.*

2 Writing assignments

In line with Graham and Perin's instructional technique *(8) Inquiry activities* (2007, 19), learners get a set of concrete data they have to analyze and integrate in their text. When they write a report, learners must analyze and integrate key words. Key words are important concepts of the domain of study, e.g., *le bénéfice*/ profit for economics or *la précarité* / insecurity for sociology. For summarizing, the data to be analyzed come out of an authentic text dealing with a topic relevant to the domain of study: an example can be found in Appendix 10.1. For graph description, the starting point of the writing assignment is an authentic graph dealing with a domain-related topic (see Appendix 10.2). Selection of appropriate data—in this case, keywords, texts, or graphs—entails the necessity of a needs analysis by the teacher. Careful needs analysis will have a positive impact on learners' motivation (Graham and Perin 2007, 24).

Furthermore, as is shown in the examples in Figure 10.2, students get detailed guidelines as to the content and length of the text. This feature of the writing assignments fits instructional technique *(4) Specific Product Goals*. Specific and reachable goals are explained to the learner by means of the analysis of good texts. This corresponds to Graham and Perin's instructional technique *(10) Study of Models*. Yet, teachers have to bear in mind that reading and writing are not simply mirroring processes. One does not automatically become a good writer by only observing good models (Graham and Perin 2007, 7–8). In order to continue fostering the writing process, pre- and post-writing activities have been developed (see next sections).

Figure 10.2: Writing assignments

Assignment for reporting

[Instructions for all writing assignments are presented to the learners in French.] Write an original and coherent text of 15 lines, reporting on the activities and/or results of the activities of one of the two companies. Integrate the three key words in the text. Divide the text into paragraphs and use linking words. You may adapt a key word to fit the grammatical context (conjugate the verb, make nouns and adjectives agree (masculine/feminine; singular/plural)), but you are not allowed to change its grammatical category (use the corresponding noun instead of the verb, for example). Figures presented in the text may be fictitious but have to be acceptable in the overall argumentation of the text.

Option 1: IKEA
détenir – restructuration – saturé
(to have (a market share) – (corporate) restructuring – saturated (market))

Option 2: Volkswagen
s'implanter – gestion – performant
(to establish (on the market) – management – performing, successful)

Assignment for summarizing

Read the article "Les cités du futur. Routes solaires, agriculture urbaine verticale et ultra-connectivité: à quoi ressembleront les villes de demain?" (text in Appendix 11.1), then summarize it in your own words by means of a text of 20 lines. First, draw a schema that visualizes all the essential elements of information in a clearly structured way. You may make your argumentation more coherent by altering the order in which the ideas are presented in the original text, but you are not allowed to transform ideas nor to add your own ideas. In order to avoid copy-pasting fragments of the original text, start from your schema to write your own text. Do not forget to divide the text into paragraphs and to use linking words and vocabulary appropriate for summaries.

Assignment for describing graphs

Describe in a single text of 18 lines all essential elements of information of the graph "Les migrants traversant la Méditerranée" (graph in Appendix 2). First, draw a schema that visualizes all the essential elements of information in a structured way. You have to summarize trends, but you may not leave out entire parts of the graph. Use the schema for writing your text. Do not forget to divide the text into paragraphs and to use linking words and vocabulary appropriate for graph description.

3 Pre-writing activities: organizing and verbalizing information

For the three text types, a written step-by-step procedure is provided to the learners. This procedure called *Schema technique* (Figure 10.3)[3] helps them to plan and revise the structure and cohesion of the text. Learners who must systematically spell out a schema before they start writing learn to gather and organize information and summarize. Furthermore, the teacher is able to consistently comment on argumentation problems by referring to the schema. The *Schema technique* covers at the same time key elements *(1) Writing strategies, (2) Summarization,* and *(7) Pre-writing* (Graham and Perin 2007, 15–18).

Figure 10.3: Basic text schema

Introductory paragraph

Frame of reference = what? where? when?
One-line statement on the current situation = problematic, promising or both
Announcement of main steps of argumentation = 1 of 3 options: see body of the text

Paragraphs making up the body of the text

Option 1: logically organized argumentation in terms of goals/methods, causes/consequences, advantages/disadvantages, problems/solutions, pros/cons or different aspects of a topic = 1 paragraph / logical category

---

[3] The technique was developed by Slootmaekers on the basis of observations of the quality of the structure and cohesion of students' texts and is presented in French in the students' courseware.

> **Option 2:** chronologically organized argumentation in terms of stages of an evolution in the past or in the future = 1 paragraph/stage
>
> **Option 3:** geographically organized argumentation in terms of comparison of different locations, in a broad sense: geographical locations, e.g., Europe versus United States; or sociological locations, e.g., urban zones versus rural zones; or economic locations. e.g., big companies versus small family businesses = 1 paragraph/location
>
> ## Concluding paragraph
> Main message of the previous argumentation
> Broader implications or related questions

Although the basic ingredients for a schema are the same for the three text types, learners are taught to accommodate for differences in task requirements and thus to develop a flexible writing competence depending on the task. When asked to integrate three key words in a business report, learners are first taught to analyze in detail the three keywords not only for their linguistic features but also for possible links between them in the larger context of a full report. Creating associations between given keywords prompts learners to think about text structuring more carefully. As shown in the example of Figure 10.4, the same keywords may give rise to different text structures that are equally good. Therefore, exercises on the arrangement of keywords into the overall structure of the text aim at developing flexibility in structuring the writing process. In line with Graham and Perin's key element *(3) Collaborative Writing*, these exercises are completed in the classroom. They allow learners to discuss different views of how to organize the same information and to consciously motivate their choice by comparing different options.

Figure 10.4: Example of three potential schemata for the same writing assignment

> ## Example of Ikea & key words *détenir – restructuration – saturé*
> ### What? When? Where?
> *Ikea est une multinationale suédoise qui vend des meubles dans beaucoup de pays*
> Ikea is a Swedish multinational, selling furniture in many countries
>
> ### Logical argumentation:
> Problem: *Ikea détient la plus grande part de marché, mais le marché est saturé.*
> Ikea holds the largest market share, but the market is saturated.
>
> Solution: *Une restructuration de la société est nécessaire.*
> The company needs restructuring.
>
> ### Chronological argumentation:
> Until last year: *Ikea détenait la plus grande part de marché.*
> Ikea was holding the largest market share.

This year:	*Ikea a dû céder des parts de marché à des jeunes entreprises. Le marché des meubles prêts à monter est ~~saturé~~ et les jeunes consommateurs cherchent d'autres produits.* Ikea lost shares to the benefit of young companies. The market of ready to assemble furniture is saturated and young consumers are looking for other products.
Next year:	*Ikea lancera une nouvelle gamme de produits écologiques. C'est pourquoi une ~~restructuration~~ de la société est en cours.* Ikea will launch a new line of ecological products. That means a restructuring of the company is going on.

Geographical argumentation:

In Europe:	*Le marché européen des meubles prêts à monter est ~~saturé~~.* The European market of ready to assemble furniture is saturated.
In Africa:	*Par contre, le marché africain a beaucoup de potentiel. Si la société veut ~~détenir~~ aussi une part de marché importante dans les pays africains, une ~~restructuration~~ sera nécessaire.*

At home, learners watch a video published by Slootmaekers on YouTube in 2013, showing the correction and evaluation of a report written by a fellow learner. Problems of structure and cohesion of this text are laid out in terms of the (lack of the) same planning strategies as the ones discussed in the classroom. Before they start watching, learners get a questionnaire that is not only intended to guide their attention towards these strategies but also to provide valuable information to the teacher on remaining problems of text planning. This activity meets key element *(9) Process writing approach*, whereby a supportive writing environment is created with more extended and systematic instruction (Graham and Perin 2007, 19). The responses to questionnaires that were administrated in 2015–2016 showed that video instruction—in addition to classroom instruction—is very useful because learners can watch it as many times as necessary and can stop and listen again if something is unclear to them. Furthermore, the use of a student text rather than an expert text in the video is very motivating for the learners. In her research, Wingate makes the same observation (2012, 7–8).

When summarizing texts, learners are trained in drawing the same type of schema as for reporting. While reading a text, they learn to use the logical, chronological, or geographical categories of the schema as queries to identify the essential elements of information in the text. For example, if the text presents the causes of a problem, will it also present consequences (logical argumentation)? Or if the author describes a situation of the past, does he or she also present projections for the future (chronological argumentation)? Just like for report writing, a typical exercise that is completed in the classroom is the comparison of different schemata for the same text. This comparative approach is not only meant to teach to distinguish good from bad schemata, but also to acquire the same kind of flexibility in organizing ideas as for the reporting. As has already been pointed out, discussions on the basis of student and not expert models have a positive motivational effect. Schemata are also valuable tools in another series of exercises aimed at avoiding plagiarism. As soon as learners understand that a schema is a more useful starting point for writing their summary than the original article itself, problems of copy-paste or plagiarism diminish drastically. The schema thus acts as a protective screen between the original text and the learner's summary.

For describing graphs, the major challenge is to fit complex, visually presented information into a linearly organized text. Again, a schema with linearly organized logical, chronological, or geographical categories seems to be a very effective tool for organizing the writing process. An example of a logical schema for the graph in Appendix 10.2 is presented in Figure 10.5. Since presenting complex visual information in words seems to be the most challenging one of the three writing tasks, pre-writing activities whereby learners assess each other's schema are extended for this text type. Graham and Perin's key element *(3) Collaborative writing* seems to be a good approach to help learners to organize their graph description. A video published by Slootmaekers on YouTube in 2014 showing pitfalls of planning a graph description wraps up the training in planning strategies. Again, key element *(9) Process writing approach* is put into practice, creating opportunities for more extended and systematic writing instruction based on student texts.

Figure 10.5: Logical schema for the graph of Appendix 10.2

What? Where? When?	*Evolution du nombre de migrants traversant la Méditerranée entre 2015 et 2017*
	Evolution of number of migrants crossing the Mediterranean between 2015 and 2017
Parameter 1	*Nombre total de migrants*
	Total number of migrants
Parameter 2	*Nombre de migrants en fonction du pays d'origine et du pays d'arrivée*
	Number of migrants according to the land of origin and the land of arrival
Parameter 3	*Nombre de migrants décédés ou disparus*
	Number of migrants deceased or disappeared

Another difficulty typical of rendering graphical information in a text is the verbalization of figures. Learners very often struggle to find the right words to summarize trends shown by figures and try to present the information of the graph just by means of a series of figures. By doing so, they force the reader to do the summarizing work, i.e., infer trends from figures. As is shown in the examples in Figure 10.6, L2 writers must learn to verbalize trends, i.e., present a series of figures by means of words.

Figure 10.6: Verbalization of the graph of Appendix 10.2

Lack of verbalization:
En 2015 le total de migrants s'élève à 1 011 712 personnes. En 2017 il est de 85 105.
In 2015 the total number of migrants is 1 011 712. In 2017 it amounts to 85 105.

Verbalization:
Entre 2015 et 2017 le nombre de migrants a chuté de plus d'un million à plus ou moins 85 000.
Between 2015 and 2017 the number of migrants has dropped from more than a million to more or less 85 000.

L2 writers not only seem to have difficulties with planning the structure and cohesion of the text but they also have to acquire lexical and grammatical structures that lie at the heart of a text for specific purposes (Slootmaekers 1996). The use of a classical (monolingual or bilingual) dictionary that is merely an alphabetical list of words presented in isolation yields a lot of problems and even problems that would not have occurred if the learner had not consulted a dictionary. An emblematic example of this type of mistake is in Figure 10.7:

Figure 10.7: Linguistic error: example 1

Mistake: **L'acte français Total, actif dans le secteur pétrolier, se porte bien.*
Target: *L'entreprise française Total, active dans le secteur pétrolier, se porte bien.*
Translation: The French <u>company</u> Total, operating in the oil sector, is doing well.

In a bilingual Dutch-French dictionary, the user can indeed find two French equivalents for the Dutch word *een bedrijf* / a company, namely (1) *une entreprise* / a company and (2) *un acte* / an act (as part of a theatre play). The lack of relevant contextual information induces some learners to pick the wrong translation. When semantic differences are more subtle, mistakes due to the transfer of L1 meanings occur very often for all grammatical categories of words, like in Figure 10.8:

Figure 10.8: Linguistic error: example 2

Mistake: *Les employés *méritent en moyenne 2500 euros.*
Target: *Les employés gagnent en moyenne 2500 euros.*
Translation: The employees <u>earn</u> 2500 Euros on average.

The same Dutch verb *verdienen* is used in both contexts of (1) *gagner de l'argent* / to earn money and (2) *mériter une récompense* / to deserve a reward.

Besides a lack of contextual information at the semantic level, classical dictionaries also display limited and rather cryptic grammatical information. As a consequence, incorrect grammatical embedding occurs for all categories of words, as shown by the following examples in Figure 10.9:

Figure 10.9: Linguistic error: examples 3 and 4

Mistake: *Une solution *pour ce problème ne semble pas être évidente.*
Target: *Une solution à ce problème ne semble pas être évidente.*
Translation: A solution for this problem does not seem to be obvious.

Mistake: *L'immigré est discriminé sur le marché du travail et les services gouvernementaux ne *l'offrent pas assez d'aide afin de trouver un emploi.*
Target: *... et les services gouvernementaux ne lui offrent pas assez d'aide ...*
Translation: The immigrant is discriminated against on the job market and government services do not offer him/her enough support in order to find a job.

By means of corpus studies, linguistic reference materials have been developed, aiming at the presentation of lexico-grammatical structures used in a specific context: future economists make use of the *Dictionnaire contextuel du français économique* (Verlinde et al. 1993–1996). For future sociologists the same type of lexico-grammatical structures is presented in the students' courseware. These reference materials present target words in short stories. Each story presents a topic of a larger content area and shows the most frequent word combinations typical of the topic at hand. For example, for the topic of competition among companies, the story starts with a company that wants to compete with other companies (*entrer en concurrence avec*) and must develop competitive goods or services (*des biens ou des services concurrentiels*).

An encompassing semantic framework lies underneath the short stories. By means of a table of contents, the learner is led to the different topics which can be studied independently. A classical dictionary with an exclusively alphabetical list of words does not allow for a quick tour or a systematic study of the most relevant words of a topic. Furthermore, the contextual dictionary is organized in a way that its odd-numbered pages present the short stories whereas the corresponding even-numbered pages show the key words of the short stories with their morpho-syntactic characteristics. This layout allows the learner not only to study the semantic context of a word (odd-numbered page) but also its relevant grammatical properties (even-numbered page). For example, the key word *la concurrence* of the short story on (economic) competition is shown together with the noun *un concurrent* / a competitor, the verb *concurrencer* / to compete and its constructions *concurrencer une autre entreprise, deux entreprises se concurrencent* / to compete with another company, two companies compete with each other, and the adjectives *concurrent (une entreprise concurrente* / a competing company*) and concurrentiel (une entreprise concurrentielle* / a competitive company*)*. Thanks to a bilingual alphabetical list with the French keywords and their Dutch equivalents at the end of the contextual dictionary, learners can quickly find a word they need for receptive or productive purposes. Unlike a classical bilingual dictionary that offers the full range of possible translations of a word, this bilingual list only presents the L1 equivalents that are relevant to the content area.

During a two-hour workshop, students learn to make use of what for them is an unfamiliar type of dictionary. An important goal of the workshop is to convince the learners to study new L2 words or meanings by memorizing short stories in the target language instead of studying endless lists of isolated words with their L1 equivalent. They understand the benefits of this new learning method as soon as they are asked to complete exercises focusing on errors that are the result of learning isolated words by means of bilingual lists. In a French-Dutch bilingual list, they would find the following example (Figure 10.10):

Figure 10.10: Target words presented without context

(1) *le bilan / de balans*	for the balance sheet of a company
(2) *la balance / de balans*	for the trade balance of a country

Since in Dutch only one and the same word form is used for both meanings (*balans*), studying the French words (*bilan* and *balance*) only from a bilingual list will inevitably lead to mistakes. But if learners memorize the two target words in an originally French context of two clearly distinct short stories, they will not be tempted, or at least not tempted so easily, to use one word instead of the other. For the two words at hand, the learning goal then becomes to memorize the example in Figure 10.11:

Figure 10.11: Target words presented in context

(1)	*Une entreprise publie son bilan annuel.* A company publishes its annual balance sheet.
(2)	*Un pays présente une balance commerciale excédentaire.* A country has got a trade surplus.

For the writing program, contextualized language exercises were conceived and arranged in a blended-learning method: some exercises are systematically reserved for classroom work and others as homework via a digital learning environment. Typical classroom exercises comprise complex sentences. Earlier research (Slootmaekers 2017) led to the conclusion that learners were looking for more intensive training in sentence analysis in particular. Presenting problems of sentence analysis in less complex exercises than a full text is an attempt to respond to their needs and corresponds to Graham and Perin's instructional technique *(6) Sentence Combining*. The same exercises also allow the teacher to introduce a correction tool that is used in a post-writing activity, i.e., the *Carrousel* correction grid (see next section). By presenting the same grammatical issues in simpler exercises and in a more complex post-writing assignment, they can be addressed in an embedded and process-oriented way (cf. key element *(9) Process Writing Approach*). The design of the contextualized language exercises has indeed been adapted to match the questions raised by the *Carrousel* correction grid and by the online writing aid *Inlato* (see next section), and so learners are systematically trained in monitoring their own language production even if they are not writing a full text yet. As word-order rules are fundamentally different in French and in Dutch, sentence structure calls for specific attention in the pre-writing activities. The example in Figure 10.12 shows an exercise whereby learners first translate individually a Dutch sentence into French and then work in pairs in order to discuss their mistakes by classifying them into one of the categories of grammatical problems listed by the *Carrousel* correction grid (see Figure 10.14).

Figure 10.12: Classroom language exercise

Original Dutch sentence: *Van 2015 tot 2017 heeft het bedrijf, ondanks de slechte vooruitzichten, geïnvesteerd in de ontwikkeling van een innovatief product dat aan de behoefte van de veeleisende consument voldoet.*

English translation: From 2015 to 2017 the company invested in the development of an innovative product meeting the needs of the demanding consumer, despite poor economic prospects.

Target French translation: *Depuis 2015 à 2017, <u>la société a investi</u> dans le développement d'un <u>produit innovateur</u> qui répond au besoin du <u>consommateur exigeant</u>, <u>malgré les mauvaises prévisions</u>.*

Typical mistakes related to word order: *Depuis 2015 à 2017 *<u>a la société</u>, *<u>malgré les mauvaises prévisions</u>, <u>investi</u> dans le développement d'un *<u>innovateur produit</u> qui répond au besoin de *<u>l'exigeant consommateur</u>.*

Homework exercises focus on less complex problems for which learners can easily find a solution themselves on condition they are provided with model answers. These answers are accessible via KU Leuven's digital learning environment Toledo. For this series of exercises, learners are asked not only to look up the correct answer but also to systematically classify their individual, and sometimes very different, language problems in the same *Carrousel* grid. Systematic use of the *Carrousel* grid, just like systematic use of the *Schema* technique, seems to help the learners become aware of potential writing problems. Filling in gaps by means of a word derived from the underlined word is an example of a typical home exercise (Figure 10.13). Before the learners start completing these exercises, they are told to study word families (noun, verb, adjective, adverb) instead of isolated words. Knowledge of word families is very useful in order to be able to write a cohesive argumentation on a topic.

Figure 10.13: Online language exercise

Exercise:
Les prix <u>ont diminué</u> fortement. .... (substantif) des prix a surpris les producteurs.
Prices went down dramatically. The decrease of the prices surprised the producers.

Mistake: *La *diminuation des prix a surpris les producteurs.*
Target: *La <u>diminution</u> des prix a surpris les producteurs.*

4 Post-writing activities: revising and editing the text

Implementing key element *(9) Process Writing Approach* not only means "creating extended opportunities for writing" but also "stressing personal responsibility and ownership of writing projects" (Graham and Perin 2007, 19). Once learners have finished writing, they tend to see revising and editing their text as the teacher's responsibility. In order to actually create ownership and thus to make learners also participate actively in this important stage of writing, an online writing aid named *Inlato (Interactive Language Toolbox)* and a question grid for *Carrousel* peer assessment were developed. Both tools are systematically used for the three writing assignments and are intended to help learners revise and edit their own texts themselves in an autonomous and collaborative way.

The online writing aid *Inlato*, developed by Verlinde, Peeters, and Wielandts in cooperation with Rymenams and Slootmaekers (2010–2012), exclusively focuses on language problems and is designed for individual, autonomous work. It is not a classical spelling and grammar check that identifies errors and presents instant solutions. It rather offers a guided analysis of the text at sentence level, breaking down the sentences into their different linguistic components. It presents grammatical and lexical resources the user might need to improve the text, according to the analysis of the sentences. The tool is well known by the students since it offers help not only for their French classes but also for their English and Dutch classes and is readily accessible in and outside university.

The question grid for *Carrousel* peer assessment developed by Slootmaekers (2017) broadens the revision scope by focusing not only on language problems but also on problems related to the structure and cohesion of the text. Furthermore, it is intended to facilitate "high levels of student interactions" which is also an important feature of the key element *(9) Process Writing Approach* according to Graham and Perin (2007, 19). In small teams of four to five people, each learner gets the same question grid with four sets of questions. Figure 10.14 shows a fragment of the linguistic questions related to word order problems. The text of all *Carrousel* participants is then passed on from one reviewer to another whereby each reviewer comments on each text by answering the questions of one of the four question sets. This *Carrousel* technique, whereby each reviewer focuses on a series of questions related to one aspect of a text, makes the revision task bearable for inexperienced L2 writers. At the same time, the Carrousel participants discuss each other's comments and therefore can learn from each other.[4] As described in the previous section, the *Carrousel* grid is introduced to the learners as part of their pre-writing activities. In the whole training program, a considerable amount of time is thus devoted to pre- and post-writing activities. As has been pointed out by Wischgoll (2016), writing quality can be enhanced by the combination of pre-writing strategies, such as planning and structuring, and post-writing activities aimed at monitoring text production.

Figure 10.14: Fragment of the Carrousel grid with questions related to word order problems[5]

Is the word order correct? **Subject Verb Object (SVO)**
e.g. *L'année passée * a l'entreprise accusé une perte.*
    L'année passée > l'entreprise a accusé une perte.
    Last year the company recorded a loss.

Is the word order correct? **Time / Place / Manner – SVO – Time / Place / Manner**
e.g. *L'entreprise * a en 2018 réalisé un bénéfice.*
    > *En 2018 l'entreprise a réalisé un bénéfice.*
    In 2018 the company made a profit.

Is the word order correct? **Noun - Adjective**
e.g. *la concurrente société > la société concurrente
    the competing company

Conclusion

Teaching writing is as much an ongoing process as learning to write. In order to provide support in writing that is individualized and process-oriented, constant revision is mandatory. In my approach, it is the outcome of our learners' writing that is used to improve teaching. The overall design of activities are revised, language materials are refined, exercises adapted, and guidelines made more coherent by observing learners' needs while writing and by analyzing their texts and responses to questionnaires. The development of appropriate writing assignments, lexico-grammatical materials, exercises for planning and revising, language exercises, video instruction, correction tools such as the *Carrousel*, and the online writing aid *Inlato* took about six years, at a rate of approximately one aspect per year. While one aspect was under

---

[4] A detailed description of the architecture of *Inlato* and of the *Carrousel* peer grid and of the use of both tools in the writing program and their impact on text quality can be found in Slootmaekers (2017).

[5] The original questions are presented to the learners in French and are illustrated by means of examples of mistakes (marked by symbol *) and their correction (marked by symbol >).

construction, classes in learning to write took place. Therefore, the teacher's role was and still is crucial to the further development of the program.

A future goal of research is the impact of different types of mistakes (morphological, syntactic, semantic) and of argumentation problems (lack of information or cohesion) on the readability of a student text. The outcome of this type of study, which broadens the scope to include the reader as well, will hopefully help the teacher make decisions on the urgency of problem treatment. It will also provide him or her with a more solid basis for weighted assessment. Another area that needs further research is Graham and Perin's key element *(5) Word Processing*. Since Graham and Perin (2007, 17) point out that word processing is particularly effective with lower-grade learners of primary and secondary schools, this instructional technique has not been thoroughly investigated with the university students involved in this writing program. In fact, students are free to use their laptop or not for their writing assignments. More recently though, the increasing number of online tools and activities has put the investigation of the effects of online collaborative writing high on the research agenda.

References

Dupont, Valérie. 2017. "Débordée par les arrivées de migrants, l'Italie met l'Europe en demeure d'agir" [Overwhelmed by Migrant Arrivals, Italy Calls on Europe to Act]. *La Libre Belgique*, June 30. Accessed January 20, 2021. https://www.lalibre.be/international/debordee-par-les-arrivees-de-migrants-l-italie-met-l-europe-en-demeure-d-agir-595551f9cd706e263e871154.

Graham, Steve, and Dolores Perin. 2007. *Writing Next: Effective Strategies to Improve Writing of Adolescents in Middle and High Schools. A Report to Carnegie Corporation of New York.* Washington, DC: Alliance for Excellent Education.

Loumaye, Jérôme. 2018. "Routes solaires, agriculture urbaine verticale et ultra-connectivité: à quoi ressembleront les villes de demain?" [Solar Roads, Vertical Urban Agriculture and Ultra-connectivity: What Will the Cities of Tomorrow Look Like?]. *La Libre Belgique*, March 18. Accessed January 20, 2021. https://www.lalibre.be/economie/entreprises-startup/routes-solaires -agriculture-urbaine-verticale-et-ultra-connectivite-a-quoi-ressembleront-les-villes-de-demain-5aaadd07cd709bfa6acd3b2c.

Slootmaekers, An. 1996. "Learning to Describe Graphs." In *Theories, Models and Methodology in Writing Research,* edited by Gert Rijlaarsdam, Huub van den Bergh, and Michel Couzijn, 299–313. Amsterdam: Amsterdam University Press.

Slootmaekers, An. 2013. "Evaluation Rapport Economique: procédure d'évaluation de rapports économiques rédigés par des apprenants de français langue étrangère" [Evaluation Economic Report: Evaluation Procedure of Economic Reports Written by Learners of French as a Foreign Language]. https://www. youtube.com/watch?v=GTYBzogTe8w.

Slootmaekers, An. 2014. "La description d'une représentation graphique: en 5 étapes les apprenants néerlandophones de français apprennent à décrire une représentation graphique" [The Description of a Graphic Representation: In Five Steps Dutch-Speaking Learners of French Learn How to Describe a Graphic Representation]. https://www.youtube.com/watch?v=DkMRosd9MuA.

Slootmaekers, An. 2017. "The Reception of Coaching Tools for Writing by Students of L2 French for Specific Purposes." In *Languages for Specific Purposes in Higher Education—Current Trends, Approaches and Issues*, edited by Martina Vránová, Dita Gálová, and Dagmar Červenková. 60–67. Brno: VUTIUM. http://www.uj.fme.vutbr.cz/lspct/cd/pdf/P14-Slootmaekers-Reception.pdf.

Verlinde, Serge, Jean Binon, Jacques Folon, and Jan Van Dyck. 1993–1996. *Dictionnaire contextuel du français économique* [Contextual Dictionary of Business French]. Volumes A, B, C, D. Leuven-Apeldoorn: Garant.

Verlinde, Serge, Geert Peeters, and Joeri Wielandts. 2012. "Interactive Language Toolbox: (Almost) Everything You Always Wanted to Know about … Texts, Words and Word Combinations in Dutch, English and French." https://ilt.kuleuven.be/inlato.

Wischgoll, Anke. 2016. "Combined Training of One Cognitive and One Metacognitive Strategy Improves Academic Writing Skills." *Frontiers in psychology* 7 (187). https://doi.org/10.3389/fpsyg.2016.00187.

Wingate, Ursula. 2012. "Using Academic Literacies and Genre-Based Models for Academic Writing Instruction: A 'Literacy' Journey." *Journal of English for Academic Purposes* 11: 26–37. https://doi.org/10.1016/j.jeap.2011.11.006.

Appendix 10.1

LES CITÉS DU FUTUR

Routes solaires, agriculture urbaine verticale et ultra-connectivité: à quoi ressembleront les villes de demain?
Un dossier de Jérôme Loumaye
La Libre Belgique, le 18 mars 2018

Depuis la sédentarisation de l'Homme durant le Néolithique, les modèles des villes et villages n'ont cessé d'évoluer. Nombreuses furent les inventions qui ont agi comme moteur de ces changements. Il est maintenant impensable d'envisager nos cités modernes sans la motorisation des véhicules, l'eau courante ou encore un réseau tentaculaire de routes et chemins. Mais qu'en est-il des inventions qui, d'ici vingt ou trente ans, paraîtront à leurs tours indispensables ? À quoi ressembleront les villes de demain ?

Un futur irrémédiablement métamorphosé en bien... ou en mal.
Surpopulation et projections

Selon les experts, d'ici 2050, près de 70 % de la population mondiale vivra dans des villes. Début du siècle, nous avons assisté à un passage de cap significatif, désormais plus de la moitié de l'humanité habite en zone urbaine.

Avec cet afflux massif qui semble irrémédiable dans les décennies qui arrivent, les villes vont dès lors devoir s'adapter. On estime à 2,5 milliards le nombre d'individus voués à migrer vers les villes d'ici 2050. Le défi de la surpopulation sera l'un des grands enjeux de ce siècle et façonnera le paysage de demain, reste à voir si cette métamorphose forcée pourra être maîtrisée par l'homme et la technologie ou verra diminuer drastiquement les conditions de vie de la population.

La métamorphose des zones urbaines, suite à cette croissance de population, est irrémédiable. Il reste alors à voir si l'Homme tentera de sortir de la boucle infernale de surconsommation des ressources de la Terre, ou continuera ce que beaucoup considère comme une course se dirigeant droit dans le mur.

La suite de ce dossier sera une projection optimiste de ce que pourrait être le futur de nos villes. Pour cela, rien de mieux que de partir à la rencontre de concepts et inventions venant des quatre coins du monde et qui pourraient bien transformer à jamais le paysage urbain.

Cité futuriste...en Gangnam Style

Première étape de notre périple : la Corée du Sud ! Plus précisément la ville de Songdo à une heure de Séoul. Une ville pas comme les autres, car elle est « intelligente ».

Une ville intelligente, ou Smart City en anglais, est un terme un peu vague qui désigne un environnement urbain « augmenté » grâce aux nouvelles technologies. Les différents capteurs et caméras qui quadrillent ces villes permettent alors une meilleure gestion des ressources, une sécurité - et une surveillance - accrue, mais aussi une gestion du trafic plus fluide, les feux de signalisation réagissant, par exemple, aux besoins de la circulation routière.

Songdo, inexistante il y a 15 ans, impressionne par sa modernité. Métro ne produisant aucun rejet de CO2, taxis fluviaux, système de gestion des déchets qui les évacue automatiquement vers les centres de tri, feux de signalisation intelligents et toits recouverts de végétaux ne sont que quelques exemples de l'ultra-modernité de cette ville. Pour l'anecdote, une partie du clip de la célèbre chanson Gangnam Style de PSY a été tournée dans cette ville.

Le prix de la modernité

Un projet qui, malgré tout, n'a pas que des aspects positifs. La construction de cette ville artificielle aurait fait disparaître la « vasière » qui s'y trouvait, un refuge naturel utilisé par de nombreux oiseaux migrateurs.

Après la Corée du Sud, prochaine étape encore plus dépaysante : direction le Nord-Ouest de la France !

En route pour le photovoltaïque !

En décembre 2016, Ségolène Royal, alors ministre de l'Écologie, inaugure la toute première route solaire au monde. Une avancée technologique qui, plus d'un an après, a presque tenu ses promesses avec un rendement entre 85 et 90 % de ce qui était annoncé : elle devait théoriquement alimenter en électricité une ville de 5000 habitants.

Cette route solaire longue d'un kilomètre et la technologie qui tourne autour de ce concept restent par ailleurs encore perfectibles. Un projet ambitieux mais aux nombreux points négatifs : le prix 17 fois plus élevé qu'une installation photovoltaïque classique, la vitesse limitée de circulation par-dessus suite aux nuisances sonores produites par les véhicules roulant sur ce dernier ou encore les nombreux problèmes techniques encourus pendant l'expérience.

Cette technologie une fois développée à son plein potentiel pourrait bien être une solution à la disparition des stocks d'énergies fossiles. Une alternative pleine de promesses quand on sait que la Belgique abrite plus de 150 .000 kilomètres de routes, ce qui équivaut à plus de trois fois la circonférence de la Terre.

Dernière étape

Depuis 2012, c'est du côté de Singapour que le futur de l'agroalimentaire est en marche. Une petite révolution qui pourrait bien doucement métamorphoser le monde de l'agriculture. Un concept qui pourrait être la réponse à la surpopulation et à la demande grandissante de denrées alimentaires.

Il faut savoir que Singapour est le deuxième pays le plus dense au monde avec 7 829 habitants/ km2. En Belgique on recense un peu plus de 350 habitants au kilomètre carré. Une possibilité d'effectuer de la production alimentaire au sein même du pays permettrait une émancipation progressive du pays par rapport aux importations de l'étranger.

Sky Greens c'est un système rotatif qui permet de faire pousser des légumes dans des tours de 9 mètres de haut. L'installation peut produire jusqu'à une demi tonne de légumes par jour, et ce sur uniquement 3,65 hectares de terrain. Pour produire une quantité équivalente, sur une plantation horizontale classique, il faudrait un terrain dix fois plus grand et le double de travailleurs.

Alors que les innovations précédentes risquent fortement de métamorphoser nos villes occidentales, du côté des pays en voie de développement - les principaux pays touchés par l'explosion démographique actuelle et future - l'avenir semble précaire.

Appendix 10.2

Figure 10.15: La Libre Belgique: "Débordée par les arrivées de migrants, l'Italie met l'Europe en demeure d'agir" (Dupont 2017)

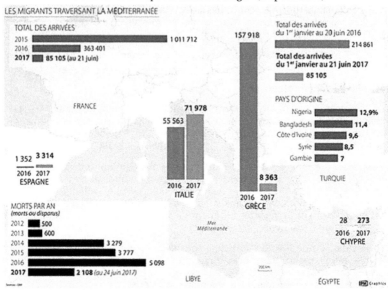

CHAPTER 11

Twenty-first-century methods for twenty-first-century skills: Developing students' ESP competencies through virtual exchange projects

Rita Kóris

Budapest Business School, University of Applied Sciences, Hungary

Abstract

Internationalization, employability, and twenty-first-century skills development have been given key priority in the twenty-first-century higher education (HE), just as the application of innovative pedagogies in ESP language teaching and the use of Web 2.0 tools in the classroom (European Commission 2013, World Economic Forum 2016). New technologies enable the implementation of online international collaboration and virtual exchange projects, which have become a new means of foreign language competence development in HE (Belz 2003, O'Dowd 2018). Despite these new trends and educational policies, international online collaboration has not yet formed an integral part of HE curricula (Guth and Helm 2010, Hagley 2016, Helm 2015, Milhauser and Rahschulte 2010, O'Dowd 2011, World Economic Forum 2016). This chapter presents the results of a qualitative study conducted among second-year BA students at a Hungarian university on their perceptions of intercultural, international collaboration projects incorporated into their ESP course curriculum. Students participated in a series of international virtual exchange projects, during which they communicated online with their international peers and had to perform various tasks and activities in mixed teams. Not only does the chapter argue for the results and advantages of international online collaboration projects from the students' perspective (high motivation; development of students' intercultural competence, ESP competence, collaboration skills; problem-solving skills; use of technology; simulation of work-life communication; active foreign language use with international peers; global teamwork), but it also details the challenges of such projects (managing deadlines and time zones, differences in intercultural communication, technical issues, team-building, and team cohesion).

Keywords: ESP competencies, twenty-first-century skills, virtual exchange, international collaboration, online cultural exchange

***

Introduction

Internationalization, employability, and transversal skills development have become key priority areas at higher-education institutions in the twenty-first century (Deardorff et al. 2012; European Commission 2013, 2017; World Economic Forum 2016). Alongside the physical mobility programs, international and European initiatives (e.g., Erasmus+ Virtual Exchange, EVALUATE, EVOLVE, INTENT, ICCAGE, GEE, Soliya Connect Program) have been launched in the past decades and even so in recent years, which have offered new alternatives for internationalization at home. These projects provide opportunities for educators and students of HE institutions to gain international experience without leaving their classrooms. Along with the organized, formal inter-university partnerships and programs, bottom-up initiatives also gain ground where instructors implement successful international projects themselves using their own professional network. "Disciplinary and multidisciplinary networks can be vehicles for staff exchanges and for internationalisation of the curriculum" (European Commission 2013, 6); as a result, these international projects will eventually be integrated into the university course curricula. There are excellent international and local best practices and sample projects that offer adaptable means and methods for educators (e.g., Guth and Helm 2010; Jager, Kurek, and O'Rourke 2016; Koris 2019; Koris, Oswal, and Palmer 2020; Koris, Hernández-Nanclares, and Mato Díaz 2020; Koris and Vuylsteke 2020; Loch and Pál 2018, O'Dowd and Lewis 2016) who are open to launch international collaboration projects within their university English for Specific Purposes (ESP) courses.

English language competence development is an integral component of any internationalization approach, just as the application of innovative pedagogies in ESP language teaching and the use of Web 2.1 tools in the classroom (Deacon, Parkin, and Schneider 2017). As it is stated in the EU white paper, "digital learning and the widening use of ICT technology [...] can open up the curriculum to knowledge, materials and teaching methods from all over the world, fostering new forms of partnerships, synergies and exchanges across disciplines and faculties that would otherwise be difficult to establish" (European Commission 2013, 7). Making use of ICT and Web 2.1 tools allows university instructors and students to implement international collaboration projects remotely in the online digital space, which calls for a new pedagogic approach and teaching methodologies.

Online collaboration or telecollaboration or virtual exchange projects can be applied in any disciplinary area; yet it has been used more frequently as a means of intercultural, foreign language, and ESP competence development in education (Belz 2003, O'Dowd 2018). Despite these new trends of internationalization of the HE and educational policies, the international online collaboration projects do not yet form an integral part of the HE curricula (European Commission 2013, 2017; Guth and Helm 2010; Hagley 2016; Helm 2015; Milhauser and Rahschulte 2010; O'Dowd 2011; World Economic Forum 2016). This chapter aims to reveal students' perspectives of intercultural, international online collaboration projects incorporated into their ESP course curriculum, to discuss the advantages of such projects by shedding light on the results and challenges, and to argue for the need of wider application of virtual exchange projects in ESP teaching at HE institutions. While a large body of research is available on the internationalization strategies of HE (e.g., Altbach and Knight 2007; Apple, Kenway, and Singh 2007; Deardorff et al. 2012; Leask 2015) and on international online collaboration practices (e.g., Belz 2003; Guadamillas Gómez 2017; Guth and Helm 2010; Helm 2015; Jager, Kurek, and O'Rourke 2016; Koris, Oswal, and Palmer 2020; Koris, Hernández-Nanclares, and Mato Díaz 2020; Koris and Vuylsteke 2020; Loch and Pál 2018; O'Dowd 2007; O'Dowd and Lewis 2016), a smaller amount of research tends to focus on students' or teachers' perspectives (e.g., Jones 2009; McKinnon, Hammond, and Foster 2017; O'Dowd 2015; Parks 2017), and little research has been devoted to the perceptions of students participating in international online collaboration projects at Hungarian HE institutions. Therefore, this study aims to fill this gap and sets out to answer the following research questions:

1. What are the Hungarian students' attitudes towards intercultural, international online collaboration projects?

2. From the Hungarian students' perspectives, what are the benefits and challenges of the international online collaboration projects?

3. What are the Hungarian students' perceptions of the knowledge and skills fostered through the international online collaboration project?

1 Characteristics of virtual exchange projects

Global trends and the digital revolution of the twenty-first century pose new challenges for the future workforce. To take on these new challenges and meet the needs of the international labor market, students need to acquire and develop a new set of skills, abilities, and competences. There is a growing tendency for universities to provide courses that target the development of students' twenty-first-century skills to increase students' future career prospects, thereby increasing the competitiveness of the institution and attracting more students (Álvarez-Mayo, Gallagher-Brett, and Michel 2017). Among the expectations of the labor market, an increasing emphasis has been placed on the so-called 4C Skills: communication, collaboration, creativity, and critical thinking (World Economic Forum 2016). For the successful application of communication and collaboration skills at a global and international level, it is essential to have a high level of foreign language proficiency. International curricula, innovative courses, and new teaching methods are indispensable for developing students' ESP language skills. Virtual exchange projects provide students with the opportunity to apply and develop intercultural communication and collaboration skills, professional language skills, as well as creativity and critical thinking.

Terms like online collaboration project, online intercultural exchange, telecollaboration, or virtual exchange project all refer to the same concept and are used as synonyms in this paper. Virtual exchange projects are established between teachers and students of two or more institutions located in different countries. These projects typically involve a longer-term collaboration that lasts several weeks, but often it is extended to an entire semester. During the project, students work in international teams and solve a complex sequence of tasks. At the end of the project, student groups usually prepare a final assignment (e.g., presentation, video, report, study). One of the main goals of virtual exchange projects is that students engage in intercultural communication using a foreign language; hence, they can acquire and develop their intercultural competence. During the project, instructors and students use online tools and applications and communicate online with their virtual groupmates. Most of this communication takes the form of written messages and online correspondence, but synchronous sessions using an online videoconferencing tool are also frequent.

Very important elements of virtual exchange projects are project-based learning and teamwork. The solution of the project assignments requires the team's joint knowledge and skills; hence students must collaborate effectively throughout the entire project if they want to complete the project successfully. Not only do students need to learn how to work and collaborate with their local team members but also how to work at a distance with their global peers on the other side of Europe or the world. Through intensive teamwork, students can take the opportunity to argue, engage in constructive debate, use their cooperative and collaborative skills, and exercise leadership and decision-making in a foreign language. It is important that educators assist their students assuming the roles of coordinators, facilitators, mentors, and counsellors (O'Dowd 2015, 198–99) to promote learner autonomy and maximize students' engagement in the project. Acquiring global group dynamic experience and developing the foreign language competence required for successful team communication are essential skills for future employees and will most likely increase students' career opportunities.

2 Aims and description of the project

The international online collaboration project took place in the spring semester of the 2017/2018 academic year between a group of students studying at a Hungarian university and another group of students at a university in the US. The Hungarian students were international relations majors enrolled at an English for International Studies course while the American students studied international business communication. This interdisciplinary project aimed to develop students' intercultural competence, critical thinking, debating, online collaboration, and communication skills in an international setting. A further aim of the project for the Hungarian cohort was to practice professional communication in English and develop their English language competence in professional contexts.

During this four-week project, students had to work in virtual teams on a series of tasks and activities. The teams were composed of both Hungarian and US students. First, they engaged in ice-breaking activities which provided an excellent opportunity to get to know each other. In the second phase of the project, both student groups in Hungary and in the US were given tasks which related to their own disciplines. The Hungarian students had to select a hot topic in international relations and politics which concerned the two countries and do background research on this topic. Based on their research, Hungarian students had to prepare a set of questions related to their chosen topic and interview their US peers by asking about their personal opinions and insights. On the other side of the Atlantic, the US students had to compare business communication practices in the US and in Hungary (or Europe). To gain insight into the business life in Hungary and Europe, they also prepared a questionnaire for the Hungarian students. During a series of email exchanges, students had to express their thoughts and opinions, argue and debate, and reflect on each other's perspectives. Following the exchange of information, both cohorts had to report back to their virtual team members and present their findings to their respective classes. The students were mainly using asynchronous communication in the project due to the time zone differences between the two universities.

3 Method

The study involved five second-year BA students majoring in International Studies at a Hungarian university in Budapest. The participants were randomly selected out of the second-year BA student community who had previously taken part in the collaboration project. The sample size and selection procedure were determined following the guidelines by Cohen, Manion, and Morrison (2007). The participants (four females: Emma, Klára, Barbara, and Judit; and one male: Robert) in the study are referred to by pseudonyms.

To gain an insight into the students' personal experiences, the challenges they faced, their views of and attitudes to international online collaboration projects, "semi-structured life world interviews" (Kvale 1996, 5) were conducted with the participants. The interviews followed the interview guide approach (Cohen, Manion, and Morrison 2007; Kvale 1996) using an interview schedule with a list of questions and guiding prompts. The interview schedule was not shown to the participants; it merely helped the researcher keep the interviewees focused on the given topics and make data collection systematic for every interviewee yet allowing enough space for free conversation.

Prior to beginning the data collection, the participants were contacted, they were briefly informed of the aims and procedures of the study, and their consent was obtained. Any information presented in this article is published with the authorization of the participants. As the interviewer and the participants' mother tongue is Hungarian, the interviews were conducted in Hungarian and lasted approximately 30 minutes. During the interviews, a friendly atmosphere and rapport was established, and the participants could express their opinions and views openly and honestly. The interviews were recorded digitally with the consent of the interviewees, and after the interviews took place, the recordings were transcribed following the transcription conventions put forward by Mackey and Gass (2005). The transcripts were analyzed, coded, and main categories were identified by applying the constant comparative method (Maykut and Morehouse 1994). To increase the trustworthiness of data collection and analysis, and thus of the overall research study, the concept of Lincoln and Guba's taxonomy of quality criteria (1985) was followed.

4 Findings

The main categories that were identified during data analysis were allocated to the corresponding research questions and the findings are presented accordingly. First, the interviewees' attitudes towards intercultural, international online collaboration projects are summarized, then the advantages and challenges of such projects are described. Finally, the knowledge and skills that the students gained through online collaboration projects are touched upon. The quotes inserted here have been translated into English from the Hungarian text of the interviews.

What are the Hungarian students' attitudes towards intercultural, international online collaboration projects?

All five interviewees have a very positive attitude towards intercultural, international online collaboration projects, and they welcome all kinds of international projects and initiatives that are built into their university courses. Students believe that online collaboration projects enrich their learning experience, increase their motivation, activate their creativity, and promote learner autonomy. At the interviews, they compared their ESP course involving international online collaboration to other university courses without international collaborative parts, and they expressed an opinion that courses with virtual exchange were more interesting and engaging.

> Klára: *I really liked that we had completely different tasks, not just exercises in the books.*

> Judit: *Finally, something new, something else than the usual seminar.*
> Tamara: *This [collaboration project] is really exciting. Much more interesting than the traditional teaching approach as it carries the students away.*

> Emma: *I was very happy to participate in the project and gain hands-on international experience. I really think that today's HE in Hungary is built on theory and not practice. This is a very rare opportunity; we usually just listen to the instructors and take notes in class.*

Emma pointed out that it would be even more important to include virtual exchange projects into the university curriculum for International Studies majors as these students will work on the international scene and will need to interact with culturally different people in their future workplaces. The students argued for the importance of gaining intercultural experience, communicating with foreign students, learning about different perspectives and worldviews. As Barbara thought, international collaboration is a great opportunity to exchange our—sometimes opposing—views and opinions and practice intercultural and professional communication. As Robert put it:

> Robert: *Sharing your own opinion and get to know others' [opinion] across cultural boundaries is what intercultural communication is all about.*

Despite the students' positive attitude, Klára and Barbara admitted that they both felt surprised and a little worried when they first heard about the collaborative tasks they had to complete.

> Barbara: *I was surprised to hear [that we must work with foreign students online] and I was even a little scared.*

The students added that these initial fears disappeared later when they started to work with their partners and started to feel confident about their own involvement in the project. All five interviewees said that their partner students were very friendly, and they could eventually build a positive rapport.

From the Hungarian students' perspectives, what are the benefits and challenges of the international online collaboration projects?

When students were asked to elaborate on the advantages of international, intercultural collaboration projects, the two most important outcomes of such projects were: (1) getting to know foreign students' individual perspectives and (2) the idea of practice over theory. Barbara, Klára, and Judit argued for the importance of expressing personal opinion:

> Klára: *We had the opportunity to learn how students think about certain issues and problems in other countries, which widens our own perspectives.*

> Barbara: *It was great to realize that they [partner students] think differently.*

> Judit: *I can read the daily news and learn about facts on the internet, but I cannot get people's own opinions. It was much better to discuss our own opinions.*

Although students emphasized the importance of theoretical foundations, they believed that gaining practical experience during their university education is also of high importance. As Klára and Barbara explained:

> Klára: *We can learn about a lot of stuff by reading our textbooks, but it is another story to discuss it with students from other countries.*

> Barbara: *The ability of expressing our own opinions on global issues and topics and practising the skills of agreeing or disagreeing are something we need in our future workplace. So we need to practice it a lot.*

Among the advantages of collaboration projects, students mentioned their increased motivation, building foreign relations with students from different countries, learning about cultural differences, and practicing professional communication in English. Judit and Robert were also highlighting that they liked working with foreign students in international teams. As for team building and good personal relations, the students expressed the importance of allowing time to get to know each other at the beginning of the project. Some students even mentioned that introducing themselves to each other helped a lot to ease communication and to interact openly and honestly with their peers. Judit, Emma, and Klára also favoured face-to-face online communication with their international partners.

Establishing good rapport between the partners and building a good working environment were also among the challenges that students had to face. Interviewees said that it was sometimes difficult to work with people that they did not know, and online interactions cannot replace face-to-face physical contact. Interdisciplinarity posed a further challenge for students; all the participants stated in the interviews that they found it difficult to work with students majoring in different disciplines.

> Emma: *I had to look up things I was not familiar with or I asked a friend who studied business and he helped me out.*

> Judit: *It was sometimes difficult to relate their discipline to ours.*

Intercultural differences also meant some challenges during the collaboration projects. Interviewees reported differences in directness, different approaches to project tasks, the level of openness towards different cultures and people, and positive versus negative attitudes to problem-solving.

What are the Hungarian students' perceptions of the knowledge and skills fostered through the international online collaboration project?

According to the participants, content knowledge can be reinforced much better by participating in international collaboration projects and putting theory into practice. It was very important for Klára, Judit, and Emma to deepen their subject knowledge within their own disciplinary area. Emma even highlighted the advantages of gaining interdisciplinary knowledge during an interdisciplinary project, which—she said—was not possible within their standard university curriculum. Barbara, Emma, and Robert also claimed they gained a different worldview and openness due to the international project experience. Participants were given the opportunity to practice intercultural communication and develop intercultural competence and skills. Judit even mentioned her positive experience with cultural stereotypes that were proved to be wrong due to her project experience.

A major benefit of international collaboration projects is the students' active English language use in meaningful, real work-life contexts. Emma, Robert, and Barbara said that professional communication in English with people outside the classroom was not possible for them. There is no opportunity to discuss disciplinary topics, issues, and problems and get an insight into other students' views outside university contexts. Therefore, an international collaboration project presents a great opportunity to step out of the classroom and engage in professional communication with diverse student cohorts. Judit and Emma also reflected on their own English language use during the project assignments, and they recalled instances of vocabulary development and genre use. Besides content knowledge and language skills development, students reported that their collaboration skills also developed, and they were given the opportunity to practice teamwork and decision-making.

5 Discussion

The interviews with university students yielded rich data on their attitudes, the benefits, and challenges of virtual exchange projects, as well as the knowledge and skills fostered through online collaboration projects. The results of the present study will be discussed in the order of the research questions.

Students' attitudes towards international online collaboration

Despite globalization trends in all walks of life, very few students have the opportunity to participate in international mobility programs, few students are able to participate in international projects, and many do not even have the opportunity to practice English professional communication in an international context. Therefore, they are unable to acquire and develop intercultural competence (European Commission 2013, 2017). This lack of international experience is probably the primary reason for the interviewees' very positive attitude towards international online collaboration projects. Students participating in virtual exchange projects tend to have very high motivation, they understand the immediate and long-term benefits of the project for their own personal and professional development.

Another reason for the students' positive attitude is the highly theoretical approach in the studies of Humanities and Social Sciences in Hungary. Most of the courses tend to be theoretical in form of lectures, and even seminars that are meant to be more practical may not follow practical teaching methods. While university language courses provide very active linguistic practice and proficiency development, real-life or work-life communication is rare. Therefore, the students' attitude welcoming any forms of new teaching approaches and methods that involve project-based learning, promote learner autonomy, and follow the learn-by-doing principle (Reese, 2011) is understandable.

Benefits of international online collaboration

Through a virtual exchange project, students gain a wealth of knowledge and lasting experience while they are also given the opportunity to develop employability skills they will need when they access the world of work. By implementing online collaboration projects as part of the university curricula, HE institutions can keep up with the demand of the globalized labor market as employers are looking for the twenty-first-century skills that can be acquired through virtual exchange projects. Participating students can develop their teamwork, cooperation, communication, problem-solving, and organizational skills, which is a very important result of a virtual exchange project. In such an international project, students can test themselves in a multicultural environment, learn about cultural differences, and experience working in global teams. They learn how to communicate with their peers around the world and get an insight into their views and personal opinions in professional contexts. Furthermore, interdisciplinary projects tend to be successful in widening students' perspectives and raising awareness of the interrelatedness of disciplines.

Challenges of international online collaboration

One of the biggest challenges is to bring students together from two or more universities into a single virtual classroom. Throughout the project assignments, students are challenged to deal with misunderstandings resulting from different professional communication practices or intercultural differences. Not all teams work effectively, and in some cases, participants have to cope with students' dropouts or longer response times in team communication. While being part of an online student community and working with peers from other universities are advantages of virtual exchange projects, online interaction cannot replace face-to-face communication. It also hinders initial team building and establishing a positive working environment within the team.

Most interviewees reported that they found it difficult to work on a cross-disciplinary virtual exchange project. As some of the discussion topics were not directly related to their own majors and disciplines, they did not feel competent enough to give their opinion on the subject and had to find alternatives and seek help from outside the team to be able to solve the tasks. While students rate the interdisciplinary aspect of the virtual exchange project as a negative challenge, it can be considered a moment of learning from the educator's point of view.

Despite some of the key challenges the students faced, they failed to mention the difficulties resulting from the use of digital tools and online applications. This may result from the fact that most participants took part in a virtual exchange project where they were mainly using email communication to collaborate within their virtual teams. In other projects, however, students are required to use new tools and online applications that they had never used before during their education.

Students' learning and skills development

Interviewees evaluated the interdisciplinarity of the international collaboration projects differently. While some students considered the interdisciplinary nature of the project a disadvantage, others believed that raising awareness of other disciplines and interdisciplinary subjects was a unique opportunity for learning. Participants of the study claimed that the online collaboration projects gave way to the development of a large variety of skills that would not happen otherwise within a regular ESP course where the instructor is using traditional teaching methods. These projects promote an active use of intercultural communication and English professional communication in an online environment, which requires students to become confident users of Web 2.1 tools. All of these skills increase students' employability prospects and give them hands-on international experience.

Developing students' ESP competence

When the virtual exchange project is embedded into an ESP course, one of the most important aims is to develop students' ESP competence. Following the concept of learning-by-doing (Reese 2011), a virtual exchange project allows students to engage in meaningful work-life communication where they can discuss professional content in English. As a first step, students were presented and became familiar with the vocabulary elements and terminology needed for the project work through real-life examples from professional communication and simulation exercises. By the time students had to use specific vocabulary items, they had been integrated into their own vocabulary sets, and students could easily apply the appropriate terminology in project communication.

Professional communication is increasingly prioritizing the communication skills that are essential for global collaboration and successful teamwork (Waldeck et al. 2012). English oral communication elements (such as chairing meetings, negotiating, proposing, brainstorming, reasoning, persuasion, constructive discussion, commenting, evaluating) and their online written forms (in emails, messages in social media, and posts) are actively used by students during virtual exchange projects. Digital skills and the efficient use of online tools and platforms in English contexts also constitute the students' ESP competence. After having completed an online collaboration project, students tend to communicate in English more effectively and with greater confidence in digital spaces.

Conclusion

International and European initiatives have been launched to internationalize HE, and many universities are consciously incorporating online international collaboration projects into their educational programs. As international online collaboration projects do not yet form an integral part of tertiary education curricula, the promotion and dissemination of institutional best practices are paramount. Such institutional best practices can easily be adapted to other disciplinary areas and other university courses by linking two partner classes in the virtual space and assigning collaborative tasks to the two student cohorts. With little investment, virtual exchange projects bring considerable benefits for both the students and the HE institution. They provide students with twenty-first century skills including digital skills and high level of ESP competence; hence they gain a competitive edge in the future labor market. In the case of HE institutions, international collaboration projects raise the quality standard of education, strengthen the international character of the university, and contribute to the institution's international reputation and global competitiveness.

References

Altbach, Philip G., and Jane Knight. 2007. "The Internationalization of Higher Education: Motivations and Realities." *Journal of Studies in International Education* 11 (3–4): 290–305.

Álvarez-Mayo, Carmen, Angela Gallagher-Brett, and Franck Michel, eds. 2017. *Innovative Language Teaching and Learning at University: Enhancing Employability.* N.p.: Research-publishing.net. https://doi.org/10.14705/rpnet. 2017.innoconf2016.9781908416506.

Apple, Michael W., Jane Kenway, and Michael Singh, M., eds. 2007. *Globalizing Education: Policies, Pedagogies, & Politics.* Bern: Peter Lang.

Belz, Julie A. 2003. "Linguistic Perspectives on the Development of Intercultural Competence in Telecollaboration." *Language Learning & Technology* 7 (2): 68–99.

Cohen, Louis, Lawrence Manion, and Keith Morrison. 2007. *Research Methods in Education.* Sixth edition. New York: Routledge.

Deacon, Amanda, Lucy Parkin, and Carolin Schneider. 2017. "Looking beyond Language Skills—Integrating Digital Skills into Language Teaching." In *Innovative Language Teaching and Learning at University: Enhancing Employability*, edited by Carmen Álvarez-Mayo, Angela Gallagher-Brett, and Franck Michel. 137–44. N.p.: Research-publishing.net. https://doi.org/10.147 05/rpnet.2017.innoconf2016.9781908416506.

Deardorff, Darla K., Hans de Wit, John Heyl, and Tony Adams, eds. 2012. *The Sage Handbook of International Higher Education.* Thousand Oaks, CA: SAGE. https://doi.org/10.4135/9781452218397.

European Commission. 2013. "European Higher Education in the World." White Paper 52013DC0499. Accessed September 30, 2020. https://eur-lex.europa.eu/LexUriServ/LexUriServ.do?uri=COM:2013:0499:FIN:en:PDF.

European Commission. 2017. "Renewed EU Agenda for Higher Education." White Paper 52017DC0247. Accessed September 30, 2020. https://eur-lex.europa.eu/legal-content/EN/TXT/?uri=CELEX%3A52017DC0247.

Guadamillas Gómez, Mª Victoria. 2017. "Building Global Graduates and Developing Transnational Professional Skills through a Telecollaboration Project in Foreign Language Education." In *Innovative Language Teaching and Learning at University: Enhancing Employability*, edited by Carmen Álvarez-Mayo, Angela Gallagher-Brett, and Franck Michel. 49–58. N.p.: Research-publishing.net. https://doi.org/10.14705/rpnet.2017.innoconf2016. 97819084 16506.

Guth, Sarah, and Francesca Helm, eds. 2010. *Telecollaboration 2.0: Language, Literacies and Intercultural Learning in the 21st Century*. Bern: Peter Lang.

Hagley, Eric. 2016. "Making Virtual Exchange/Telecollaboration Mainstream— Large Scale Exchanges." In *New Directions in Telecollaborative Research and Practice: Selected Papers from the Second Conference on Telecollaboration in Higher Education*, edited by Sake Jager, Malgorzata Kurek, and Breffni O'Rourke. 225–30. N.p.: Research-publishing.net

Helm, Francesca. 2015. "The Practices and Challenges of Telecollaboration in Higher Education in Europe." *Language Learning & Technology* 19 (2): 197–217.

Jager, Sake, Malgorzata Kurek, and Breffni O'Rourke, eds. 2016. *New Directions in Telecollaborative Research and Practice: Selected Papers from the Second Conference on Telecollaboration in Higher Education*. N.p.: Research-publishing.net

Jones, Elspeth, ed. 2009. *Internationalisation and the Student Voice: Higher education Perspectives*. New York: Routledge.

Koris, Rita. 2019. "Három egyetem—Két kontinens—Egy tanterem: Szaknyelvi kompetenciák fejlesztése nemzetközi interkulturális, interdiszciplináris projekt keretében" [Three Universities—Two continents—One Classroom: Developing University Students' Professional English Language Competence through an International Intercultural Interdisciplinary Project]. *Porta Lingua 2019*: 69–77.

Koris, Rita, Núria Hernández-Nanclares, and Francisco Javier Mato Díaz. 2020. "Virtual Exchange for Teaching EU Economics: Building Enriching International Learning Experiences for European Students." In *Designing and Implementing Virtual Exchange: A Collection of Case Studies*, edited by F. Helm and A. Beaven. 93–103. N.p.: Research-publishing.net.

Koris, Rita, Sushil K. Oswal, and Zsuzsanna B. Palmer. 2020. "Internationalizing the Communication Classroom via Technology and Curricular Strategy: Pedagogical Takeaways form a Three-Way Online Collaboration Project." In *Internationalizing the Communication Curriculum in an Age of Globalization*, edited by Paaige K. Turner, Soumia Bardhan, Tracey Quigley Holden, and Edda M. Mutua. 235–242. New York: Routledge.

Koris, Rita, and Jean-François Vuylsteke. 2020. "Mission (Im)Possible: Developing Students' International Online Business Communication Skills through Virtual Teamwork." In *Designing and Implementing Virtual Exchange: A Collection of Case Studies*, edited by F. Helm and A. Beaven. 69–79. N.p.: Research-publishing.net.

Kvale, Steinar. 1996. *Interviews: An Introduction to Qualitative Research Interviewing*. Thousand Oaks, CA: SAGE.

Leask, Betty. 2015. *Internationalizing the Curriculum*. London: Routledge.

Lincoln, Yvonna S., and Egon G. Guba. 1985. *Naturalistic Inquiry*. Beverly Hills, CA: SAGE.

Loch, Ágnes, and Ágnes Pál. 2018. "Úton a nemzetköziesítés felé—az ICCAGE projekt (2015–2017) a nemzetköziesítés szolgálatában" [On the Road of Internationalization—The ICCAGE Project (2015–2017) in Service of Internationalization]. *Porta Lingua 2018*: 29–40.

Mackey, Alison, and Susan M. Gass. 2005. *Second Language Research: Methodology and Design*. Mahwah, NJ: Lawrence Erlbaum.

Maykut, Pamela, and Richard Morehouse. 1994. *Beginning Qualitative Research: A Philosophic and Practical Guide*. London: Falmer Press.

McKinnon, Sabine, Angela Hammond, and Monika Foster. 2017. "Reflecting on the Value of Resources for Internationalising the Curriculum: Exploring Academic Perspectives." *Journal of Further and Higher Education* 43 (1): 138–47. https://doi.org/10.1080/0309877X.2017.1359506.

Milhauser, Kathy L., and Tim Rahschulte. 2010. "Meeting the Needs of Global Companies through Improved International Business Curriculum." *Journal of Teaching in International Business* 21(2): 78–100.

O'Dowd, Robert. 2007. "Evaluate the Outcomes of Online Intercultural Exchange." *ELT Journal* 61 (2): 144–52.

O'Dowd, Robert. 2011. "Online Foreign Language Interaction: Moving from the Periphery to the Core of Foreign Language Education?" *Language Teaching* 44 (3): 368–80.

O'Dowd, Robert. 2015. "The Competences of the Telecollaborative Teacher." *Language Learning Journal* 43 (2): 194–07.

O'Dowd, Robert. 2018. "From Telecollaboration to Virtual Exchange: State-of-the-art and the Role of UNICollaboration in Moving Forward." *Journal of Virtual Exchange* 1: 1–23.

O'Dowd, Robert, and Tim Lewis, eds. 2016. *Online Intercultural Exchange: Policy, Pedagogy, Practice*. New York: Routledge.

Parks, Elinor. 2017. "Content Modules in UK and US Universities—Their Unique Contribution towards the Development of Intercultural Competence and Criticality." In *Innovative Language Teaching and Learning at University: Enhancing Employability*, edited by Carmen Álvarez-Mayo, Angela Gallagher-Brett, and Franck Michel. 59–66. N.p.: Research-publishing.net.

Reese, Hayne W. 2011. "The Learning-by-doing Principle." *Behavioral Development Bulletin* 17 (1): 1–19. http://dx.doi.org/10.1037/h0100597.

Waldeck, Jennifer, Cathryn Durante, Briana Helmuth, and Brandon Marcia. 2012. "Communication in a Changing World: Contemporary Perspectives on Business Communication Competence." *Journal of Education for Business* 87 (4): 230–40. https://doi.org/10.1080/08832323.2011.608388.

World Economic Forum. 2016. "New Vision for Education: Fostering Social and Emotional Learning through Technology." Accessed September 30, 2020. https://www.weforum.org/reports/new-vision-for-education-fostering-social-and-emotional-learning-through-technology.

Contributors' biographical information

Emma Abbate is a teacher of Latin, History, Art, Geography and, CLIL in Cambridge International IGCSE® High School Armando Diaz (Caserta), trainer and author of digital content, and freelance researcher. She cooperates with University of Napoli Orientale as a teachers' trainer and expert in CLIL Master-degree courses. She has gained specific expertise in Erasmus+ project management as a coordinator of projects funded by the European Commission. She holds a BA in Literature, Latin, History, and Geography teaching, MA in e-Learning and CLIL, and PhD in History (University Federico II-Napoli). She has far-reaching experience in continuous professional development for teachers, teacher trainers, head teachers (e-Learning courses, blended courses, on-the-job training, workshops) in the Italian context, and in international communities of peers on CLIL language teaching and Technology-Enhanced Language Teaching (TELL). She has presented papers at national and international conferences and published articles in peer-reviewed journals. Her areas of expertise include transnational cooperation, international project planning and management, higher education, school education, CLIL, ICT, historical research, language learning, Languages for Specific Purposes, Italian as a foreign language, e-Learning, blended learning, TELL, CALL, EFL, MALL, teacher training, and school innovation.

Loredana Bercuci is Junior Researcher at the Department of Modern Languages of the West University of Timișoara in Romania where she also teaches ESP in the Political Science Department, as well as Applied Linguistics and American cultural history in the English Department. She holds a Ph.D. in American Cultural Studies. In 2016–2017, she was a visiting Fulbright scholar at the State University of New York in New York City. She previously taught English for Specific Academic Purposes at the University of Nottingham in the United Kingdom. Her research interests include English for Specific Purposes teaching, corpus linguistics, American Studies, and critical theory. Her recent publications in the field include "Calibrating Digital Method Integration into ESP Courses According to Disciplinary Settings" (*New Trends and Issues Proceedings on Humanities and Social Sciences* 7 (1): 20–29) and "A Corpus Analysis of Argumentative Structures in ESP Writing" (*International Online Journal of Education and Teaching* 6 (4): 733–47).

Klára Bereczky, PhD, is Senior Lecturer at the Department of Languages for Finance and Business Management at the Faculty of Finance and Accountancy of Budapest Business School, University of Applied Sciences. She has been teaching English for Information Technology, Aircraft, Business, Management, Human Resources, Ergonomics and Work Safety, Presentation Skills and Business Communication. She wrote her PhD dissertation on Teacher Development for Business English Instruction at Eötvös University, Budapest, Hungary. She was awarded a Dennis Gabor Innovation Award by Dennis Gabor College Foundation for Innovation in Distance Education in 2005. She is a patron of Dennis Gabor Talent Point. Her research areas are English for Business and Information Technology, CLILL, ESP teacher training, presentation skills, and business communication. She is particularly interested in understanding the professional identity of ESP teachers. Recently, her work has focused on developing complex problem-solving skills and digital ESP course materials.

Mădălina Chitez is Senior Researcher in Applied Corpus Linguistics at the West University of Timisoara, Romania. She obtained her PhD in English Philology with a specialization in corpus linguistics from Albert-Ludwig University of Freiburg and worked as a researcher in Germany and Switzerland, with research stays in Italy and the UK, investigating topics in learner corpora, academic writing, and contrastive rhetoric. Since returning to her home country, Romania, in 2017, she has been conducting research in corpus-related academic writing, digital humanities, and CALL. Her current project, ROGER, aims at identifying salient linguistic and rhetoric features of the Romanian student academic writing from a Romanian-English contrastive perspective with the help of a bilingual comparable corpus of student texts. She is the Founder and Director of the CODHUS research center (Centre for Corpus Related Digital Approaches to Humanities), which has a strong interdisciplinary and applicative character.

Dita Gálová is Director of the Institute of Foreign Languages at the Faculty of Mechanical Engineering. She has been teaching English as a foreign language at Brno University Technology since 2002 and was a coordinator of Business English courses at the Faculty of Business and Management from 2002 to 2016. She received her master's degree in English and Russian at the Faculty of Education, and Ph.D. in Philology at the Faculty of Arts, Masaryk University in Brno. Her research interests include LSP/EAP, blended learning, and assessment of English as a second language.

Katherine Guertler is Professor of Intercultural Communication and English and academic head of the foreign languages program at Ostbayerische Technische Hochschule Regensburg, a technical university of applied sciences in Germany. Her research deals with the scholarship of teaching and learning in the context of ESP, most prominently the competence-oriented education of university students of engineering regarding interpersonal and intercultural technical communication skills. Her teaching includes Technical English for a range of disciplines as well as EAP.

Elis Kakoulli Constantinou (PhD in ESP Teacher Education, MA in Applied Linguistics, BA in English) is an English language instructor and former Acting Director at Cyprus University of Technology Language Centre and a teacher trainer at the Cyprus Pedagogical Institute of the Cyprus Ministry of Education, Sport and Youth. Her research interests revolve around ESP and Teacher Education, curriculum development, teaching methodology, the integration of new technologies in language teaching, and action research. Her work has been published in peer-reviewed journals and volumes and presented at academic conferences. She is a co-editor of the volumes *Tertiary Education Language Learning: A Collection of Research* (2021), *ESP Teaching and Teacher Education: Current Theories and Practices* (2019) and *Professional Development in CALL: A Selection of Papers* (2019), and a member of various professional organizations.

Eric Koenig is Professor of Technical and Business English and academic head of the Language Center at Technische Hochschule Nuremberg, a technical university of applied sciences in Germany. Originally an engineer with nearly three decades of experience in industry, he has been teaching EFL and ESP at the tertiary and adult level since 2005. His current research interests include learner motivation as well as multimedial methodology and content of tertiary-level English for technical majors, particularly with regard to their relevance to actual practice. The ability to provide communicative, task-based curricula for Technical English courses lies at the focus of these research efforts.

Rita Kóris is Associate Professor at Budapest Business School University of Applied Sciences, Hungary, where she teaches courses on International Business and Management. She has been involved in several international collaboration and virtual exchange projects in higher education for more than ten years. She has given several presentations and held workshops in Hungary and abroad on the internationalization practices and virtual online collaboration in HE. She was involved in the Erasmus+ Virtual Exchange Project as a co-trainer helping university educators in their professional development to learn how to develop and implement transnational virtual exchange projects. Her research interests include the use of technology and online collaboration practices in HE, innovative teaching practices, development of twenty-first-century skills and competences, and academic development.

Viktória Lázár (MA) has completed her doctoral studies in the Language Pedagogy Program (ELTE, Budapest). At present, she is working on her dissertation entitled "LSP Needs Analysis in Tertiary Education." She has conducted research on goal setting and belief-formation among language learners and language teachers. She teaches Business English, English for Tourism, and Presentation Skills at Budapest Business School (Hungary). Her main concern is to help young people achieve their goals and find purpose in their lives. She therefore joined the mentoring programs both at the university where she works and the church community where she belongs.

Lucía López Risso is currently pursuing her bachelor's degree in Psychology at Universidad de la República, Uruguay. As an undergraduate student, she has been involved in various projects as a research assistant, such as a research project which looked into English reading comprehension in graduate and undergraduate students at her university. She has also worked for the National Agency of Research and Innovation assisting in a project that analyzed teaching practices regarding reading instructions in public primary schools at Montevideo, Uruguay. She is particularly interested in language education and language contact phenomena.

Salomi Papadima-Sophocleous (DProf, MEd, MLitt, PostGrads in: CALL, TESOL, TFrench&GreekSOL, BA in French) is Assistant Professor in Applied Linguistics and Director of Cyprus University of Technology (CUT) Language Centre, CUT LC Director and coordinator of MA in CALL (retired May 31, 2021), currently a Researcher at CUT Cyprus Interactive Lab (CIL), has extensive language-teaching experience (secondary and tertiary level, and teacher training in L2 teaching, curriculum development, CALL, and CALAT), both onsite and online. She is a co-editor of *International Experiences in Language Testing and Assessment* (2013), *CALL Communities and Cultures* (2016), *Professional Development in CALL: A Selection of Papers* (2019), and *ESP Teaching and Teacher Education: Current Theories and Practices* (2019). Her recent co-edited volume is on *Tertiary Education Language Learning: A Collection of Research* (2021) and her recent co-authored book is on *Formative Assessment in L2: A Systematic Review and an Annotated Bibliography* (2021). Her current research examines online language teaching, CALL and ESP teacher education, L2 CALAT.

Yliana Rodríguez is currently working in the Center for Foreign Languages in the Faculty of Humanities of Universidad de la República, Uruguay, and is a researcher of the National System of Researchers of Uruguay. She is the coordinator of the Academic Reading Comprehension Courses in Foreign Languages of the Faculty of Psychology, where she has been teaching the English course for nine years. Rodriguez holds a PhD from Leiden University (The Netherlands), an MA in Human Sciences and a BA in Linguistics from Universidad de la República. She is interested in studying the language-learning mechanisms of adults as well as the most efficient teaching techniques. She argues that interdisciplinary studies between sociolinguistics and educational and cognitive sciences are necessary to achieve better results in language teaching. Her research interests apart from language education are language contact phenomena, language attitudes, conflict linguistics, and language awareness.

Christian Rubio is Associate Professor of Spanish at Bentley University, where he is also the Chair of the Modern Languages Department and the Director of Honors Program. He holds a PhD from Columbia University, an MA from Teachers College, Columbia University, and a BA from CUNY Queens College. He has published in the field of Peninsular Studies, including his most recent book, *Krausism and the Spanish Avant-Garde: The Impact of Philosophy on National Culture* (2017). He was part of the Modern Languages Association (MLA) ad-hoc committee that drafted the Guidelines for Evaluating Publicly Engaged Humanities Scholarship in Language and Literature Programs. Dr. Rubio was appointed permanent member as a correspondent at the Academia Norteamericana de la Lengua Española.

An Slootmaekers studied Roman Philology at Leuven University (KU Leuven) and is working for the Interfacultair Instituut voor Levende Talen (Institute for Living Languages) of the same university. She has developed courses for French for Specific Purposes in various areas: economic sciences, social sciences, and philosophy. All the courses are based on studies of LSP combined with studies of language acquisition. In the context of the courses for economic and social sciences, special domains of interest are vocabulary acquisition, listening comprehension, and writing competence. The course "French for Reading Knowledge" as part of the international program of the Institute of Philosophy also turned reading comprehension into a topic of regular study. For all target groups, different forms of blended learning, in particular tandem language learning and online language learning, are put into practice and studied.

Jolana Tluková is Assistant Professor of technical English at the Faculty of Architecture and the Faculty of Civil Engineering at Brno University of Technology, a technical university of applied sciences in the Czech Republic. She has been teaching EFL, ESP and EAP at Brno University Technology since 2006 and has been a coordinator of ESP courses at the Faculty of Architecture since 2015. In 2012, she received her Ph.D. in English studies/linguistics at the Faculty of Arts, Palacký University in Olomouc, Czech Republic. Her research interests include ESP, EAP, blended learning, and assessment of ESP. Her research focuses on terminology acquisition in ESP courses, and she has created an online Czech-English glossary of technical terminology for civil engineering students.

Martina Vránová was a recipient of the Hlavinka Fellowship from the Czech Educational Foundation of Texas at Texas A&M University, College Station, Texas, USA, where she earned her MA degree in English. In 2010, she received her PhD in Comparative Literature at Masaryk University, Brno, Czech Republic. She is currently Assistant Professor of English at the Institute of Foreign

Languages, Faculty of Mechanical Engineering, Brno University of Technology. She has taught ESP at various levels and areas for almost fifteen years. Her other research interests include academic writing, rhetoric, and contemporary fiction. She has co-edited conference proceedings, *Languages for Specific Purposes in Higher Education* (2017), and a volume of literary and cultural studies papers, *Crime and Detection in Contemporary Culture* (2018). She has also published two novels in Czech.

Index

A

activities
  classroom, xx, 30, 78, 107, 108–10, 131–46, 150, 155
  communication, 70
  content-focused, 143
  context-embedded, 150
  corpus-based, 183
  discussion, 156
  group, 156
  in class and take home, xxi
  in class communicative, 137
  kinesthetic, 141, 143
  learning, 71
  reading, 156, 158, 159
  research, 67
  speaking, 137–38
  targeted, 142
  task based learning, 141
  writing, xxiii, 138–39
adult
  education, 29, 41, 43
  learner, 30, 40–42
  learning, 31, 41
annotation tools, xxii, 155, 156, 159
applied linguistics, xvii
assessment, 39, 74, 117, 124, 127, 204
  peer, 202
awareness
  language, 118, 127
  metalinguistic, 152

B

best practice, xvii, xviii, 131–46, 210, 220
Bloom's taxonomy, 150
Business English (BE), 24, 26, 89, 101–14

C

CALL, xvi, 41
CLIL, xvi, xxii, 147–67, 190
cloze-test creator, xxii, 154
cognates, xxi, 122–27
cognitive
  dissonance, 37, 43
  process, 150
  skills. See skills
collaboration
  and networking, 16
  international, xxiii, 209–23
  online, xxiii, 209–23
  with subject teachers, 4, 9, 16, 25, 39, 63
communication
  activities. See activities
  classroom, 135
  dialogic, 70, 71
  intercultural, 209–23
  online, 162, 216
  oral, 137, 143, 220
  process, 30
  professional, xxiii, 17, 66, 209–23
  skills. See skills
  team, 213, 219
  technical, 138

Lightning Source UK Ltd.
Milton Keynes UK
UKHW021925180123
415590UK00015B/308/J